Advance Praise

"Nancy Giordano has given us in Leading *a fascinating book that inspires and informs. This is an important book for all of us who know that a world of part-nerism is possible if we leave old thinking behind and use our enormous creativity, full of leading-edge examples of what forward-looking people all over the world are doing to build a more caring and equitable world."*

—Riane Eisler, President, Center for Partnership Studies;
author of *The Chalice and the Blade, The Real Wealth of Nations,*
and *Nurturing Our Humanity*

"*Sustainability and prosperity are not at odds—they are mutually reinforcing. Thank you, Nancy Giordano, for demonstrating how leadership is not something one is, but something one does—with others. Leading is a team sport."*

—Douglas Rushkoff, Founder, Laboratory of Digital Humanism;
Professor of Media Theory and Digital Economics, Queens College, CUNY

"*Applying old thinking to new tools is both naive and dangerous.* Leading *offers us a compelling case why we must reset our approach to business to ensure we build a thriving future for all."*

—Chip Conley, *New York Times* bestselling author;
hospitality entrepreneur; Strategic Advisor, Airbnb

"*Giordano is an intellectual powerhouse, and this book upends every cherished notion we have about what it means to lead. A must-read for anyone serious about building a future that includes everyone."*

—Sunni Brown, social entrepreneur;
bestselling author, *Deep Self Design*

LEADER*ing*

THE WAYS VISIONARY LEADERS PLAY BIGGER

WAKE
WONDER
NAVIGATE
CONNECT
CONTRIBUTE
BE AUDACIOUS
THRIVE

NANCY GIORDANO

A *FORBES* TOP FEMALE FUTURIST

COPYRIGHT © 2021 NANCY GIORDANO

LEADERING

The Ways Visionary Leaders Play Bigger

ISBN   978-1-5445-0880-1   *Hardcover*
        978-1-5445-0879-5   *Paperback*
        978-1-5445-0878-8   *Ebook*

For my children, Hugo, Zane, and Harper—
darlings, you are the future that inspires me most. xo

Contents

Prologue

"Never let a good crisis go to waste."
—Winston Churchill, British prime minister and statesman

On a Friday afternoon in March 2020, I was receiving feedback on what I had expected was the final version of this book's manuscript when my phone suddenly started pinging with news from friends and colleagues. They were crushed to learn that SXSW (aka South by Southwest)—the global technology, music, and arts festival held annually in my current hometown of Austin—was being canceled for the first time in its thirty-four-year history. The culprit: COVID-19. That was the moment I'll think back on when we all begin telling stories about how and when we realized life as we knew it was shifting radically.

That was the last day students in the U.S. saw their classrooms. And the one on which many offices moved into homes. Despite warnings from China, Italy, and Spain, we did not really comprehend what was coming our way, how much sadness and support we would simultaneously experience. Or how suddenly it would catapult us all into the future.

In the six months since, we have all had to make major changes. We have had to absorb new information, statistics, and protocols related to keeping ourselves and our communities safe. We have been cheering huge manufacturers who redeployed time, materials, and talent to quickly increase the supply of hand sanitizer, face masks, and ventilators in order to support brave essential workers—from healthcare providers to grocery store team members to teachers—all over the world. Most business leaders have been simultaneously diving in to keep their teams and customers secure while suddenly realizing they must reinvent their paths to the future.

After that phone call, and as I write this now, in September, it is clear that the world has fundamentally shifted. Alongside the COVID-19 pandemic, we're coming to understand Black Lives Matter, not just as a march but as a movement—and not just in the U.S. but around the world. We are witnessing erratic geopolitical decision-making and ineffective regulatory reviews. There is a great deal of uncertainty over what the economic recovery path will really look like, despite Wall Street exuberance. There is no just "getting to the other side" of this and reverting back. There are important things we will never be able to unlearn. Nor should we. While a majority of this book was written prior to these cataclysmic global events—because the seeds of what is needed in the future were already sown—it is critical we don't let this crisis go to waste.

There simply is no more outrunning what's to come.

Ready or not, remote work isn't an experiment; it's survival. Digital delivery isn't cannibalistic; it's now the expectation. Virtual meetings, telemedicine, and digital classrooms offer us entirely new, necessary, and intimate ways to connect...around the entire globe. As such, we are learning quickly what works and what doesn't. We are witnessing the role that organizational culture and design have on the success of these new efforts. We are now seeing who has the infrastructure for this digital lifestyle and who doesn't, which tools are still missing, and how this is impacting our personal relationships and sense of self.

These new activities and economic realities are forcing us to acknowledge and finally reckon with the glaring and historical inequities that exist in technology access, medical care, stable jobs, and emotional and financial safety nets. It's putting a compassionate spotlight on formerly radical ideas such as universal basic income (UBI) and other financial scaffolding for those suddenly thrust out of work. It also is opening the keyhole to the next wave of peer-to-peer (P2P) mutual aid initiatives as well as helping us much better prepare for the technology-accelerated job displacement looming ahead.

Similarly, as planes were grounded, roads became quieter, factories took a rest, and stores limited access, the planet took a huge cleansing breath. This gave us an extraordinarily clear view of the impact our consumptive behaviors have on the planet's health. Will this allow our environments to heal a bit? A lot? Completely? Will it extend our 2029 tipping point climate crisis warning? Will this finally change some of our behaviors and make us think twice about booking a flight or wasting food?

Most poignantly, how will we look at the value of life as we all are daily calculating the risk of death?

When we look past the fear and inevitable losses of this difficult moment to compassionately embrace the humanity in each other, we will be in such a strong place to actively and bravely build a safer and more thriving future— for all of us, as individuals, as organizations, as industries, and as a much more connected society. With a greater reverence for life and deeper faith in our own resilience and ability to change, I believe the huge disruptions of 2020 are making much more visible the new solutions and more caring investments needed to shape a human-centered economy ahead. This crisis presents an opportunity.

Leadering is our answer to this call. And in the coming pages, through examples of audacious leaders and responsive organizations around the world, I'll show you the authentic and inventive ways we can all step up to this challenge.

Welcome to *Leadering*. I am very grateful you are here.

Change Your Mindset, Change the World

"The most difficult thing is the decision to act, the rest is merely tenacity."

—Amelia Earhart, American aviation pioneer and author

Despite only having locations in Texas and Mexico, H-E-B is one of the most beloved grocery chains in the U.S., beating out giants like Costco and Amazon.[1] And because I live in Austin, I am lucky enough to be a customer. Founded in 1905, H-E-B is still privately held and, with around four hundred stores, ranks as the twentieth-largest retailer in the U.S. by revenue. When the pandemic hit, H-E-B teams were ready, having taken the role of community first responder seriously during past hurricanes and the previous virus scares, doing whatever was necessary to ensure folks had a reliable source for food and water[2] (though the pandemic run on toilet paper caught them off guard too). It tops the list of favorite grocery stores by shoppers because we are convinced every day that our store really cares about what we want and need—from their high-quality produce and private-label products, to their investments in sustainability, their communities, and supporting their workers.

Their continued success, however, is not simply about extraordinary crisis management. Or being deeply committed to their customers' wellbeing. Or investing in digital preparedness with an extensive new tech hub. It is about all of this and more. While the grocery industry has been slow to wake up to the winds of change—operating nearly the same way since the first modern supermarket was opened over a hundred years ago—H-E-B is working hard to be prepared for the future. They know change is coming fast.

Kroger, the second-largest U.S. grocery retailer, has made aggressive investments in digital transformation, including opening six Ocado-robot-run automated warehouses to fulfill online delivery orders faster. Amazon is

---

1   Dom DiFurio, "H-E-B Is Rated the Top U.S. Grocery Retailer in New Study, Beating Costco and Amazon," *The Dallas Morning News*, January 8, 2020.

2   Dan Solomon and Paula Forbes, "Inside the Story of How H-E-B Planned for the Pandemic," *Texas Monthly*, March 26, 2020.

expanding its cashier-less checkout and integrating Alexa help stations throughout their new Amazon Fresh stores, while the number one retailer in the country, Walmart, just teamed up quickly with Oracle to buy a 7.5 percent stake in controversial social video platform TikTok. Game on. We can already see how data changes food shopping in China with Hema, a store that requires all shoppers to use the app, and how 5G is reshaping a leader like e-mart in highly urban South Korea. As sensors in both our refrigerators and Tupperware take inventory of what we eat (and what we don't), and drones and self-driving delivery vehicles respond quickly to our needs, tomorrow's grocery stock-up is going to look entirely different.

So what will it take to navigate this kind of big change?

Many leaders now recognize that for many years they spent too much time looking backward and only considering near-term goals. This has left them unprepared to move forward in what is rapidly emerging as an extraordinarily transformative, highly ambiguous future.

It is clear that disruption can erupt from anywhere, jump across markets, and quite suddenly challenge service and product delivery, business models, and the entire ways we live, learn, work, and shop. A worldwide pandemic, societal justice movement, and escalating global tensions are calling into question most of our assumptions about how things get done and how we can do things better. But even aside from such global phenomena, we know that a scrappy startup can swiftly change how your customers seek out or interact with your offering. A new technology or acquisition in an unrelated field can send waves through your industry (think Amazon's unexpected purchase of Whole Foods). Even more daunting, innovators far outside our industry—and field of vision—now have the opportunity to radically transform it. It is amazing how a delivery service like Instacart is impacting the auto industry and the desire for car ownership. And as business becomes more digital, it is data versus heavy infrastructure that becomes the moat that protects us. We have to approach things differently now.

For years, corporate strategists and futurists have been encouraging organizations and government leaders to become more adaptive, to try new approaches, and to shift behaviors to address things like climate change as well as growing societal and economic inequities. From most, we heard back some combination of "It's too hard," "Too expensive," "Too disruptive," "Too impersonal," and "Too insecure." Often, inertia won the day. So, one of the most stunning and lingering things about this shocking moment in history is that suddenly *everyone* is being thrust into this new era *together*.

Now that we are all more awake, this book will clearly present the kind of dynamic "leadership" necessary for this brave new world.

As we imagine our place in this moment of significant transformation, we find ourselves confronted by a lot of new questions, which often swarm in simultaneously. The concerns I commonly hear from leaders are:

Does my current business model still hold? Do I have the right team in place? Who should we partner with, and how? How do I reduce fear and instill confidence in my teams, colleagues, bosses, and investors? What new technologies should I invest in? How do we fill the growing gap in the skills we need? How do I manage investor expectations while leading my company through transformation? How do I wrap my arms around unpredictable global demands and shifts? How can I drive change when there are so many regulations in my industry? How do I collect enough data to make good decisions yet ensure I do it respectfully? How should I respond to competitors with a different playing field or moral compass? How do I create a culture that enables people to learn versus feel like they're failing all the time? **How can I get my "real" work done when there is so much change to manage?** *How do I manage information overload as I try to stay up to date?* **How do I better integrate my values with the choices I'm making at work?** *How can I get folks to move faster when the organization isn't ready?* **How do I prepare my kids for a world in constant flux?**

And, of course...this one:

How should I navigate my role in a future that is constantly changing?

The future *will* look very different from the way things have operated until now. Some have declared that retail will change more in the next five years than it has in the past fifty, and society will change more in the next fifty years than it has in the last three hundred. A recent headline declared that "We are approaching the fastest, deepest, most consequential technological disruption in history."[3] Major industries, from medicine to energy to travel to entertainment, are radically transforming, putting pressure on others, such as manufacturing, construction, transportation, finance, education... frankly, all of it.

None of us can afford to sit on the sidelines. Now is the moment we must all play bigger.

We have the insight to build an even better next. We have the opportunity to carve a clear, galvanizing path forward—today and tomorrow. But to do so, we need to cultivate the mindset, capacities, and internal compass that enable much more sustainable and powerful decision-making.

---

3   Tony Seba and James Arbib, "We Are Approaching the Fastest, Deepest, Most Consequential Technological Disruption in History," *Fast Company*, October 5, 2020.

Through years of work helping organizations and teams embrace and build a thriving future, I have come to clearly appreciate that we don't need to change *what* we think as much as we must change *how* we think.

WHY WE ARE FAILING TO MEET THE DEMANDS OF CHANGE

Our conventional version of leadership—the traditional one practiced de facto in most organizations today—was built to fit the demands of the Industrial Revolution. It is *that* outdated. It is ill-equipped for the challenges of our increasingly digital and transforming world. Leaders have traditionally been taught to think and operate in centralized, siloed, hierarchical structures, to focus on efficiency and predictability in order to scale reliable, consistent delivery of products and services. Despite talk of double and triple bottom lines and innovation hubs, many leaders are still being measured by narrow definitions of success and taking only incremental steps forward. And in most companies today, leaders are so focused on (and wholly incentivized toward) short-term thinking that they often don't invest in long-term potential. Which is all at odds with today's mandate for breakthrough responsive thinking.

A study by Duke University and the University of Washington provided an example of how distorted our thinking has become when the researchers asked business leaders the following question: "If you knew you could invest in an initiative that would offer a huge financial benefit to the company in the long term, but you would have to take a hit in the short term, would you do it?"[4] Their response was startling:

---

4 "Why Leaders Should Focus on Long-Term Growth," *Knowledge at Wharton*, May 8, 2018.

Eighty percent of respondents said they would decrease value-creating spending on research and development, advertising, maintenance, and hiring in order to meet (short-term) earnings benchmarks. More than half the executives would delay a new project even if it entailed sacrificing value.

Why? Especially when the scenario assured a massive financial reward for the organization down the road?

Because we have been taught that leadership is about creating steady, consistent growth while controlling for risk, and because we have been increasingly incentivized to protect the status quo. Sadly, such conventional thinking sacrifices huge advances for the sake of short-term comfort and security. If we continue to use a twentieth-century industrial playbook, we will be put at ever-greater peril—especially as the speed of change accelerates and the stakes become higher. Facing radical change with our current leadership approach will cause the breakdowns to increase, severely compromising our success (and wellbeing) ahead. We must evolve beyond outdated leadership beliefs that lead us to:

- Resist change and maintain the status quo.
- Keep the power at the center.
- Compete alone, win alone.
- Extract value.
- Be incremental to reduce risk.
- Rigidly commit to a single plan.

It's time to ditch the old playbook and develop a set of dynamic practices that improve our abilities to orient, innovate, and create long-term, caring solutions.

LEADERING: THE MINDSET WE NEED TO BUILD THE FUTURE WE WANT

"Leadership," the noun, is often synonymous with management: it's static, directive, exclusive, and hierarchical. It is focused on month-over-month sales growth, share price, market valuation, and an ever-expanding GDP.

"Leadering" offers clarity and urgency around what twenty-first-century stewardship demands. It shifts our approach to a *verb*: the continual practice of sensing and responding rather than seeking best practices. This new mindset, required to face the future, challenges entrenched thinking about how success is actually created and rewarded in enterprises as we move ahead.

To do this, we need to understand why our outdated playbook is now dead (discussed in detail in Chapter 1) and commit to shifting our mindsets to:

- **Wonder (versus Resist).** As technology is advancing, information is growing, and culture is shifting exponentially, we must be willing to expand our current understandings, approaches, and beliefs. A constantly changing future requires a constantly learning person, team, or organization. In Chapter 2, we explain why wonder and curiosity are essential for innovation and should be prioritized and incentivized as important. "What if..." must become a point on our compass.

- **Navigate (versus Replicate).** To thrive in a state of permanent ambiguity and opportunity, leadership must shift from command-and-control best practices to an ability to sense and respond in real time. In an environment that demands continuous innovation and on-demand delivery, we need to build the capacity to rapidly design, test, iterate, and collaborate. This is the thrust of Chapter 3.

- **Connected (versus Alone).** In an increasingly complex world, no single individual or organization will have the capacity to build everything alone. In Chapter 4, we describe how we'll need to leverage the resources and strengths of external partners and internal teams—even, on occasion, our competitors—to innovate and ensure harmony within the environments of which we're a part.

- **Contribute (versus Extract).** As the environmental and societal breakdowns become more evident, it is no longer sustainable to simply extract resources for the benefit of a small number of investors or shareholders. In Chapter 5, we cover in detail how future success of business will be dependent on generating value for a much broader set of stakeholders; this includes current and future societies.

- **Be Audacious (versus Incremental).** Given we are about 1 percent into what exponential technologies will make possible, a vastly different future is being built as we speak. In Chapter 6, we offer a motivating call to address escalating gaps as you imagine the boldest contribution your organization can make and orient your teams toward that North Star.

- **Thrive (versus Die).** Rather than going all in on one uncertain future and building a solid plan, only to get it wrong, we must commit resources to multiple eventualities that prepare us for the unexpected. In Chapter 7, we offer tangible ways to cultivate the practices that ensure we are ready and able to harness the potential of the moment. And the one that comes after that.

As we have experienced so viscerally these past few months, dramatically changing conditions require a completely different way of leading: one that allows organizations and teams of all sizes to drive rapid transformation and respond quickly and collaboratively to new pressures and opportunities. Leadering makes it possible to confidently shift from reading routes on the well-worn map to having confidence in being guided by a reliable compass and a motivating North Star. It requires we adopt a mindset relentlessly committed to human-centric innovation, building relationships in mutually dependent ecosystems, and creating sustainable value.

We are standing in a unique moment in time in which we have huge opportunities to impact our world in far-reaching ways. Even better, these are not way out there in some distant future—they are waiting for us right now. Today it is possible to 3D-print a solid house for only $7,000 in twenty-four hours. It is possible to grow healthy food with 95 percent less water and 390 times the efficiency of conventional farming.[5] It is even possible to perform robotic heart surgery from miles away. All of which will dramatically broaden access to those essentials—food, energy, housing, medical care—that determine the quality of our lives.

This points out another—highly important—reason to shift our thinking. Applying old mindsets to new, exponentially more potent technologies can create damage at a scale we never considered. The consequences of twenty-first-century mistakes will be even more difficult to clean up than the twentieth-century ones we are dealing with now. To enable radical change, we need radical solutions. Accepting radical solutions requires a radical openness of mind...and heart. We need to shift to a mindset framed by

---

5   Mark Esposito, Terence Tse, Khaled Soufani, and Lisa Xiong, "Feeding the Future of Agriculture with Vertical Farming," *Stanford Social Innovation Review*, December 27, 2017.

audacity and ingenuity as well as by compassion and humility; the innovations and technologies of the future will demand nothing less.

I believe the future is rich with potential. By marrying exponential technological advances with the mindset that can turn these opportunities into practical solutions to our problems, it will become increasingly possible to reduce suffering and provide *more* than enough for everyone.

A client beautifully summarized my thinking on Leadering this way: "To change what's out there, we need to change what's in here. And to change the future, we need to change the present."

THE JOURNEY TO THIS BOOK

My own professional journey played a major role in how I chose to write this book. I spent the first half of my career working in top-tier ad agencies to build and launch iconic brands and then consulting with prominent organizations such as Nestlé, the Coca-Cola Company, Sprint, and Acumen. I saw visionary leaders who could sense change was happening and were committed to real transformation...and many more who denied it and struggled to absorb and respond to new information about what the future holds. While I sometimes met executives who were confident and ready to adapt to the expectations ahead, I confronted many more who were simply looking for the next intervention they could quickly put into action. I often felt as though I was trying to explain the world is round to those who couldn't imagine it as anything other than flat.

Fortunately, I've found frustration to be a great source of motivation. Whenever I have become stuck trying unsuccessfully to inspire a clear (to me) improvement in an organization I was working with or in, my impulse has been to get closer to the source of resistance. What is *really* getting in the way here, I often wondered?

After many years of working with Fortune 500 leaders and seeing up close that current approaches to facing change were rapidly losing their effectiveness, I decided to join the disruptors themselves. I dove into the tech world to help form an artificial intelligence startup and began actively working alongside the designers, technologists, and entrepreneurs who are building the code, the solutions, and the structures shaping our collective future. My curiosity about what's to come led me to help launch the global TEDx movement, band together with extraordinary thinkers at Singularity University, and learn from organizations of all kinds about what it takes to confront change—internally and externally. I have delivered close to eighty keynote talks around the world these past few years, each time learning something new from the organization and audience about the concerns they are facing.

Today, I'm part of another AI startup dedicated to empowering organizations of all sizes to harness the power of their data in effective and ethical ways. I am also contributing to global teams passionately applying what I call "horizon technology" that will deliver a distributed internet and new economic accountability metrics that can dramatically improve the ways we create and coordinate resources ahead—from food and financing to labor and energy, and so much more.

I wrote this book to link these worlds: to connect the leaders who are seeking to reorient resources and implement innovation in thoughtful and valuable ways today with the confident, visionary people who are building the technologies and emerging societal structures of tomorrow. Together we become more empowered to shape a future in which all thrive.

Despite all this preparation, I'll admit that it is damn tricky writing a static book about a dynamic world in complete flux. I have been experiencing firsthand the stress of learning and leading simultaneously, for, while I am very clear on the future I want to live in, I'm learning more each day about the systemic weaknesses and risks that are informing it. The future is fluid, and so is my thinking. It has to be. So I invite you to stay in the conversation and join me at *leadering.us* for updates and gatherings that allow us to explore together how to apply this new thinking.

THIS IS THE MOMENT

As we think about the individual roles each of us will play in the big transformations of the future, it's easy to get caught in a flurry of insecurities. We ask ourselves, Am I good enough? Am I bold enough? Am I smart enough? Am I (fill in the blank) enough to drive this future forward? The place to start is in believing we can.

I am calmed by this quote from Steve Jobs:

> *When you look around and see that everything around you that you call life is made up by people who are no smarter than you; and you can change it, you can influence it, you can build your own things that other people can use—once you learn that, you'll never be the same again.*[6]

The current constructs in which we and our businesses operate have all been created and invented by real, flawed people—and they can just as easily be questioned and reconceived by *you*. Are the current structures in your industry serving you? Go even bigger: are the constructs of work, education, food systems, energy, healthcare, or any of people's basic needs

---

6   *Steve Jobs: Secrets of Life*, Santa Clara Valley Historical Association, 2012.

working for you and others? Can you imagine improving each of these in the future?

Leadering is the crucial shift we need to navigate our way to the healthy, accessible, safe, and inclusive future we all want. It advocates for a new mindset that allows you to embrace possibility and recognize your *agency to act*. This one change can have a massive impact on how you orient toward the future and ensure your organization navigates confidently—and even enthusiastically—forward.

Throughout this book, we'll examine specific ways this new mindset takes shape. Through stories and statistics, concepts, and charts, we'll discuss how you and your organizations can understand and begin practicing Leadering. Starting *now*.

LET'S BEGIN WITH A BREATH

Here is the critical bit: embracing ambiguity and complexity requires heavy doses of self-awareness and self-care. As we get ready to dive in together, I invite you to start this exploration with a deep breath.

Seriously. Allow yourself to take a deep inhale right now.

And an even bigger exhale...

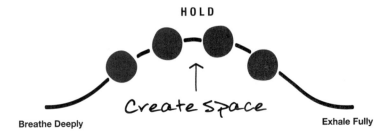

Now, with your eyes closed, take a couple more as you imagine clearing a wide-open space among all these competing thoughts and worries. Slowly exhale each time. Sit tall and feel yourself calmly making each next decision with clarity and confidence. Use this moment to congratulate yourself on all you have *already* learned and created.

Each time you pick up this book—and, ideally, as you start and close each day—I invite you to take a deep breath or two just like this and reconnect with your strength, your compassion, and your own sense of purpose.

I sincerely hope *Leadering* gives you the confidence and practical guidance you need to be the visionary leader you are ready to be—no matter your age or tenure. None of us can afford to sit on the sidelines. Now is the moment we must all play bigger.

The future is counting on you.

CHAPTER ONE

Why the Playbook Is Dead

"The Visionary starts with a clean sheet of paper and reimagines the world."

—Malcolm Gladwell, author

Walking down Sixth Avenue in downtown Seattle, you're surrounded by traditional, square-edged skyscrapers of concrete, steel, and glass. One after the other...until you cross Lenora Street, and then—*whoa!* Suddenly there's a structure in front of you that challenges all the rules of what an urban office building should look like.

In the middle of an expanse of green sit three geodesic domes. Curved girders wrap around the domes in a network of lacy steel. Through the glass, you can see a rain forest of plants in green walls of foliage that climb from floor to ceiling. These unconventional buildings, called The Spheres, house Amazon's headquarters.

As a company, Amazon has challenged the rules of business by reinventing retail—in speed of delivery, brand orthodoxies, and their business model—so it's fitting that their HQ buildings are a complete departure from the structures around them. The Spheres use land very differently than the office towers that loom nearby. The domes are surrounded by green space that dominates the city block. And the interior office space is filled with forty thousand plants from fifty countries around the world, creating a focal point around nature and diversity that is so often absent from sterile work environments. This was not an afterthought; there are so many plants in and around The Spheres that it took over six hundred full-time workers to design, install, and maintain the greenery on campus. The building's lighting, air, and water systems incorporate sophisticated technologies designed to support not just the human inhabitants but the flora as well.

Simply looking at the building from the street makes one wonder: What is the very deliberate design of a building like this intended to provoke and nurture? How might that impact and enhance both wellness and productivity? Note: it took just five years for The Spheres to spring from initial design to being open and in full use.

This is the kind of audacity of vision and execution the future expects.

Of course, not every Amazon building looks like this, and not all of Amazon's business practices have such a humanistic focus. Many of their warehouse operations are currently under fire for driving efficiency and productivity at the expense of employee wellbeing. Despite phenomenal business results, Jeff Bezos has also been excluded from *Harvard Business Review*'s most recent tally of top-performing CEOs due to a disturbing gap in environmental, social, and governance leadership (ESG). Amazon is succeeding and failing simultaneously by not considering the needs of all stakeholders.[1]

The Spheres represent a driving need of the future—to be bold, unconventional, and audacious—however, the future will demand that there is an equally important need to hold each other well.

WHAT'S MISSING ABOUT MODERN LEADERSHIP

Recently, an informal post about a touching moment in an airport went viral, and it caught my attention. The post told the story of a young pregnant woman traveling alone with a toddler.[2] It was late in the afternoon, and the toddler was having a tough time, running wild around the gate area and refusing to listen to his mother. She was doing her best to manage the situation but, at some point, felt completely overwhelmed. She sat down in a seat and burst into tears.

In the next moment, six women independently took notice. Each of them stopped what they were doing—stepping out of the line they were standing

---

1   "The Best-Performing CEOs in the World, 2019," *Harvard Business Review*, 2019.
2   "Women Encircle a Crying Mom Whose Toddler Was Having a Meltdown at the Airport," *Good News Network*, February 15, 2018.

in or getting up from the chair they were sitting in—and together, they quietly encircled the distraught mother. None of them had met each other before this moment, but here they were, collaborating to provide comfort and de-escalate the moment.

When they got down low with the mom, the curious toddler came over to sit in her lap. One woman began singing "The Itsy-Bitsy Spider." Another woman pulled a snack out of a bag for the toddler. Another gave him a toy and a blankie. Another helped the mother with a sippy cup. Their efforts worked: the toddler stopped screaming. Mother and son took a deep breath. When it came time to board, the two calmly walked onto the plane together.

These women recognized a need, and they stepped in to fill it. They instinctively came together—they didn't need permission or direction from anyone to help. They coordinated organically, without a handbook or specific rules of engagement. And they just as comfortably came apart; once the scenario was resolved, the women simply disbanded. They went back to their separate seats, back to the airport bookstore, back to their own flights. No one expected credit or promotion for their success. They didn't go on to form a group or go on vacation together.

I've thought of this story a lot during the pandemic—and it is inspiring to see organizations similarly jump in to help. But this isn't just a crisis stance. Audacity. Empathy. Agency. Cooperation. Adaptivity. These are the expectations of the future.

To better understand the combined insight of the Amazon and airport stories, we have to take a closer look at the big shift we are heading into.

THE FIRST PRODUCTIVITY REVOLUTION (1PR)

New technologies and the breadth of data we will now be able to access will give us an extraordinary ability to solve complex problems and build more-resilient structures, but these developments also raise more questions than we are able to answer—for the most part, because our thinking hasn't kept up with the exponential pace at which new technologies are shaping and disrupting the world as we know it. As a World Economic Forum article noted:

> We stand on the brink of a technological revolution that will fundamentally alter the way we live, work, and relate to one another. In its scale, scope, and complexity, the transformation will be unlike anything humankind has experienced before. We do not yet know just how it will unfold, but one thing is clear: the response to it must be integrated and comprehensive, involving all stakeholders of the global polity, from the public and private sectors to academia and civil society.[3]

Throughout our industrialized past, there have been several big shifts in the way we have leveraged resources and organized societies. Here, on the cusp of the next one, let's take a look at what has come before.

In the First Industrial Revolution, the technologies of mechanization, steam power, and waterpower suddenly enabled us to use machines to replace much of the demand for human "muscle" labor and to travel much further, faster, and more safely.

During the Second Industrial Revolution, we gained the capabilities for mass production using assembly lines and electricity. Suddenly it was

---

3   "The Fourth Industrial Revolution: What It Is, How to Respond," *World Economic Forum*, January 14, 2016.

possible to have refrigerated train cars, which meant we could transport something as perishable as food from one far-off location to another. Communities didn't have to organize around a single nutritional resource. Families didn't need to own their own cows; milk could be refrigerated and delivered. Meat could be butchered and shipped across the country. The ability to more efficiently produce and distribute resources impacted where people could work and live, as well as the kinds of jobs they could do. The shift from an agricultural focus to an industrial one also required whole new structures in the form of labor laws, education systems, environmental and safety regulations, and urban planning.

The Third Industrial Revolution was spurred by computers, automation, and digitization. As far back as 1959, Peter Drucker coined the term "knowledge worker" to describe people who could work and produce value entirely in data and digital formats. Being liberated from physical infrastructures meant people could decouple their work from a specific corporation, store, or employer; they could create their own careers on the web. People turned to entrepreneurship in greater numbers, and in just ten years, we have seen many startups develop into billion-dollar businesses. Facebook has grown to 2.7 billion monthly active users as of the first quarter of 2020,[4] WhatsApp now has two billion monthly active users,[5] Instagram has one billion, and while Airbnb's value has dropped during the COVID-19 pandemic, it is still valued at $18 billion and operates in more than 100,000 cities worldwide. The list goes on.

Though it is currently being spoken about as the Fourth Industrial Revolution, we are actually moving into an age of "cyber-physical systems,"

---

4   J. Clement, "Facebook: Number of Monthly Active Users Worldwide 2008-2020," *Statista*, August 10, 2020.

5   J. Clement, "Number of Monthly Active WhatsApp Users as of 2013-2020," *Statista*, April 30, 2020.

where products all around us are imbued with mechanisms to capture, control, or monitor behaviors to enhance and improve user experiences. Executive chairman of the World Economic Forum Klaus Schwab describes this new era we're entering as "characterized by a fusion of technologies that is blurring the lines between the physical, digital, and biological spheres."[6] Our ability to collect and understand vastly more data is allowing us to learn and grow exponentially. What's more, having these cyber-physical systems means we can outsource more to robots and AI, and this capability is yet again dramatically shifting the nature of work. How we create value, exchange goods and services, and coordinate and

6   Klaus Schwab, "The Fourth Industrial Revolution: What It Means, How to Respond," *World Economic Forum*, January 14, 2016.

communicate with one another to produce value—even our cultural structures and lifestyles—will all continue to look different. These technology waves don't just allow us to do things faster or more cheaply—they change the ways we live.

As such, I propose that using the word "industrial" to describe a digital future is part of the outdated mindset we need to change. As we move from a society of manufacturing and consumption to one of innovation and regenerative value exchange, I offer the "First Productivity Revolution" (1PR) as the more accurate description. One that will put us on a much steadier, more inclusive and sustainable path.

THE DISRUPTION MANDATE

What makes the twenty-first century so different from the previous one? Simply put, there are five very big shifts reshaping business and society that require equally big shifts in how we respond, especially if we intend to remain relevant in the years ahead. These include:

- Escalating consumer expectations
- The calculus of exponential change
- Shifting to an emphasis on stakeholders (versus only investors)
- The need for long-term versus short-term thinking
- Redressing systemic injustice

Let's take a look at what these five shifts entail.

ESCALATING EXPECTATIONS

The rise of the web in general, and social media specifically, has empowered today's shopper. Prior to the pandemic, 87 percent of buying decisions began with research conducted online, usually on Amazon or Google; and we learned that 84 percent of consumers trust online reviews as much as personal recommendations. These numbers have skyrocketed over the past several months as all of our habits and behaviors are being redirected.[7]

We want more: more quality, innovation, personalization, transparency, speed, discovery, and flexibility. And we want it for less: less time, energy, loyalty, attention, trust, and money (unless you make it super convenient or give me an extraordinary experience). We are now much more discerning in all these decisions.

The kicker is that the tension between escalating expectations and reduced investment will not at all slow down as emerging technologies create entirely new ways to have our needs and wants met. This presents huge opportunities—if we're paying attention—as there remains a big disconnect between what customers desire and what companies are delivering. A 2019 global survey by Acquia across more than five thousand businesses and five hundred marketers confirms that, while 87 percent of marketers believe they are delivering engaging customer experiences, nearly half of consumers say brands don't meet their expectations.[8]

The vast amount of data we're collecting every second can produce valuable insights to help close this experience gap. We've already reached a point where every day, according to IBM, we create 2.5 quintillion bytes of data.[9] We've gone from logging 100 GB of information *per day* in 1992, to 50,000 GB *per second* in 2018. And that's before our toothbrushes can sense

---

7   Ryan Erskine, "20 Online Reputation Statistics That Every Business Owner Needs to Know," *Forbes*, September 19, 2017.
8   "Closing the CX Gap: Customer Experience Trends Report," *Acquia*, 2020.
9   "Every Day Big Data Statistics—2.5 Quintillion Bytes of Data Created Daily," *Vouchercloud News*, April 5, 2015.

when it's time to get our teeth cleaned or our smart Tupperware alerts us that our leftovers should be eaten today. Increases in computational power and cheaper and accessible cloud data storage will make it possible to put all that data to good use (we hope), exponentially changing every domain of our lives.

This isn't just hype. If fifteen years ago I had told you the next decade would give rise to a $20 billion company based on the selfie, you would have asked me, "What's a selfie?" And yet, here we are, watching the valuation of Snap fluctuate at astronomical levels. We underestimated the ability of a photo to shift from a memory device to a means of dynamic, highly emotional communication. As Snap, Inc. founder and CEO Evan Spiegel described it, "Snapchat really has to do with the way photographs have changed. Historically, photos have always been used to save really important memories: major life moments. But today...pictures are being used for talking."[10]

The digital photo isn't the only innovation that demonetized an entire industry. As we continue to demand *more* while being willing to give *less*, companies are having to look with fresh eyes at what their customers are actually willing to pay for, who wants to actually own what, and the impact this has on each and every model of business currently. It is impossible to fully imagine what shape our lives will take when all these technologies emerge and converge.

Blockchain, Bitcoin, and peer-to-peer payments encourage us to connect more directly with one another. With big data, we can now glean insights into markets and behaviors that we never had access to before—again challenging many assumptions about both human behavior and enterprise business models. Additive manufacturing and virtual reality will necessarily

---

10   "What Is Snapchat?" *YouTube*, June 16, 2015.

provide on-demand satisfaction. How do we become better at spotting these changes and burgeoning opportunities? How does this shape current business models and open space for new ones entirely?

THE CALCULUS OF EXPONENTIAL CHANGE

Back to the stat about the 2.5 quintillion bytes of data we create each day: That's about four Eiffel Towers' worth of Blu-ray discs stacked on top of each other. According to a recent NPR story, there are now more transistors that exist on this planet than there are leaves on trees.[11] As my friend and fellow futurist Steve Brown once described it, "The planet is growing a digital nervous system."

We get excited by the potential of technologies such as artificial intelligence, augmented reality, and additive printing, then get disappointed by their slow rate of implementation. Analog businesses rely on linear growth and distribution models. Digital ones—which rely on network adoption and create hordes of data—operate with an entirely different physics. They expand (and contract) exponentially.

There's an ancient Indian legend of an exchange between a mathematician and a king that perfectly illustrates the effect of exponential growth. The king is a chess enthusiast and challenges the mathematician to a game. To incentivize the mathematician, he grants him a reward if he wins. The mathematician requests that the king place a single grain of rice on the first square of the board, then two grains of rice on the second square, and so on, doubling the number of grains on each successive square. The mathematician asks to be paid only the amount of rice on the final square. The king agrees, thinking this a paltry fee. But in the punchline of the story, the king goes bankrupt.

11   "After Moore's Law," *The Economist*, March 12, 2016.

Think of the king's predicament: On square sixteen, he probably still thinks he's made a good deal. On square twenty, perhaps he begins to see his hubris. On square twenty-two, however, he's painfully aware of what a raw deal this really is and the danger this puts his kingdom in.

Where are we on the board? Futurist and entrepreneur Byron Reese believes that, as a society, we could be on day sixty-two of a sixty-four-square chessboard. Let that sink in for a moment.

I believe we are further back on the board than that, but the path seems clear, and as such, deserves a lot more of our attention. Exponential advances are already vastly shifting the playing field all over the world. Recognized as one of the one hundred ideas pioneering change by the World Economic Forum, fintech company ZestMoney in India is using the best of mobile technology, artificial intelligence, and digital banking to disburse credit to customers who need it most in every corner of the country within seconds and without human interference.[12]

The confluence of growing data availability, faster processing power, and cheaper, accessible cloud storage is enabling developments that seem small when they first arrive on the scene but quickly become disruptions that shake the ground under our feet.

SHORT-TERM TO LONG-TERM THINKING

It's often difficult for established enterprises to reprioritize the steps of their approach. Typically, large organizations have conservative boards of directors and legal structures that tether them to their old processes and products. Though most large enterprises were originally formed

---

12 "ZestMoney," *World Economic Forum*, 2020.

around an inspiring mission—to deliver value to customers—corporations have increasingly been forced to focus on growing as much profit as possible for a small pool of demanding, short-term-focused investors. With shareholder pressure to stay profitable across every single quarter, many times these companies encounter resistance to diverting profits into developing innovations that may take longer to seed and recoup.

Validating the Duke study of short-term decision-making, I often hear even visionary CEOs describe with frustration how they feel whipsawed by the quarterly expectations of investors. They feel hamstrung to make the bold decisions necessary for the healthy future of their companies. Yet they are the very people responsible for setting the course of their organizations. How do they find the agency to support and drive innovation in their businesses amidst these pressures?

Global CPG giant Unilever is an encouraging example. During Paul Polman's ten-year tenure as CEO, the company delivered consistent top- and bottom-line growth ahead of market expectation. Committing to a new model of sustainable growth served the needs of its many stakeholders and created excellent returns for its shareholders, delivering a total shareholder return of 290 percent over that period. A key part of their strategy was the move to suspend quarterly reporting, with the belief that "Frequent financial reporting forces executives to think short-term rather than long-term, causing them to put off long-term investment in order to please short-term investors," as one *Inc.* article reported.[13] This is the imperative of new-economy leaders.

---

13 Geoffrey James, "Why Unilever Stopped Issuing Quarterly Reports," *Inc.*, January 23, 2018.

SHAREHOLDERS TO STAKEHOLDERS

As we take a closer look around us, we see the need to explore the impact of business in a much broader way. "Externalities" is the term economists use when they talk about the side effects—or in the positive case, the spillover effects—of a business's operations.[14] They are the impacts that a business has on its broader environment, either directly or indirectly, but is not obliged to pay for or otherwise take into account in its decision-making. This word opens growing questions in a new era of business leadership. What responsibility do enterprises have to consider "externalities?"

As Republican president Calvin Coolidge warned back in the exuberance of the late 1920s:

> *No enterprise can exist for itself alone. It ministers to some great need, it performs some great service, not for itself, but for others; or failing therein, it ceases to be profitable and ceases to exist.*

How will our sense of responsibility shift as an increasingly empowered civil society takes stock of the impacts of massive industrial growth and what is possible with potent new technologies—and thus continues to shine a bright spotlight on corporate decision-making?

And what are the boundaries? On the one hand, we want to hold someone responsible for societal assaults we're all paying increasing attention to, such as rising rates of obesity, inequality, anxiety, addiction, rising sea levels, forest fires, and more. But this also raises complex questions

---

14 Christopher Meyer and Julia Kirby, "The Big Idea: Leadership in the Age of Transparency," *Harvard Business Review*, April 2010.

around what is fair to hold enterprise leaders accountable for.[15] What constitutes a "responsible corporation" in an era of shifting sensibilities and capabilities?

In his 2019 letter to fellow CEOs, BlackRock's Larry Fink offered this perspective:

> As divisions continue to deepen, companies must demonstrate their commitment to the countries, regions, and communities where they operate, particularly on issues central to the world's future prosperity. Companies cannot solve every issue of public importance, but there are many—from retirement to infrastructure to preparing workers for the jobs of the future—that cannot be solved without corporate leadership.[16]

Larry is not alone in his perspective. A survey by Deloitte highlighted that 63 percent of millennial workers believe that the primary purpose of businesses should be improving society versus generating profit.[17]

One thing is clear: it is no longer enough for organizations to consider shareholders alone. Leaders need to regard the needs of *stakeholders* as they make decisions, which includes any person who is impacted by an organization's choices, including customers, communities, suppliers, partners, and even the environment.

In his book, *Conscious Capitalism*, John Mackey describes how businesses have the capacity to impact the societies in which they operate:

---

15 Michael Schrage, "Embracing Externalities Is the Road to Hell," *Harvard Business Review*, April 21, 2010.

16 Larry Fink, "Profit and Purpose," *BlackRock*, 2019.

17 "The Deloitte Global Millennial Survey 2019," *Deloitte*, 2019.

We believe that business is good because it creates value. It is ethical because it is based on voluntary exchange; it is noble because it can elevate our existence, and it is heroic because it lifts people out of poverty and creates prosperity.[18]

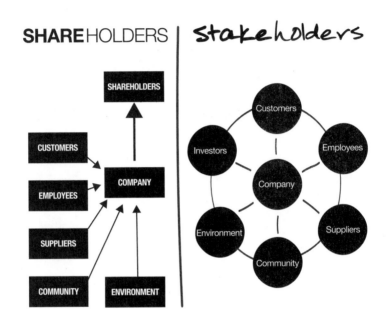

I would submit that the idea of a "responsible corporation" is as simple as this: the public regards a company as responsible when they perceive that it is steadily internalizing externalities—prioritizing its ability to measure and positively manage its impacts on society.

Conversely, when the public perceives that a company is producing an externality that it could take greater responsibility for—but isn't—stakeholders move into action. We boycott, we protest, we create new regulations

18 John Mackey and Raj Sisodia, *Conscious Capitalism* (Brighton: Harvard Business Review Press, 2014).

and write new laws. As the quote from President Calvin Coolidge above reminds us, this isn't new thinking. We have always rewarded the companies we think are holding us well, and we have found ways to punish the ones that aren't. The difference now is that, in the face of extreme breakdowns, our radar is more sensitive. And in our hyper-connected world, we have infinitely more ways to make our views and values known.

As we continue, we'll see how digital advances create a need for even greater responsibility. For instance, employees of Salesforce, Microsoft, Amazon, and Google have recognized the impact and potential damage that exponential technologies could create if used for discrimination and persecution—an issue that raises bigger questions about how to apply these technologies to shape an inclusive, thriving, and humane future rather than a divisive, oppressive one. Then there's CVS's willingness to forgo potential profits to align more fully with their purpose, which we'll hear more about in upcoming chapters. Such actions cause us to wonder about the role of business in a shifting society and what will be the shape (or maybe even need) of capitalism ahead.

REDRESSING SYSTEMIC INJUSTICES

"While we are all in the same storm, we are not all in the same-sized boat." This was the way our school superintendent compassionately framed things as he opened a Zoom meeting in July to explain the back-to-school plan of the moment. The pandemic has certainly made this truth much more visible and rapidly widened an already growing gap. We are collectively learning to appreciate a challenging reality: that access to quality medical care, healthy food, safe jobs, technology-savvy schools, and even clear air is not evenly distributed by race or ethnicity. Women around the world are also paying a steep economic price as childcare and in-person schooling are closed.

These systemic biases in access, opportunity, and justice have existed for a very long time. That which was intentionally designed into our systems hundreds or even thousands of years ago continues to permeate our lives and social fabric today: in everything from law enforcement and criminal justice; to college admissions and access to capital to start or fund a business; to simply being able to get, and then hold, a job...especially while raising a family. As Darren Walker, president of the Ford Foundation, put it in a recent *New York Times* op-ed:

> *Inequality in America was not born of the market's invisible hand. It was not some unavoidable destiny. It was created by the hands and sustained effort of people who engineered benefits for themselves, to the detriment of everyone else. American inequality was decades in the making, one expensive lobbyist and policy change at a time. It will take a concerted effort to reverse all of this, and to remake America in the process.*[19]

What is new is the awakening of those in positions of privilege to stories like the Tulsa massacre in 1921, the rampant sexual abuse across industry sectors, and the long-biased aspects of our market economy that permeate business today.

The #MeToo and #TimesUp campaigns on behalf of women and #BlackLivesMatter movements have raised attention across the globe, with sympathetic marches from Brazil and Syria to Paris and Australia—and it seems these are contributing to big shifts in the way we now consider our economic opportunities and social mobility.

In early 2020, the Pew Research Center did a survey showing that in the U.S., we are rapidly shifting our core belief in what it takes to achieve

---

19   Darren Walker, "Inequality and Our Capitalist System," *New York Times*, July 25, 2020.

financial success.[20] As recently as 2017, a similar survey showed people were pretty evenly split, with 45 percent believing that hard work drove financial rewards, 43 percent believing that wealth was a result of having more advantages than others, and 12 percent unsure. Yet by January 2020 (before the pandemic hit the U.S.), only 33 percent believed being rich was a result of hard work, with nearly double (65 percent) now believing that one was rich because "they have had more advantages in life than most other people." Almost no one was unsure how they felt this round.

So, as we wake up, how do we channel our frustration and anger into proactive steps ahead? Author James Baldwin reminded us, "Not everything that is faced can be changed, but nothing can be changed until it is faced."

In the U.S., these shifts in empathy and understanding will hopefully help level the playing field with universal childcare and paid family leave (the U.S. is the only country among forty-one nations that does not mandate any paid leave for new parents, according to data compiled by the Organisation for Economic Co-operation and Development).[21] Personally, I also hope this finally makes possible the passing of a federal amendment protecting the rights of women in the Constitution, which it astonishingly still does not.

Paramount is addressing an already alarming disparity in access to technology and education—both in the U.S. and around the world, as this could reverberate for generations to come. Exponential growth is not always positive.

There are more inclusive ways to redistribute productivity, such as a guaranteed income or digital dividends for our data. Following the lead

---

20 Robin Moriarty, "Is a Fundamental Culture Shift Happening?" *Forbes*, April 21, 2020.
21 "PF2.1. Parental Leave Systems," *Organisation for Economic Co-operation" and Development Family Database*, August 2019.

of Sweden and other curious countries such as France, Canada, and Mexico, Hawaii has proposed a post-pandemic "feminist recovery plan" that includes a variety of recommendations, including no cuts to funding for domestic violence services and shifting the state's reliance away from the tourism industry that offered women precarious, low-paid jobs.[22] Meanwhile, Massachusetts is considering a bill that would invest nearly $1 billion in programs and services to address health, education, and economic disparities in communities of color. Many more private and public efforts are surfacing to ensure much more access to funding for anyone with the gumption to start a business or advance a new technology solution.

The pandemic has shaken us awake in some very significant ways, but as these five transformative shifts point out, more changes are definitely ahead.

THE END OF LEADER*SHIP*

By now, you can appreciate how fast the future is taking a radically new shape. Which is why we need an equally new way to describe or label how to navigate our work ahead. To become a successful "bionic company"— capable of integrating people and technology—Boston Consulting Group puts it this way: "In order to survive, thrive and compete successfully, companies now have only two years (or less) to get to where they might otherwise have hoped to be in five. Companies require a new kind of leadership and significant leap beyond the old paradigms."[23]

---

22 Alisha Haridasani Gupta, "What Do Sweden and Mexico Have in Common? A Feminist Foreign Policy," *The New York Times*, July 28, 2020.

23 Diana Dosik, Vikram Bhalla, and Allison Bailey, "A Lot Will Change—So Must Leadership," *Boston Consulting Group*, July 31, 2020.

As the 2010 *Wall Street Journal* article "The End of Management" anticipated, the management practices we have historically used to lead organizations are no longer holding up:

> *The reasons for this are clear enough. Corporations are bureaucracies
> and managers are bureaucrats. Their fundamental tendency is toward
> self-perpetuation. They are, almost by definition, resistant to change. They
> were designed and tasked, not with reinforcing market forces, but with
> supplanting and even resisting the market.*[24]

The article points out that twentieth-century success was achieved by
companies that developed the techniques required for running large corporations, and management structures and hierarchies were central to
those operations:

> *Corporations, whose leaders portray themselves as champions of the
> free market, were in fact created to circumvent that market. They were
> an answer to the challenge of organizing thousands of people in different
> places and with different skills to perform large and complex tasks, like
> building automobiles or providing nationwide telephone service.*

Said another way, twentieth-century organizations—both for-profit and
not-for-profit—were built to extract value at scale as efficiently as possible. But the authors note that in the twenty-first century, "Modern management is nearing its existential moment." The evidence is mounting.
From top to bottom, the shape of our work continues to shift, creating
new challenges for leaders at all levels of an organization. This is evidenced by:

---

24 Alan Murray, "The End of Management," *The Wall Street Journal*, August 21, 2010.

- **Decreased relevance.** A corporate longevity forecast conducted by Innosight details how the life span of a company on the S&P 500 narrowed from thirty-three years in 1964 to twenty-four years by 2016, and at the current churn rate they estimate that about half of all S&P 500 companies will be replaced over the next ten years.[25] According to Boston Consulting Group (BCG), the odds of failure are increasing. Released in January 2020, just as the pandemic emerged, their study forecast that one out of three public companies will cease to exist in their current form over the next five years—a rate six times higher than forty years ago.[26] Meanwhile, a Havas Meaningful Brands survey conducted across 1,800 brands in thirty-one markets with 350,000 respondents discovered that 90 percent of consumers think that the content brands serve up is completely meaningless, and more alarmingly, 77 percent couldn't care less if brands disappeared altogether.[27]

- **New roles.** The onset of digital disruption—and the ensuing shorter business cycles—is dramatically shifting the roles and tenures of C-suite executives across the board. The median tenure for CEOs at large-cap (S&P 500) companies dropped a full year between 2013 (six years) and 2017 (only five years).[28] The BCG study reports that only 44 percent of today's industry leaders have held their position for at least five years, down from 77 percent fifty years ago.[29] Even boards of directors are no longer immune to the disruptive forces of technology—which now require them to work more intensively

25 Scott D. Anthony et al., "2018 Corporate Longevity Forecast: Creative Destruction Is Accelerating," *Innosight*, 2018.

26 "How to Thrive in the 2020s," *BCG*, 2020.

27 Sulaiman Beg, "Havas Group's Maria Garrido Shares the Highlights of the 2019 Meaningful Brands Study and Why Being Meaningful Is Good for Business," *Havas*, February 26, 2019.

28 Dan Marcec, "CEO Tenure Rates," *Harvard Law School Forum on Corporate Governance and Financial Regulation*, February 12, 2018.

29 "How to Thrive in the 2020s," *BCG*, 2020.

beyond the fiduciary duties expected in the past to include a focus on strategy, ethical considerations, and a broad range of other tasks.

- **Polarizing profitability.** Now that the game is changing and we are required to create value in more dynamic, personalized, and interconnected ways, performance is suffering. The January BCG report also points out that the gap between winners and losers is growing, with the profitability spread between top and bottom quartile companies nearly doubling over the last thirty years.[30] As we all know by now, none of this is slowing down, which requires that we dramatically rethink our approach toward leading.

IT IS TIME FOR LEADER*ING*

When my friend Peter Vander Auwera casually introduced this word "Leadering" to me, I immediately thought how well it captured the way I had been approaching my strategic work and learning to shape stronger, more engaged, and adaptive teams—ones that could move with a sense of fluidity, connection, and empowerment to meet the needs of the future.

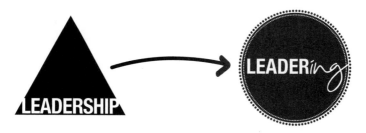

(n): a static, closed, hierarchical, organizational approach designed to scale efficiently for consistent short-term growth

(v): cultivating a dynamic, adaptive, caring, inclusive mindset which supports continuous innovation for long-term sustainable value

---

30 "How to Thrive in the 2020s," *Boston Consulting Group*, 2020.

Leadering embraces the extraordinary potential in change, the possibilities in ambiguity, and the insights in complexity. As we strive to adapt to a new and constantly moving future, we will be required to shift the way we think of leadership: from a role of control, mastery, and authority (*leadership*) to actions that are responsive, innovative, caring, and audacious (*Leadering*). Leadership is built on yesterday. Leadering confidently and thoughtfully anticipates tomorrow.

It begins by broadening the view through which we approach our work.

THREE LENSES ON THE FUTURE

Building a better "next" requires that we broaden our perspectives. We often pick up a book like this to be more effective professionals (as immediately as possible, we hope!). But the reality is that we are also humans going through extraordinary change—as people, parents, daughters, sons, and community stewards, as well as members of society and planetary citizens. This requires a new mindset in which we consider the impact of significant changes through three different yet interconnected lenses:

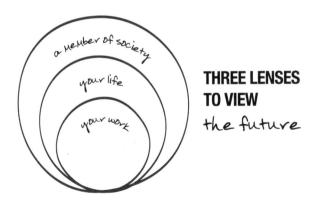

Importantly, not only are these additional dimensions becoming more visible, but the boundaries between them are becoming more porous. Our professional decisions have a tremendous impact on our lives, as well as the lives of those around us, in the present and across time.

Not surprisingly, what makes wrapping our arms around the future so daunting are the changes in speed, scale, *and* scope simultaneously. We have to respond faster, with increasing attention to the impact of our actions and our values, on a much wider group of stakeholders. So as everything is up for reinvention and redesign, what replaces yesterday's playbook? How do we navigate frequently changing terrain?

A TWO-QUESTION COMPASS

When we are willing to trade a static instruction manual (metaphorically and strategically speaking) for a dynamic compass, we have more relevant intel with which to explore a dawning horizon. It's why I emphatically believe the playbook is dead. In the twenty-first century, we need a compass. One that is calibrated by continually asking these two pivotal questions:

What does the future need and expect from us? + What are we each in a unique position to contribute to it?

These two questions have guided my strategy and innovation work for over a decade and opened new, previously unseen opportunities to put organizations on a more robust and energizing path.

Disarmingly simple, these apply to us as individuals, as team members, as organizations, as industries, and even as nations. They provide valuable insights because we each bring a unique collection of experiences, curiosities, equities, resources, and perspectives to bear in answering them.

Our answers allow us to hone our particular strengths and advantages. By focusing on our unique contributions, it's possible to step into the future with more motivation to overcome obstacles. And by checking in often, we can adjust our steps to ensure we are heading toward the right destination. These questions allow us to shift the outlook on the future from one of *overwhelm* to one of *opportunity*.

Many years ago, my strategic team was invited to help Nestlé Frozen Foods address the question "How can we get consumers to buy more frozen food?" We all quickly realized we needed more relevant questions to drive the change they wanted to see. As data showed that shopper tastes were fragmenting, we instead asked "How can we make the manufacturing process leaner so we can test new products faster and be more responsive?"

But that wasn't the only external shift impacting this business. After decades of "Big Food" growth, people were becoming savvier about nutrition needs, while bipolar income splits illuminated that wealthier and younger shoppers now wanted not only convenient, well-priced meals but also "clean," fresh, healthy food they could really trust. As a global leader in frozen food, it became clear the unique opportunity, then, for Nestlé was in asking this guiding question: "How can we rebuild trust in industrial food?" This purpose-led reframing opened many new possibilities for this business unit as they enthusiastically reconsidered all processes and approaches to better meeting the needs of this discerning shopper.

Disruption is happening all around us. Who could have imagined five years ago that cigarette manufacturer Philip Morris would become a life insurance company[31] or that fast-food White Castle burgers and KFC chicken would proudly feature plant-based versions of both meats? That Facebook

---

31 "Philip Morris International Is Now in the Insurance Business," *Sustainable Brands*, 2019.

would try to launch their own currency?[32] Or that a global virus would be able to stop us all in our tracks?

There is an abundant opportunity that arises from innovation, disruption, and change. As we have been discussing, *never* has this been more important. The question now is how to bravely answer the call.

CROSSING THE LIMINAL GAP

Years before Apple launched the first iPhone, Nokia showed a prototype phone with a color touch screen and the ability to play games and shop online. But they were unable to actually bring it to market, spending long months "strategizing" and mired in internal politics, leading to a billion-dollar loss in the second quarter of 2012—and the elimination of over ten thousand jobs that year.[33] I remember exactly where I was when I read this news story and how frustrated I felt that rather than protect shareholders and employees by acting, Nokia had actually put both at risk by failing to move forward. While they had access to the same materials and technologies as Apple to advance their projects, Nokia executives did not have a North Star—a clear vision of their purpose—that allowed them to let go of their trusted products and processes and build something new. Apple, by contrast, and with due consideration, was willing to cannibalize some of their current products to develop their next-generation offerings. And as we all now know, they went on to become one of the highest-valued companies in the world.

When we envision the shift between one economic era and another, we can see a gap form as old systems are breaking down and new systems are

---

32 Cale Guthrie Weissman, "Western Union Stock Tanks after Facebook Unveils Libra Cryptocurrency," *Fast Company*, June 18, 2019.

33 Seth Weintraub, "Collapsing Nokia May Have Had Apple-Like Hardware in Development in the 90s," *9to5Mac*, July 19, 2012.

yet to be created. I describe this as the "liminal gap:" the space between now and next; between our present ways of operating and what the future needs; and even between me, the leader, and you, my potential collaborator.

This term was inspired by Nora Bateson, a filmmaker, writer, educator, and president of the International Bateson Institute. In Nora's view, leadership isn't exercised across hierarchies; it happens between individuals, in the specific context of each relationship.[34] By recognizing this liminal space between where we came from in the past and what we must build next, we can create the practices we need to cross the gap.

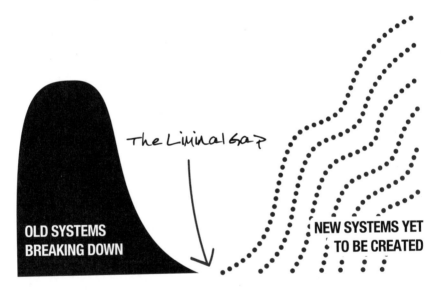

There are well-told examples of companies that failed to recognize the next opportunities and fell into the liminal gap. At its peak, BlackBerry owned over 50 percent of the U.S. and 20 percent of the global smartphone market, selling over fifty million devices per year. But when the iPhone launched, BlackBerry leadership dismissed the touchscreen, insisting

---

34 Nora Bateson, "Liminal Leadership," *Kosmos*, 2017.

that consumers wouldn't give up their keyboards.[35] We all know how that ended. Then there's the classic story of Blockbuster arrogantly declining to buy Netflix, even when presented with the opportunity more than once. Blockbuster went bankrupt in 2010, and Netflix is now worth more than ExxonMobil; valued at $196 billion, it is more than thirty-nine times what Blockbuster was worth at its peak.[36]

The pressure is on to keep up with new innovations. And fortunately, there is a growing list of *encouraging* stories that demonstrate how.

Take shipping giant Maersk. In a digital world, a company like Maersk isn't just competing with other shipping companies; they are actually defending against other logistics leaders, such as Uber. Despite their colossal size, Maersk is finding new ways to navigate through key technological shifts, using artificial intelligence to slash their fuel costs,[37] and build a blockchain-enabled digital shipping platform called TradeLens that provides supply chain visibility in real time.[38] Maersk now accounts for more than half of the world's ocean container cargo.

In May of 2019, Salesforce unveiled a new blockchain platform that extends the power of customer relationship management (CRM), helping users build and maintain complex blockchain networks, apps, and smart contracts, with simple drag-and-drop programming.[39] Gartner predicts that

---

35 Vlad Savov, "BlackBerry's Success Led to its Failure," *The Verge*, September 30, 2016.

36 Greg Satell, "A Look Back at Why Blockbuster Really Failed and Why It Didn't Have To," *Forbes*, September 5, 2014.

37 Leonora Beck, "Maersk to Slash Its Fuel Bill Using Artificial Intelligence," *ShippingWatch*, March 7, 2019.

38 "Hapag-Lloyd and ONE Join Maersk Blockchain Platform," *The Maritime Executive*, July 2, 2019.

39 Anna Baydakova, "Cloud Giant Salesforce Unveils First Blockchain Product for Business," *Coindesk*, May 29, 2019.

blockchain solutions will result in $176 billion in added business value for companies by 2025, and $3.1 trillion by 2030.[40]

There is, however, a growing lag between those who are building the new... and the rest sorting through how to adapt to it. Some leaders have already been taking on big challenges like the ethics of AI,[41] sustainable supply chains, and having a drone deliver lunch, putting them firmly ahead of the curve. In an exponential world, enterprises that continue to dive into new learning rather than snapping back to "normal" will cultivate the insight and the data that will pull them further ahead, making it even more difficult for second- and third-wave players to catch up.

Our work, then, is to learn to confidently navigate the space between the now and the next; to boldly make the leap between the old systems, practices, and mindsets of the industrial age; to move toward the dynamic, collaborative potential that the digital future offers.

DIVING DEEPER
NORA BATESON ON CONTEXTUAL RELATIONSHIPS

Nora Bateson is president of the International Bateson Institute, a Sweden-based social-benefit group founded by her father and grandfather. The institute's work is based on the question "How can we improve our perception of the complexity we live within, so we may improve our interaction with the world?"

---

40 Bianca Granetto, Rajesh Kandaswamy, John-David Lovelock, and Martin Reynolds, "Forecast: Blockchain Business Value, Worldwide, 2017-2030," *Gartner Research*, March 2, 2017.

41 S. A. Applin, "Everyone's Talking about Ethics in AI. Here's What They're Missing," *Fast Company*, June 14, 2019.

As an economist, humanist, environmentalist, and philosopher, Nora Bateson seeks to understand the changing role of leadership through a holistic lens. To lead effectively, we must collect data about how our organizations are operating—but more importantly, we must understand the *contextual relationships* of that data.

Data, Nora argues, doesn't exist outside of the context in which it was created. She calls contextualized data *warm data*. We've been trained, however, to look at cold, hard "facts": the scientific method has encouraged us to think that a finding is only worth paying attention to if we can isolate and validate it outside its original context. In reality, our ability to create a specific effect or glean new insights is sometimes very dependent upon the circumstances in which something happened. With this in mind, Nora argues, we have to think about how we gather and use data in a holistic and relational way.

When we treat data as discrete and independent from the environment in which it was gathered, we end up solving one problem, only to inadvertently create many more. Similarly, companies are used to allopathic solutions that fix one discrete piece of a problem without recognizing the implications of other parts of the system.

A holistic approach looks at the entire system to understand where the breakdowns exist and how relationships connect disparate elements to one another. This is a difficult concept for a company to grasp when they are entrenched in more mechanical processes. But when we pay attention to the relational elements of our systems, we can get greater insights into the next right move to make. Appreciating these interdependencies is actually the gift of complexity.

Nora calls these relational connections the "liminal" spaces, where individual relationships influence what happens in the greater system.

> Whatever leadership used to be—it used to be. Now, it has to be something different. Now, we all have to be more than we were. Leadership models come in many flavors. Strategic leadership, leadership from behind, organizational, innovative, creative leadership, collective leadership, transformational leadership, cross-cultural leadership, team leadership—the list goes on. But the kind of leadership that I want to explore may not be identifiable as leadership at all. I am interested in a kind of mutually alert care and attention to the wellbeing of all people and ecological systems. This kind of leadership cannot be found in individuals; rather, it is found between them. It cannot be found in organizations, nations, religions, or institutions; rather, it is found between them.
>
> —Nora Bateson[42]

THE BIG SHIFT…IN MINDSET

Radical transformation isn't solely a technology quest. Rather, it's a very human call to collaborate better within our organizations and with the communities and environments in which they exist. As we mentioned

---

42 Nora Bateson, "Liminal Leadership," *Kosmos*, 2017.

earlier, we don't need to change *what* we think, as much as change *how* we think. The acute disruption we are facing and will continue to face in our work and personal lives demands a similar shift in our way of thinking about these challenges. Meaning the "big shift" ahead is not only one of transforming economic models to meet societal expectations, but also one that requires a big shift in leadership—to a *Leadering* mindset that is dynamic, caring, inclusive, and focused on supporting constant innovation to create sustainable value.

Leadering means adopting an active posture:

- Primed to embrace opportunities among growing complexity
- That feels safer challenging the status quo and old assumptions than not
- That can comfortably handle learning and leading simultaneously
- That empowers and incentivizes individual action in service of overall success
- Able to champion and reward exploration by appreciating the greater risks of not trying
- That considers the needs of a wide range of stakeholders versus prioritizing only investors/shareholders
- That stands for long-term impacts rather than contorting to hit unrealistic quarterly targets
- That appreciates the advantages of mutually beneficial collaborations rather than relying on autonomy and silos
- That values and prioritizes diverse thinking and strives for equitable distribution
- That understands the danger of applying outdated goals and yardsticks to exponential technologies
- That sees we have to address the whole system (not just a part) in order to drive successful, long-lasting change and deliver value

- That believes it is *our* responsibility to build a human-centered, safe future in which we all thrive

This list may seem daunting or idealistic. How can we actually get to this new way of thinking, reacting, and behaving?

I believe there is a path. As we will see, there are all kinds of organizations and individuals, including the U.S. military, who inspire us with the bold, audacious leaps they are making and the ways they are rethinking their organizations, approaches, and even roles.

In order to navigate differently, however, we need to first learn to think differently. It begins with cultivating a sense of wonder that is more compelling than our resistance to change.

CHAPTER TWO

Wonder (versus Resist)

"You can't trust your judgment if your imagination is out of focus."

—Mark Twain, American writer, publisher, and entrepreneur

As a futurist sharing my perspectives on what's to come, I have been told *emphatically* over the years that Americans would never consider a concept like universal basic income, that an AI algorithm will never replace a doctor...and that a CEO would never tweet. It is just not easy to imagine how a new advance could really shake things up.

This resistance to new ideas, however, is becoming an issue, as it has been estimated that 90 percent of the world's information has been created in just the last two years. Think about the implications of that statistic. Embracing new information with wonder versus resistance opens us up to see the opportunities, advantages, and sometimes even the threats that change makes possible. Rather than reactively responding with "That will never happen," imagine if instead we instinctively wondered, "What if?" For example, what if...

- You could visit an unstaffed kiosk at the mall to have an illness diagnosed by AI?
- You could print a perfectly optimized nutritious meal for each member of your family?
- You could have your prescriptions (or Slurpee) delivered to your door across any terrain within an hour?
- You could embed a small chip in your hand that would eliminate the need to ever carry a wallet, an ID card, or a building keycard?
- You could work just five hours a day for a full-time paycheck?

Behind each of these questions is a solution that is in development at the time of this writing. As quickly as new capabilities are taking shape, even these cutting-edge innovations could be old news by the time you're reading this paragraph, but here is what's in development at the moment:

- In China, healthcare platform Ping An Good Doctor unveiled its first staff-less medical "One Minute Clinic" and digital pharmacy at the Wuzhen World Internet Conference in 2018. You can simply sit in what looks just like a photo booth to receive an AI-enabled diagnosis, then be given access to whichever of the one hundred common medicines are available safely (we presume) through the kiosk vending portal.[1]

- The wonderfully named Foodini food printer has been on the market since 2016. And for the past several years, the U.S. Army has been experimenting with ways to create highly tailored rations that meet a soldier's real-time nutritional needs and preferences.[2] Using these facts to expand our imaginations further, at a future-forward ideation session, a team of food executives envisioned one day being able to use a food printer at home to print an Oreo cookie—making us further wonder whether the branded recipe could be transmitted cryptographically directly to the smart machine?

- As of this writing, Walgreens has signed up with Wing, the new drone delivery service owned by Alphabet and granted FAA approval in 2019, to begin home delivery trials in Virginia.[3] And in Reno, Nevada, on July 10, 2019, 7-Eleven partnered with privately held company Flirtey to deliver the first drone meal delivery, even beating Amazon to the punch.[4]

---

1   Dean Koh, "Ping An Good Doctor Launches Commercial Operation of One-Minute Clinics in China," *Mobi Health News*, January 7, 2019.

2   Diana Macovei, "Exploration of 3D Food Printing and Its Application for Tailored Military Rations—Presented by Mary Scerra, U.S. Army Natick Soldier Research," *3D Food Printing Conference*, 2018.

3   "Walgreens Will Be First Retailer in U.S. to Test On-Demand Drone Delivery Service with Wing," *Walgreens*, September 19, 2019.

4   Lora Kolodny, "7-Eleven Delivers by Drone in Reno Including, Yes, Slurpees," *TechCrunch*, July 16, 2016.

- A company in Sweden has been incentivizing its employees to micro-chip their hands in order to make their work lives more convenient, leading to a surge of chipping parties in Sweden, and now, due to a curious American business owner, also in Wisconsin.[5]

- A small German technology firm recently implemented an eight o'clock in the morning to one'clock in the afternoon workday for its full-time staff,[6] while Microsoft has been experimenting with a four-day workweek in Japan, seeing lifts in productivity of 40 percent.[7]

Beyond the science-fiction value of these headlines, it is fascinating to stop for a moment to consider what is driving these innovations and experiments—and what their implications could be: What technologies make this possible now? How will these recalibrate expectations for your stakeholders? What are the external impacts they could have? How could this create a new opportunity for you?

Just these few stories raise a myriad of questions around new business models, digital revenue streams, intellectual property, ethical and cyber-security concerns, and the growing confusion about the kinds of skills that will be needed and eliminated. Let's take the microchipping story, as one example, and unpack all the things it makes me wonder.

First, note the strong desire for convenience, frictionless transactions, and reduced complexity that would encourage someone to opt in to become a

---

5   Jeff Baenen, "Wisconsin Company Holds 'Chip Party' to Microchip Workers," *Chicago Tribune*, August 2, 2017.
6   Cal Newport, "5-Hour Workdays? 4-Day Workweeks? Yes, Please," *The New York Times*, November 6, 2019.
7   Bill Chappell, "4-Day Workweek Boosted Workers' Productivity by 40 Percent, Microsoft Japan Says," *All Things Considered*, November 4, 2019.

cyborg. Second, this commitment certainly raises questions about the ethical and cybersecurity risks associated with a presumably always-on tracking practice. Not surprisingly, labor unions are not big fans of this move, as they see it as an invasive form of employee monitoring versus a liberating opportunity for worker convenience. Most intriguing, it makes the discussion of how likely we are to accept digital implants very real, raising even more questions about when and how such a decision should be made.

Assuming we do someday find this enhancement valuable and safe, will implanting microchips be something we decide individually as we become adults, or will it be a consideration at childbirth, the same way vaccination and circumcision decisions are made currently in the U.S.? And what if one nation decides it's an ethical practice and one does not (similar to cell engineering or cloning advances)—how does that change global competitiveness?

Even one headline like this creates a cascading list of new things to be curious about. Taken together, this small sampling of emerging innovations stands as a gale-force warning that current approaches are not likely to hold up under the winds of new demands. They should have us all wondering the implications of "What if?" and "How fast?"

ONE PERCENT OF THE WAY IN

I've often wondered: If we were standing in Florence at the front end of the Renaissance, would we recognize the movement taking shape as art, politics, immigration, economics, science, and philanthropy converged to propel Europe out of the Dark Ages?

At the dawn of 2020, when we spoke with those actually building the applications of tomorrow and asked how far into this new era we were, almost universally the reply was, "Only 1 percent." Navigating the pandemic has certainly accelerated our appreciation for the digital tools currently available, but we have yet to see the explosion of innovation this period will no doubt inspire. Imagine, then, if we're only around 1 percent of the way into the First Productivity Revolution, where will we be ten years from now? How about fifty?

The fascinating part is that things can shift very quickly, as we have witnessed before. *New York Times* financial columnist and bestselling author Thomas Friedman documented how symbiotic technologies emerged in 2007. Observing the sudden and significant wave in cultural shifts this ushered in, he wondered, "What the hell happened in 2007?" Digging in, he found that in just this *one* year:

- The first iPhone was launched.
- Facebook opened from a closed student network to anyone with an email address.
- One-year-old Amazon Web Services got traction.
- The internet crossed one billion users, and the API (application programming interface) market was created as microservices came into being and apps took off.
- In 2007, Hadoop, "the most important software you have never heard of" according to Thomas, began expanding the ability of any company to store and analyze enormous amounts of unstructured data. This helped enable both big data and cloud computing. Indeed, "the cloud" really took off in 2007.
- The cost of making solar panels began to decline sharply in that year. As did the cost to sequence the genome.
- Airbnb was conceived in 2007.
- GitHub, now the world's largest open-source software-sharing library, was opened in 2007 (and has recently been purchased by Microsoft).

- The Kindle kicked off the e-book revolution.
- Microfinancing took off when two-year-old Kiva.org caught fire.
- Google introduced Android.
- And in 2007 IBM started Watson, the world's first cognitive computer.

As all of these innovations advanced and their impacts converged, entirely new possibilities and new power took shape. As Thomas summed:

> *What happened around 2007 was that connectivity and computing got so fast, cheap, ubiquitous, and leveraged that they changed three forms of power—in really differentiated ways—all at once: The power of one, the power of machines and the power of ideas.*[8]

Our first smartphones changed our concept of what could be accomplished in the palms of our hands. Once we understood what an "app" was, we could begin to appreciate the possibilities for "software as a service." Since then, Google Maps has changed the way we get around the world. Square has enabled anyone to become an instant credit-card-accepting retailer. Banking has been disrupted by Venmo; music by Spotify; dating by Tinder; hospitality by Airbnb; communications by WhatsApp, WeChat, and FaceTime; transportation by Uber and Lyft—the list goes on. Daily life has been reconstructed by Zoom, new functionality available on our phones continues to shape entirely new business models, and rapid changes in consumer behaviors have simultaneously eroded—and created—billions of dollars of value.

We arguably didn't pay enough attention to the giant shifts that took place that year because the recession hit hard in 2008. It took several years for businesses to realize their old operating systems were losing relevance and

8   Thomas Friedman, "Why the World Changed in 2007," *Today*, November 21, 2016.

would not hold in this new normal. Though it all makes sense when you look back, it is so very difficult to imagine what is possible as we look ahead. As Bill Gates once said, "Most people overestimate what they can do in one year and underestimate what they can do in ten years."

THE TEN TECHNOLOGIES RESHAPING EVERYTHING

Digital technologies are the major forces that will shape the 1PR. This also means they evoke pivotal strategic questions. To awaken your sense of wonder and fuel your imagination, here is a very quick overview of the emergent tools shaping our society in the years ahead: what they are, why they matter, and where they could take us in the next five to ten years. [*Note: market size estimates are offered here to promote curiosity versus comparative business modeling, as they do not all come from the same source.*]

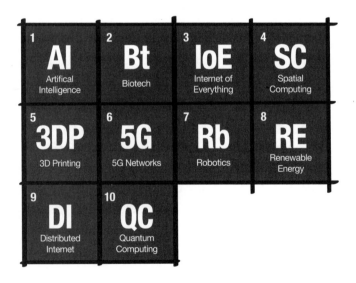

ARTIFICIAL INTELLIGENCE

AI—which, unless noted, is used in this writing as a blanket term that includes machine learning, natural language processing, and augmented and cognitive computing—is expected to be as ubiquitous and integrated into the twenty-first century as electricity was in the twentieth century. Early adopters of AI are already achieving significant benefits, including increased efficiency, cost reduction, predictability, improved customer experience, and new paths to data-driven revenue growth. The AI market is estimated to grow to a $390.9 billion industry by 2025,[9] as it is quickly becoming the foundational technology for delivering the hopes of responsive manufacturing, autonomous vehicles, precision medicine, personalized retail, and so much more.

Consider how the internet launched us into a new era as we pulled out of the 2000 recession and how mobile and social technologies did the same in 2008. Even greater potential exists with AI in a post-COVID recovery, yet reportedly, as of now, only 23 percent of businesses have incorporated AI into their processes and product or service offerings.[10] How and when will you feel it is time to jump into the AI-enabled future?

The abundance of possible applications of AI raises a long list of questions around ethical use, privacy, bias, and "explainability" (meaning, can a learning algorithm explain how it got to its answer?). Is your enterprise prepared to address worries about job security and trustworthiness? What will it take to break through organizational silos in order to successfully adopt AI solutions?

---

9 "Artificial Intelligence Market Size Worth $390.9 Billion by 2025," *Grand View Research*, December 2019.

10 "65+ Statistics about Artificial Intelligence," *Zoominfo*, October 24, 2019.

BIOTECHNOLOGY

Broadly defined, biotechnology uses living systems and microorganisms to develop or make products. Innovations such as growing human organs, vertical farming, and plant-based meat are still so new, but the global biotechnology market is set to exceed $775 billion by 2024, according to a new research report by Global Market Insights.[11]

Provocatively, the market growth of inexpensive, high-quality, tasty modern food, designed using "food-as-software" technology—in which eaters download microorganism designs, protein recipes, and molecular cookbooks from global databases to create foods based on their precise specifications—is poised to create a million new jobs and grow to $1 trillion annually by 2035. And it becomes part of the solution for feeding what could be as many as ten billion people on the planet at that point.[12] While food fads come and go, there has not been this kind of shift in the food industry since the introduction of refrigeration.

It's not surprising, then, that the industry itself is wrestling with a whole new set of questions, from whether these new products should be labeled "meat" to whether they should be sold next to animal proteins or beside vegetables? If food can literally be reinvented and printed, what are the implications for medicines? And for manufacturing anything, for that matter?

THE INTERNET OF EVERYTHING (IOE)

Digital sensors are becoming so small, powerful, and cheap that we will be tempted to embed them in everything. The "smart devices" market is

---

11 "$775 Billion by 2024: Biotechnology Market Set for Rapid Growth," *MarketWatch*, February 25, 2019.
12 "New Report: Major Disruption in Food and Agriculture in Next Decade," *RethinkX*, 2019.

anticipated to reach $1.1 trillion by 2026,[13] and a Gartner report anticipates that there will be twenty-five billion connected things by 2025.[14] We are rapidly advancing to a world in which literally everything will be intelligent and linked in real time, with or without a human involved. This gathering of data and the networks emerging to synchronize this learning are paving the way for increasingly automated responses to the world around us, allowing us to be more self-regulated and externally monitored at the same time.

From window shades suddenly closing on a sunny afternoon, to medicine cabinets that see a pattern of illness forming and pre-order medicine, to toothbrushes that automatically book an appointment with a dentist when they sense it's time, our relationship with our surroundings will be completely different. It will impact every aspect of our business systems and practices...and our relationships with others.

Again, this raises questions about privacy, cybersecurity, and how we handle insurance. As we become more reliant on algorithms and ambient technology for guidance, can we begin to imagine what life could look like when it is nearly 100 percent quantified, personalized, and increasingly optimized? What will a world with very few surprises feel like? How will we compensate?

SPATIAL COMPUTING

Currently, augmented and virtual reality—AR and VR, respectively—require some kind of hardware device, be it headgear or our smartphones, yet these two technologies work quite differently: *augmented reality* applications overlay digital information on top of an analog experience (for

---

13 Shanhong Liu, "Internet of Things—Statistics and Facts," *Statista*, October 24, 2019.

14 "Gartner Identifies Top 10 Strategic IoT Technologies and Trends," *Gartner*, November 7, 2018.

example, superimposing facts about a neighborhood as you walk down a new street), while *virtual reality* puts a user in a state of total digital immersion. It is still very early days for both, but as each continues to improve and become more ubiquitous, AR/VR will become less novel and instead will form a more integral part of consumers' everyday technology experience, morphing into what is described as spatial computing.[15] Worldwide, the AR/VR market size is forecast to grow 7.7 times between 2018 and 2022 and is expected to generate $70 billion to $75 billion in revenue by 2023.[16]

The list of applications is vast and growing. In Hong Kong, the cutting-edge mental therapy program Yes I Can is using the immersive experience of virtual reality to help people overcome social anxiety fears by walking them through everyday environments and everyday situations.[17] Augmented reality is being used on assembly lines, where workers are provided with visual displays of the parts and details to assemble and then receive information about the necessary instruments or next steps for every stage via special goggles—all hands-free. A similar approach is happening in groundbreaking surgeries that incorporate both augmented reality and virtual reality tools, helping surgeons prepare for operations, as well as providing them with the opportunity to study 3D renderings of patients to maximize efficiency and minimize risk.[18] Even firefighters are receiving real-time feedback about the speed, direction, and locations of fires from crowdsourced data via AR-enabled goggles.[19]

---

15 Blair Felter, "Emerging Technology Requires Innovative Data Center Management," *VXChange*, April 12, 2019.

16 "For AR/VR 2.0 to Live, AR/VR 1.0 Must Die," *Digi-Capital*, January 15, 2019.

17 Rachel Yeo, "Virtual Reality Mental Health Project to Offer New Option for Hongkongers Seeking Help," *South China Morning Post*, June 17, 2019.

18 Bruno Jacobsen, "How Augmented Reality Can Change Surgical Procedures," *Future Proof*, January 14, 2019.

19 Greg Nichols, "California Firefighters Use Augmented Reality in Battle against Record Infernos," *ZDNet*, August 17, 2018.

How will these technologies impact learning? Will these reskill workers faster? How will they transform the entertainment, gaming, healthcare, and manufacturing industries? How will they enhance our abilities to collaborate, design, and even shop together around the world? Importantly, how will we manage, protect, and potentially choose to monetize the way this attention data is gathered and used?

ADDITIVE/3D+ PRINTING

Being hailed as one of the most disruptive technologies of our age (you sense a theme here?), 3D printing is generally described as the process of building a three-dimensional object from a computer-generated design by successively adding material layer by layer, though these techniques are becoming more sophisticated each day. The global market for 3D printing and services—also described as additive manufacturing—is expected to grow to almost $50 billion by 2025.[20]

There is already a 3D printer on the International Space Station, and teams of scientists are imagining how to 3D print new colonies on Mars.[21] Here on Earth, we've figured out how to use other conventional materials, such as metal, to 3D print an entire bridge, which, as of this writing, will be installed over a canal in Amsterdam.[22] As impressive as those accomplishments are, 4D printing takes it further by using nanotechnology to program matter, which gives everyday materials, such as wood, carbon, and textiles, the ability to self-transform. Can you imagine that chair you ordered from IKEA assembling itself once you open the

---

20 I. Wagner, "Additive Manufacturing and 3D Printing—Statistics & Facts," *Statista*, November 18, 2019.
21 "3D-Printed Habitat Challenge," *NASA*, 2019.
22 Gunseli Yalcinkaya, "World's First 3D-Printed Steel Bridge Unveiled at Dutch Design Week," *MX3D*, October 22, 2018.

box—or your car tires automatically changing composition in response to certain driving conditions?

How will this impact the shipping, warehouse, and fashion industries as we create our own designs and have the products instantaneously manufactured for us? While additive printing technology will certainly enhance the medical industry, food production, heavy manufacturing, and more, it will simultaneously raise new questions about intellectual property, safety regulations, and waste. Could an airline print a replacement part originally created and sold by a supplier? How would that part be inspected? And should a family be stopped from printing their own "Legos"? Is it possible all buildings will someday be printed rather than built? What will the market value of these things become? How can this address sustainability and concerns around waste?

ROBOTICS

Innovations in engineering and machine learning are paving the way to an accelerated adoption of robots over the next five years. Interestingly, adoption rates vary significantly around the world. Comparing the ratio of robots to every ten thousand employees, we see a wide disparity: South Korea has the highest density of robots per capita, at 631, compared to the U.S. with 189, and India, with only three. Not only will robots be pervasive throughout the industrial farming, hospitality, caregiving, and information sectors, they will increasingly be a part of our societal fabric: as companions,[23] playing into our inexhaustible need as humans for social intimacy and friendships.

---

23 Kate Baggaley, "New Companion Robots Can't Do Much but Make Us Love Them," *NBC News*, June 23, 2019.

All these things beg the question, how will significant gaps in automation across a global landscape play out in the years to come? What will our emotional responses to robots be? And how will we feel as they replace workers, as well as take the dirty, dangerous, and demeaning jobs humans should be spared?

RENEWABLE ENERGY

As with all of these other technologies, it was hard to imagine ten or twenty years ago that clean energy from alternative, naturally replenished sources could replace fossil fuels as the world's major energy source, but that's exactly what we're on track to accomplish. Estimations show that by 2030, 30 percent of all global energy will come from a combination of wind and solar—with the hope that other less well-known technologies, such as nuclear fusion, green hydrogen pyrolysis, and next-gen biofuels, will also help increase capacity. In the U.S. specifically, solar and wind power are growing so rapidly that for the first time ever, the United States will likely get more power in 2021 from renewable energy than from coal, according to projections from the Institute for Energy Economics and Financial Analysis.[24] Already there are several countries around the world almost entirely operating on renewables, proving it can be done.

Will companies rooted in the petroleum-heavy economy transition successfully or continue to block progress? How will pricing be affected? Can you imagine what becomes possible when costs become negligible and all of humanity is connected to unlimited supplies of energy? What are the risks ahead in *not* jumping on board?

---

24 Matt Egan, "Solar and Wind Are Booming, While Coal Keeps Shrinking," *CNN Business*, January 21, 2019.

5G CONNECTIVITY

For all these advances to manifest, we will need faster connectivity and nearly 100 percent network reliability. And it's coming. By 2024, it is estimated that about 40 percent of the world's population will be connected to fifth-generation wireless technology (5G)[25] that is one hundred times faster than the 4G technology we currently have.[26] Autonomous vehicles will have an easier time driving on their own, robots will be able to safely conduct remote surgeries with no lag, and people will be able to download full-length, high-definition films in seconds. Everything from cars to refrigerators, traffic lights, surveillance equipment, utility smart meters, and phones will be interlinked on a global web of electromagnetic field (EMF) technologies.

How do we balance the advancements this will allow against the potential health or societal implications of creating a planetary nervous system that will envelop us all?

DISTRIBUTED INTERNET

The World Wide Web just celebrated its thirtieth birthday, and each day, more people around the globe are joining the three billion others already online. Yet many concerned folks—including its original inventor, Tim Berners-Lee—have questioned its structure and are eager to rebuild a better version. They advocate for protocols that disincentivize exploitative behavior, keep us and our data much safer, and provide greater civic and environmental resilience—meaning, neither a government nor a hurricane

---

25 Alex Ward, "Why the U.S. and China Are Sparring Over 5G in Europe," *Vox*, March 21, 2019.

26 Elizabeth Woyke, "China Is Racing Ahead in 5G. Here's What That Means," *MIT Technology Review*, December 18, 2018.

can knock it out. There are many ways to describe these early efforts to facilitate direct peer-to-peer coordination that include blockchain, distributed ledgers, cryptocurrencies (made famous by Bitcoin), and my favorite initiative: Holochain.

While there is a lot to understand technologically (enter a giant rabbit hole here), this is the big idea: twentieth-century progress was the result of distributing resources through centralized structures and protocols that provided access and set pricing; think banks, energy plants, email servers. In this fast-forming cryptography age, however, the fundamental way we connect to information and exchange value with one another will become direct. This will empower collective action and offer greater inclusion and access. Eventually, this will likely eliminate the need for single, centralized sources of control that are vulnerable to multiple threats.

How can this approach scale? And how will our thinking evolve as we learn to rely less on institutions and more on ourselves and each other? How can we best manage the transition between centralized and distributed systems? What kinds of new learning will be required? What kinds of societal structures will evolve (e.g., mutual aid networks)? Can this help add support and security to informal economies around the globe? What new business models will arise?

QUANTUM COMPUTING

There is no end to our imagination when we envision what might be possible with all these technologies. But how are we going to harness the computational power required to help make it all happen? That's where quantum computing comes into play. Since computers were first created, they've undergone wave after wave of increased capacity, each time giving us the ability to actualize previously unimaginable ideas. Right now, we stand at the precipice of evolving from classic computing to taking a quantum leap. In their book *The Future Is Faster Than You Think*, Peter Diamandis and Steven Kotler describe the abilities of quantum computing this way: "IBM's Deep Blue computer that beat Gary Kasparov at chess examined two hundred million moves per second. A quantum machine can bump that up to a trillion or more."[27]

And in case you think we're a long way off from that kind of computer power, Rigetti Computing has already developed a quantum computer that they've opened for anyone to access and use to write programs.

As with describing other horizon technologies, we can only imagine how the ability to solve unbelievably complex problems will literally transform all humanity. Taking it out all the way, is it possible that quantum machines will be able to match or even surpass the intelligence of humans? And if so, by when?

IMPORTANT THINGS WORTH WONDERING ABOUT

When we consider how these capabilities will converge tomorrow, we're faced with ever more complex questions about the challenges and opportunities available to us today. Here are just a few of the strategic issues my team and I are focused on as we consider the future of converging tech:

CAN WE RESKILL AN ENTIRE POPULATION?

As we imagine a world heavily influenced by AI algorithms, robotics, and on-demand 3D printing—enhanced with ubiquitous applications of spatial

---

27 Peter Diamandis and Steven Kotler, *The Future Is Better Than You Think: How Converging Technologies Are Transforming Business, Industries, and Our Lives* (New York: Simon & Schuster, 2020).

computing (via augmented, virtual, and mixed realities)—how will the concept of work and the ways we do it shift? There is a vigorous debate about whether we will have more jobs or fewer in the years ahead, with plenty of statistics that support both cases. Meanwhile, Ginni Rometty, former CEO and now chair of IBM (and champion of IBM Watson) raises an equally important issue when she forecasts that, in either of these scenarios, 100 percent of us will need to be reskilled.[28]

Skilling, reskilling, and upskilling a global population will require significant coordination between governments, businesses, and education institutions. It is also a big shift most people are unprepared for individually. Commerce expert and Harvard professor Dan O'Connor warns his research indicates that 30 to 40 percent of today's workforce will not be able to successfully cross the work-skills divide—a seriously daunting thought that deserves much more of our attention. Given the extraordinary rate of change, what kind of societal scaffolding will be needed until this supply and demand balance of talent works itself out?

WHAT ARE THE RISKS OF AI BIAS?

While AI creates an opportunity to construct critical solutions to widespread problems, a growing reliance on algorithmic decision-making will also raise important questions on how organizational structures and cultures will be impacted. How will we protect against biased algorithms as these touch every area of our lives from job placement and background checks to how work is assigned and data is collected? Will we trust AI recommendations over our experienced peers? How will we untangle and correct the mistakes made by machines that are perceived as smarter than ourselves?

---

28 Dria Roland, "Why Companies Need to Reskill the Workforce for the New Digital Economy," *Fortune*, April 14, 2020.

HOW DO WE MAINTAIN TRUST IN A "DEEPFAKE" WORLD?

It is becoming ever more possible to realistically mimic the voice and image of a person, as well as to fabricate influential text and documents. This naturally raises serious questions about how these technologies can be misused—and whether this could be detected. Can we anticipate and somehow better prepare for this? When there is a whole new information paradigm, what are the structures that need to be built to ensure integrity? Will we actually be able to "trust the science"? How do we help prepare society for the challenges these technologies pose to our collective sense of truth?

HOW WILL THE RISE OF CHINA SHAPE THE WORLD?

Are we adequately addressing the profound global imbalances as China dives full speed ahead (and develops their own ethical standards), while many others, including the U.S., take a much slower approach to adopting, regulating, and requiring any education around the use of AI?

From significant state investments in AI research to embedding it in the curricula of grade school children, in 2017, China laid out a plan to become a world leader in AI and create a one trillion yuan (nearly $150 billion) industry by 2030.[29] With the largest population on the planet and an increasingly sophisticated technology infrastructure that has launched global apps such a TikTok, China now has the ability to collect an enormous amount of data, fueling their growing lead in a complex future driven by AI infrastructure.[30] What will that mean for privacy and cybersecurity? How will their view

---

29 Arjun Kharpal, "China Wants to Be a $150 Billion World Leader in AI in Less than 15 Years," *CNBC*, July 21, 2017.

30 "China's Singles' Day Shopping Spree Sees Robust Sales," *People's Daily*, November 11, 2019.

of citizens' rights drive their competitiveness in this arena? How will this shift their global influence as they achieve significant breakthroughs in and with this technology?

WHAT HAPPENS WHEN WE REACH THE SINGULARITY?

Ray Kurzweil, one of the world's leading inventors, thinkers, and futurists, known for his almost unerring predictions around what the future holds, has forecast that, "By 2029, computers will have human-level intelligence." What if by 2045 (another date Ray forecasts), we will be able to multiply our effective intelligence a billion-fold by merging ourselves with the artificial intelligence we have created, unleashing a superhuman intelligence[31] known as "the singularity"—the name given to the moment when this superintelligence is realized, rendering humanity irrevocably changed?

While I get excited about all the possibilities these present, it is also easy to become overwhelmed by the implications of these transformational technologies. We need space to fully consider what each of those could mean for our own companies, communities, and even our personal lives. We must make room for wonder. And conversation.

LEARNING TO RIFF

If we're only a percent or two in, it is clear we will be faced with new information and new possibilities at an astounding rate. And as exponential curves grow, the longer you wait to explore, the more you will have to learn. What often keeps us on the sidelines, however, is an inability to make sense of it all. In a thoughtful read on how to tackle the world's biggest issues,

---

31   Christianna Reedy, "Kurzweil Claims That the Singularity Will Happen by 2045," *Futurism*, October 5, 2017.

Swedish futurist Laurence Van Elegum points out the paradox: "We have come to expect simple solutions to ultra-complex problems."[32] So we wait for things to get clearer in order to know which side we should be on.

It is naive—and even perilous—to believe the future is only good or bad. Hopefully, none of us is that blindly optimistic nor cynically pessimistic. Searching for a single black or white answer often draws us to polarizing pundits and puts us at greater risk in a world of interdependency and growing complexity. Especially when we're being asked to respond, react, and innovate at a breathless pace.

Updating our understanding of new topics takes more than simple exposure to a big statistic or even an astounding example. Instead, engaging often requires that we hold two or more competing narratives about what this all means—and to rely on more than "thinking." Making visible what we feel and what we believe creates the ability for a much richer form of "sense-making," which in turn informs our ability to first interpret and then to act on what we think. Allowing for ambiguity while exploring our emotions and beliefs—including conflicting ones or those that seem illogical—enables us to freely wonder.

For example, are "flipped classrooms" and personal tablets improving education or not? Are genetically modified foods bad for our health or the key to solving world hunger? Is capitalism today ensuring society's strength or eroding it? Faced with complex, often contradictory beliefs, we often freeze and do nothing until we can be sure we are doing it "right." But this paralysis isn't necessary—or sustainable.

---

32 Laurence Van Elegem, "The Two Opposing Tech Forces Behind the World's Biggest Problems—and Why We Shouldn't Try to Solve Them," *Nexxworks*, November 26, 2019.

To help us find the value in these conflicting narratives, I developed another deceptively simple tool that teases out emotional distinctions. It is especially illuminating when used with a group.

I call it the RIFF model. While it closely parallels the classic strategic SWOT (strengths, weaknesses, opportunities, and threats) analysis, in this case, we move from assessing our individual or organizational competitiveness to wrapping our arms around a more nuanced view of the future. It forces us to examine more closely what we—and ideally others—believe. Best of all, this mapping also gives us more insight into where we can uniquely put our energies: again, as a professional, a human, an organization, or even an industry.

When I look at the future, what am I most...

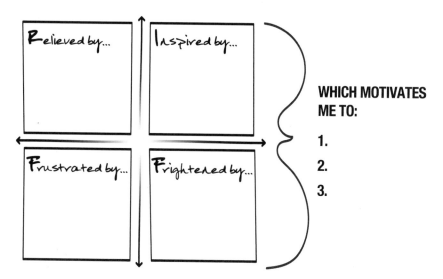

I have used the RIFF model with a wide range of audiences, from students to CEOs, and it's interesting to see how different people use the tool. Some use it to reflect externally on industry and societal shifts they can see now and on the horizon (e.g., rising youth empowerment, the growth of cryptocurrencies, climate change, 3D printed food) and what they might build in response. Others use the quadrants to write out their internal personal reactions about their own ability to move through the future (e.g., my broad network of relationships, lack of understanding about algorithms, the ability to enhance my education, lower barriers to starting my own company).

Each quadrant corresponds with one of four specific emotions we feel when confronted with new information or observations about technology, society, business, or the future in general.

I invite you to take a moment right now to write out your thoughts on each of the four RIFF questions. Think about this *externally*, draw a quadrant, and label each box with one of these emotions. In the top left, write out everything you're relieved by. Devote the top right box to everything that inspires you about the future. In the bottom left, all the possibilities that frustrate you. And finally, in the bottom right, everything you're afraid of for the future.

In general, I have found this leads to three big insights.

First, as you look over your quadrants, what can you observe? Do more of your answers fall into one quadrant or another? If you had no trouble filling in tons of responses to the bottom two quadrants, you're not alone. Many people are biased toward things that frustrate them and that they are fearful of, and we forget how things are also changing for the better. This informs our personal and/or organizational narrative of what we believe is (or is not) possible. If, overall, we believe the future is scary and/or intractable, we are less likely to move forward. If, by contrast, we see things as more optimistic or balanced, we begin to see that we have a lot of resources and possibilities to draw on. In my personal RIFF, for example, I'm relieved by a shift to systemic thinking and that I can easily find and connect with nearly any expert in the world.

Second, when you do this with a colleague or even a small team, you'll see that what may inspire *you* actually frightens someone else. For example, 3D printing a house is great for those in the business of creating safe, affordable housing but is likely scary for a Sheetrock manufacturer. This insight then creates much more empathy and the opportunity for a more compassionate response.

Recently, I was humbled to hear one participant in a RIFF session explain how even "empowered youth" could be something to be frightened by, saying, "If kids are not raised in safe environments or well educated, they will have that much more power in their hands to make scary choices, both for themselves and society." Wow! So true.

Thirdly, this means those bottom two quadrants offer a springboard for action. When we can honestly inventory the issues we are frightened about, we are then more motivated to redirect the impact they will have and instead create solutions. In my case, my fear of AI bias—and companion concern about the startling demographic homogeneity of data scientists and machine learning engineers—has me preaching nonstop about the critical need for diverse input on all AI endeavors. A similar fear about growing anxiety among youth led me to create the Career Fair For the Future, where college and high school students could actively explore how new technologies will impact the careers that they are interested in—positively and negatively.

Taking time to develop this RIFF inventory liberates our thinking by giving us more than one camp (i.e., optimist versus pessimist) to stand in. It also encourages us to wonder how others see things and to consider alternative opinions. Importantly, it helps us better see the unconscious narratives we carry that actively inform our actions. You shape what you believe is possible. In turn, you inspire what becomes reality. Being able to consciously reframe our beliefs and to see things with greater empathy makes answering our Two-Question Compass even clearer. Remember:

1. *What does the future need and expect of you?*
2. *What are you in a unique position to create and contribute toward it?*

WONDER IN ACTION

Turns out that two very different professions are working to solve the same problem within their respective fields: how to safely and effectively push fluid through a pipe. So, consider for a moment the knowledge a petroleum engineer and a cardiologist might have to offer to one another.

A desire to fully explore this question led medical director Alan Lumsden and retired ExxonMobil research manager William Kline to co-found an organization in which professionals from wide-ranging fields could learn from each other. Their organization, cleverly named Pumps & Pipes, hosts conferences, hackathons, and education programs to help innovators "explore each other's tool kits." The program held its first small event in 2007 and today welcomes professionals and students in all fields of science, technology, engineering, art, and mathematics. Conferences are live-streamed to eighty-eight countries.

Being biased in wonder pays off.

Through her investment team and personal relationships, Martha Stewart was introduced to emerging leaders in the tech world, like Google's Sergey

Brin, when they were just getting started. Along with her partner at the time, who worked for Bill Gates developing Microsoft Word, she was exposed to cutting-edge innovations that were coming to the publishing industry. Insatiably curious, she paid attention to the potential of desktop publishing and wondered how it could give her business a competitive advantage. Though other magazines were still using cutters and creating "mechanicals" to design physical layouts, Martha began to use a digital process for the layout of *Martha Stewart Living*. Hers was one of the first magazines to do so.

Not all breakthroughs, meanwhile, require deep technological curiosity (though that certainly helps). At its core, wonder is about synthesizing new learning with possibility.

Creative powerhouse Brian Grazer, a successful Hollywood producer whose films have grossed over $13 billion, is literally fueled by wonder. Every two weeks for the past twenty-two years, Brian has committed to inviting someone outside his industry to lunch, simply to learn. With Carlos Slim, a Mexican businessman, Brian wondered what kinds of daily struggles does the richest man in the world face? With Jonas Salk, who famously cured polio, it was what drives a person to pursue a cure for the worst disease afflicting the world if there's no financial benefit to the discovery? With Edward Teller, the inventor, he pondered what is it like to create a weapon like the hydrogen bomb that has the capability to destroy the world as we know it? Imagine the new trends, patterns, and opportunities he has learned about through those hundreds of conversations. By regularly connecting with people outside of his usual circle, he gets a better understanding of how things work and what makes different people tick, and as a result, he's able to see new possibilities for how to invest his time and money in narratives that create more-compelling movies.

Because both Martha and Brian keep their minds open and recognize the value of investing time in conversations with seemingly little relevance to their lives, they have been able to take advantage of opportunities that might not have otherwise been in their day-to-day spheres of awareness. Investing time and resources into wondering improves our ability to navigate change. But here's the tricky part: just being able to see what is taking shape is not enough; we need to have the confidence that we know how to act on what we learn.

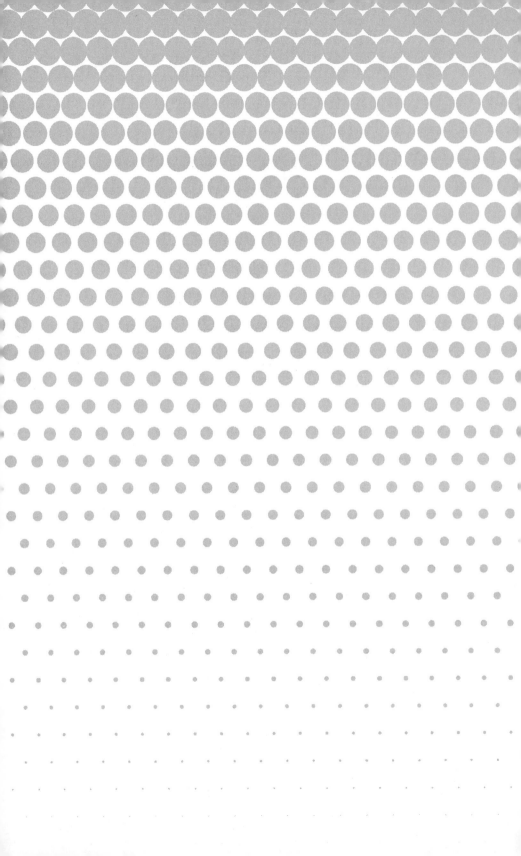

CHAPTER THREE

Navigate (versus Replicate)

"My question is how organizations can lead us not toward some predictable goal, but toward a greater and greater capacity to handle unpredictability, and with it, a greater capacity to love and care about other people."

—Margaret Wheatley, author, management consultant, and systems thinker

Last summer, I was invited to a unique conference in Bretton Woods, New Hampshire[1]—the very same place where international leaders met in the wake of World War II to establish the International Bank for Reconstruction and Development, as well as the International Monetary Fund. During this modern gathering on the economy, we explored three important issues to building a stronger, more robust future: more inclusive economic models and metrics for our increasingly unbalanced society; the role cryptocurrencies can play in building more resilient communities; and structures and ways to stem the environmental and ecological impacts of our relentless focus on growth.

On the second morning of the event, as I began walking through the historically elegant and very large resort, I held the door open for another attendee I was eager to speak with. As we walked to breakfast, my new pal from MIT Media Lab and I had a fascinating conversation.

When we got to the spot where I thought breakfast would be, no one was there; turns out the previous day's breakfast had been held in a different location, and today it had moved to the veranda. The man laughed suddenly. "You just seemed so sure," he said, while implying, "so I followed you." I was startled and suddenly embarrassed; I assumed we had been implicit collaborators and that he would have changed our course or asked me to confirm my decision if he had any doubts. Though we were walking side by side, I gave the impression that I knew where we were going. And I was wrong.

That's the thing—it's so easy to feel very sure...and also be very wrong. Perhaps at this moment, *you* are afraid of stepping out on a new edge in fear of making the wrong call. Totally fair. But you should also be aware of how much authority you give others when you let them take the lead.

---

1 BrettonWoods75.org

In a world of dynamic change, an old map is often more dangerous than none; it gives us a false sense of security and/or encourages us to default to what we assume we "know." In its place, we must develop the confidence—and humility—to learn and lead simultaneously.

FROM CONTROL TO INNOVATION

Traditional management structures are built with a top-down approach designed for rigid control and consistent, reliable, "flawless" delivery. Today, there is much less time to wait for decisions or direction from a few empowered leaders or small select committees; organizations with rigid bureaucracy miss windows of innovation (think: Nokia). The challenge all enterprises face today is the need to create adaptive processes that manage design and production cycles faster and more thoughtfully.

OLD ECONOMY expectations	NEW ECONOMY expectations
CERTAINTY	Dynamic
MASTERY	Adaptive
CONTROL	Distributed
AUTONOMY	Collaborative
AUTHORITY	Beliefs
SHAREHOLDER	Stakeholder
PROMISE	Commitment
PROCESS	Passion
CONSISTENCY	Responsive
GROWTH	Trust
TRANSACTION	Relationship

This was the issue facing Nestlé Frozen Foods as they wondered how to regain momentum and reverse a scary trend of declining sales. As all those tech advances launched in 2007, the world shifted, swiftly changing expectations. Here is how we summed up the big shift in what their consumers and their business partners now expected of them.

Like all large corporations, they used to spend years researching, testing, and rolling out new products with elaborate marketing support. But now the pressure was really on as retailers like Walmart were only giving them six or seven weeks to demonstrate demand; less than two months to prove that a new concept could be successful in the market. Responding faster meant the leadership team had to reevaluate and restructure *every* process that framed their work internally and externally: how they sourced and prioritized new ideas, their relationship with retailers, as well as other forms of distribution, even the way rooms and buildings were named on the campus. Most importantly, they had to completely shift from "only" delivering an efficient transaction to cultivating trustworthy relationships with all stakeholders. As Nestlé's story shows, we need to reorient our mindset and accept that surety will no longer come from having the answers, but instead from asking different kinds of questions and building new capacities to adapt. As CEO, author, professor, and frequent TED speaker Margaret Heffernan notes:

> *The unexpected is becoming the norm. It's why experts and forecasters are reluctant to predict anything more than 400 days out. Why? Because over the last twenty or thirty years, much of the world has gone from being complicated to being complex—which means that yes, there are patterns, but they don't repeat themselves regularly. It means that very small changes can make a disproportionate impact. And it means that expertise won't always suffice, because the system just keeps changing too fast.*[2]

2   Margaret Heffernan, "The Human Skills We Need in an Unpredictable World," *TED*, 2019.

As mentioned in this book's introduction, a common question I hear as a futurist is "How do I navigate my role in a constantly changing future?" The capability to navigate rather than replicate is both a choice and learned behavior. It is a kind of adaptivity that empowers decision-making *while* one is continuously reading, evaluating, and traversing new terrain. Encouragingly, there are several approaches and tools I've encountered that can help us better understand and cultivate this ability to navigate.

LEARNING TO SENSE AND RESPOND

The key to fostering adaptivity in ourselves and our systems is to boost our capacities to *sense* and to *respond*. Much like the example of the women from the airport story, we need to become much better at sensing what is happening around us in order to see new possibilities and threats taking shape. However, in order to make it through that liminal gap between now and next, we must also vastly improve our ability to respond with decisive action.

A direct way to strengthen the *sensing* part of the equation is to get better at collecting and valuing information we receive on the front lines. Who in your organization has the most understanding about your customers' needs? If you own a restaurant, it's likely the waitstaff. In tech services, it's the people in your call center. In many businesses, it is the salespeople or the team mining social media that get a sense of what's happening in real time. The people in these roles have a wealth of knowledge about how your company's products and services work in real applications. Too often, however, hierarchical systems within a company prevent that information from being fed back up the chain in a quick, actionable manner.

In 2019, we watched this play out with the launch of Apple's highly anticipated new credit card. As female/male couples individually applied, many found the women received lower credit limits than the men—in some cases, twenty times lower—despite similar or sometimes even stronger financial histories and credit scores. When outraged applicants called Apple's call centers to demand why, they were met with completely insufficient responses. "Sorry. It's just the way it works. Try again in six months." No further action was offered by the company, so as has become the way, angry applicants turned to Twitter to vent and quickly learned they weren't the only ones experiencing this.[3] The fervor swelled, Apple's reputation took a hit, and within a week, regulators began a probe into the Goldman Sachs algorithms used to assign creditworthiness.[4] Welcome to the future.

Now consider: where in your company is valuable information going unheard?

In this one example, we see how important it is to build ways to sense shifts and address problems quickly. Empower frontline people in your organization to listen and confidently share what they are hearing. Take seriously recommendations from the teams that run sustainability, DEI (diversity, equity, and inclusion), and "future of work." And use social media to strategically monitor customer and community sentiment in real time. AI will be a growing ally here. Recognizing the power your customers now have, it is also critical to build social capital so that if (OK, when) you need support, the community backs you up.

Of course, the *response* side of this equation is vital as well. Netflix hit a big bump in 2011 when they first announced their intent to split their slowing DVDs and growing video-on-demand streaming into two separate offerings—remember the momentary launch of Qwikster? Netflix stock plummeted as 800,000 subscribers dropped the service after learning

---

3   @DHH et al., "The @AppleCard is such a fucking sexist program..." *Twitter*, November 7, 2019.
4   "Apple's 'Sexist' Credit Card Investigated by U.S. Regulator," *BBC News*, November 11, 2019.

they would have to pay separately, and more, for DVD and streaming combined. Netflix responded quickly: they were willing to change course, issue an apology, and migrate customers more thoughtfully. As reported in a study on "adaptive resilience," it was through "empathy, transparency, and determinacy" that Netflix managed to turn its error around.[5]

By its twentieth anniversary in 2018, Netflix had 117 million streaming subscribers worldwide, up from the twenty-four million or so total members with which it closed out the third quarter of 2011.[6] And the DVD business lives on, with just over three million subscribers at last count. Though their timing and execution were off, their vision was right. And they bounced back in a much stronger position to grow in the new world of video delivery. At the close of 2019, Netflix had the best-performing S&P 500 stock of the decade, up a staggering 3,726 percent.

When we don't have cultures or structures that support open communication both within and outside the organization, sensing customers' needs takes a very long time. But when we open lines of communication to all stakeholders—and restructure the ways we create, iterate on, and deliver solutions—we build the capacity for faster, greater adaptivity; not last year, not last week, but right now. And in many cases, even today.

RETHINKING RISK

Earlier, I made the bold claim that many things put in place to mitigate risk in the old economy are now huge vulnerabilities in this new, highly connected, digital one.

---

5   Cristina Meniuc, "Adaptive Cycle of Resilience: Netflix Case Study," 2013.
6   Ashley Rodriguez, "As Netflix Turns 20, Let's Revisit Its Biggest Blunder," *Quartz*, April 14, 2018.

How can we get better at discerning what is necessary evolution versus what we fear is business suicide?

We often deny new information as a way to defend or protect the status quo—because, frankly, we discount anything we don't understand (yet). While, historically, it was considered distracting and potentially dangerous to pay attention to ideas on the edge, now that thinking *must* flip.

There are many outdated practices putting organizations at risk today. Containment might have been a smart strategy in slow-moving markets, but these days keeping our information siloed and our decisions centralized prevents collaboration and limits our visibility into what could work and where things are stuck. Similarly, the drive to be hyper-efficient stymies our ability to learn and meaningfully connect, exposing us to new problems. Ignoring externalities also puts us at risk when societal conditions or attitudes change: note the pharmaceutical executive sentenced to five years in prison for his part in the opioid epidemic,[7] or the Adidas executive who recently resigned after failing to address issues of racism and discrimination.[8] As obesity rates for children continue to grow, should high-calorie-beverage or fast-food executives be worried?

What about the ways our boards of advisors are structured? Are they protecting our companies from rash decision-making, or are they inadvertently strangling important advances? How do we weigh the input of these quarterly advisors, who may have tenured experience in the previous era of operations but who may struggle to pivot into the 1PR? How can they keep up with dynamic industry changes and what the

---

7   Pat Milton and Laura Strickler, "Drug Company Founder John Kapoor Arrested for Alleged Opioid Scheme," *CBS News*, October 27, 2017.
8   Kevin Draper and Julie Cresswell, "Adidas Executive Resigns as Turmoil at Company Continues," *New York Times*, June 30, 2020.

organization is learning *every day* in order to put their wisdom to more relevant use?

Incremental thinking, we were taught, was another way to keep the ship safe. While the Silicon Valley adage "Move fast and break things" is filled with a dangerous hubris, it *is* time to become much bolder with our leaps. Assessing and implementing small steps often keeps us blinded to the much bigger mounting shifts that can completely disrupt our carefully crafted five-year plan.

Standardization was also something many organizations strove for in the past to scale quickly, efficiently, and in ways that reduced risk. But a recent situation demonstrated how that thinking can backfire, as sadly, a relentless focus on standardization means we may potentially lose the joy of eating bananas[9]—for the second time. And by design. Back in the 1950s, the world's supply of bananas came from a tasty but not very hardy variety called the Gros Michel. The banana industry focused on a single varietal in order to standardize supply chain processes and mitigate risk, but the Gros Michel was wiped out due to disease. In desperation, farmers turned to yet another single variety, the Cavendish, and considered themselves saved. Today, the Cavendish accounts for 99 percent of the bananas imported around the world, and now it, too, is under threat from a deadly and quickly moving fungus. While monoculture may seem safer and much more efficient, we don't appreciate how this thinking instead threatens the entire system.

This story presents a cautionary tale for the tech world. We've seen how quickly a digital virus can ravage the internet. When we all rely on the same defaults and standards on our networks, we leave ourselves open to the

9   Anna Purna Kambhampaty, "What We Can Learn from the Near-Death of the Banana," *Time*, November 18, 2019.

same vulnerabilities. This realization has led many technologists to use artificial diversity in the systems they create. They, too, are learning that diversity is key to breeding resilience.

We bring greater vulnerability and risk to our organizations when we try to circle the wagons to maintain an industrial-era competitive advantage, rather than when we open ourselves to new information, new people, and new ideas that don't just better serve us but actually empower us in the face of ambiguity.

Just as one learns to use a compass, there are several ways we can get more adept at reading dynamic, often unknown, terrain, including:

- Getting serious about diversity and inclusion
- Inviting dissent
- Designing in empathy
- Seeking uncommon partnerships
- Reframing ambiguity
- Championing curiosity

Let's take a look at each of these in turn.

GETTING SERIOUS ABOUT DIVERSITY AND INCLUSION

To navigate with more confidence, we need more perspective because the leadership profiles of most large industries are still shockingly homogenous. Out of the S&P 500 firms, there are more CEOs named John (and Robert, and William, and James) than there are women CEOs—four times as many, to give a sense of scale.[10] Directors younger than fifty make up

---

10   Justin Wolfers, "Fewer Women Run Big Companies than Men Named John," *The New York Times*, March 2, 2015.

6 percent of the seats on S&P 500 boards—drop the age to forty-five, and it's less than 2 percent. There are more directors seventy-five or older than those fifty or younger. And only a third of companies in the S&P 500 have at least one director younger than fifty who is not also the company's CEO. Though these norms are changing slowly, they hold especially true in finance, medicine, transportation, and energy sectors, where 76 percent of jobs are held by men, and 95 percent of the workforce is white.[11]

Research shows that companies with diverse teams of people are more innovative, which puts many male-dominated organizations at a growing disadvantage. In a study of companies across a range of industries, those with the most women in top leadership positions had a 35 percent higher rate of return on equity than those with less diversity. Financial metrics lined up, too, with a 34 percent higher total return to shareholders.[12] Other studies have shown that diverse work environments lead to happier, more engaged employees,[13] and result in better decision-making 87 percent of the time.[14] So is it risky to diversify our organizations or not to?

While performance metrics are motivating, there are even more critical reasons to get on this train, pronto! Consider the example from Fitbit, the enormously popular wearable tech company. Fitbit's functionality is based on a technology that reads information through our skin to determine a sense of motion and deliver performance results. It turns out the company only tested the product on a small group of people and then went forward on their development anyway. This led to the discovery that the platform

---

11 Lisa Winning, "It's Time to Prioritize Diversity across Tech," *Forbes*, March 13, 2018.

12 "Report: The Bottom Line: Connecting Corporate Performance and Gender Diversity," *Catalyst*, January 15, 2004.

13 Lydia Dishman, "What America's Happiest Workplaces Have in Common," *Fast Company*, October 19, 2015.

14 Erik Larson, "New Research: Diversity + Inclusion = Better Decision Making at Work," *Forbes*, September 21, 2017.

doesn't read darker skin as effectively as lighter skin...all of which then called into question the reliability of Fitbit's technologies.

Similarly, when technologist Joy Buolamwini was a master's student at MIT Media Lab, she was startled to find the facial recognition technology she was using for an art project, which projected digital masks onto faces, was able to detect a white face (especially a man's) but not her dark skin.[15] Looking out further, when Joy learned how these error-prone algorithms are used in law enforcement, she took on the task of fighting for their much more thoughtful design and application by founding the Algorithmic Justice League. Twitter also has begun investigating why photos shared on their platform favor white faces over dark ones when auto-cropped for smaller screens.[16]

These errors in decision-making have the potential for a huge impact as technologies gain wider adoption. As Apple's credit card team is learning, these are biases one wants to catch before a product launches—not after—and certainly before they have the potential to compound rather than redress significant social justice concerns.

This is the lesson: simply by their nature, any homogenous team or environment is subject to unconscious bias. Without a sensitivity or perspective that can question things, we end up with skewed results. Without a diverse team building, testing, and monitoring these ideas, we likely won't know where the bias is baked in. This goes far beyond gender or race. Teams are strengthened, and resilience is born of contributions from those with diverse backgrounds, education, geographical origins, hobbies, and so on.

---

15 Tom Simonite, "Photo Algorithms ID White Men Fine—Black Women, Not So Much," *Wired*, February 6, 2018.

16 Sam Shead, "Twitter to Investigate Racial Bias in Its Picture-Cropping Algorithm," *NBC News*, September 21, 2020.

Importantly, inclusion—the capacity for an organization to actually listen to diverse voices and input—is just as important as inviting a diverse group around the table. Women in President Obama's first cabinet found this especially vexing and developed a strategy of "amplification" that went viral: the idea was that if a woman said something that was ignored by the men in the room, another woman would repeat it, thank her colleague for the comment, and so on, until the president and others in the room acknowledged the point. Eventually, Obama himself caught on and was grateful to have been called out.[17]

The payoffs are worth it, as diversity is also becoming a successful economic strategy. Christopher Louras, the mayor of a small Vermont town, leveraged ethnic diversity to resurrect his floundering local economy. The population of his community was declining, leaving behind vacant housing and unfilled entry-level jobs. To solve this problem, Louras collaborated with a resettlement agency to welcome Syrian refugees to town, an initiative that has been repeated in other small towns in Montana and Georgia.[18] Rutland, Vermont, has now become an enclave for refugees, to positive economic effect.

Diversity and inclusion will become especially critical as new, complex technologies are promising to give us seemingly superhuman powers.

INVITING DISSENT

To reap the full benefits of diverse input, we need to create environments in which teams and leaders alike are empowered and encouraged to engage

---

17 Juliet Eilperin, "How a White House Women's Office Strategy Went Viral," *The Washington Post*, October 25, 2016.

18 Tim Henderson, "Shrinking Small Towns See Hope in Refugees," *PEW*, August 5, 2016.

in constructive dissent. We must be able to handle challenges to the orthodoxy or majority opinion, particularly since modern business is increasingly complex, making cooperation and openness to new perspectives essential if breakthroughs and innovations are to be thoughtfully made.

In her book *In Defense of Troublemakers*, psychologist Charlan Nemeth makes the point:

> *Repeatedly we find that dissent has value, even when it is wrong, even when we don't like the dissenter, and even when we are not convinced of his position. Dissent...enables us to think more independently and also stimulates thought that is open, divergent, flexible, and original.*[19]

More and better ideas come from organizations where people are able to exchange unfamiliar points of view. However, having someone with a very different background question a decision or long-held practice often requires sophisticated development of the culture inside our organizations, as well as our own sense of self. It requires frameworks that foster psychological safety and teams where people feel comfortable being genuine, speaking up, and being themselves. In the end, it's not about *who's* right; it's about *what's* right. To paraphrase the scientist Jacob Bronowski, no society or organization died from dissent, but plenty have perished from conformity.

So how do we create inclusive communities that hold a diversity of experience or opinion rather than incentivize a dangerous culture of conformity? How do we learn to have difficult conversations and still move collaboratively ahead? In an increasingly polarized society, how do we create more empathy while ensuring decisions get made?

---

19 Charlan Nemeth, *In Defense of Troublemakers: The Power of Dissent in Life and Business* (New York: Basic Books, 2018).

As you're reading this book and thinking about which future you want to create, it's worth noting that strong, inclusive business cultures have one foundational quality at their core—empathy.

DESIGNING IN EMPATHY

While traditional research and development processes are now too slow and expensive, for more than a decade, the process of *design thinking* has been advancing as a fast-moving practice built to incorporate the flow of new information. Historically, design was thought of as an aesthetic process to create an artifact, such as a car or dress. But it has now taken on a very different meaning, as "design" is an iterative process of creation and innovation.

Design thinking starts by empathetically listening to what is needed—rather than building something just because we can. What is the pain point? Where is the human-centered need? Then we consider: What can we quickly build to meet that need and get some immediate feedback? Is there a quick way to prototype the idea?

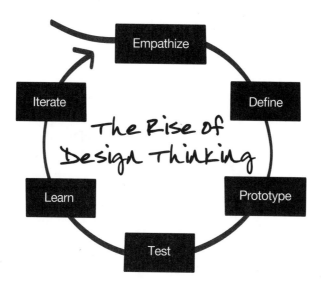

When real users are putting new concepts to work in everyday settings, we can get more meaningful and faster feedback. And in a world of quickly escalating expectations, it isn't easy to see what will catch fire until you try. Seeing users actually apply a solution gives us insights on the features they love and the real needs they're looking to fill (or not), which may be different from what we had assumed our intended audience was seeking. This is where the concept of "pivoting" caught on.

Starbucks started by selling espresso machines and bags of whole roasted beans. Photo management site Flickr began as an online role-playing game that included a photo-sharing tool that turned out to be more popular than the game. And what about YouTube? Starting as an online video dating site, the company recognized the potential for a wider and more efficient host for people's online videos—leading to Google eventually acquiring them for $65 billion.[20]

Importantly, when we engage in the process of listening/prototyping/learning to meet needs faster, we don't have to wait for our solution to be perfect.

Let that sink in for a moment: in a world of constant change, your solutions from now on will never be "perfect."

It is incredibly difficult for many leaders to become comfortable with "good enough"; your customers are relying on you, and we are taught reliability and consistency matter most. But consider how trusted products are created in the software field: engineers are constantly building prototypes, exposing them, getting feedback, and iterating. This process is repeated many times before a product is finalized to determine what updates are

---

20 Jason Nazar, "14 Famous Pivots," *Forbes*, October 8, 2013.

needed. Development goes around and around in a cycle of constant improvement, ensuring the concept *remains* relevant and reliable.

So how do we take this model into the business world? You likely are familiar with the concept of a *minimum viable product* (MVP): the minimum version we can create in order to get feedback. The key is to make this first version truly address a need.

Before design thinking really caught on, we were taught that innovation came through a process of robust research and development that carefully mapped each stage from concept to delivery. Design thinking puts the need front and center—like how to travel faster from point A to point B—and iterates a series of concepts that accomplish that goal from skateboard to scooter to motorcycle to car. Each iteration offers value as well as room for improvement.

The iPhone presents a real-world example. The first iPhone was not nearly the versatile device it is today—when first launched, it didn't even have a "cut and paste" function. But by releasing it to the market, Apple was able to see quickly what features people used, what new capabilities they wanted, and what powerful new concepts might be possible.

It is not just about the final product or service; design thinking also helps us improve every internal process—from hiring to accounting to procurement to partnering. All of which helps make a team or business unit more responsive.

When we spend time listening, actively experimenting with potential solutions, and creating in-field prototypes to learn with, we also become aware of new questions or gaps that encourage us to partner with people outside our organization who have complementary skills or experience we need. And these alliances can come from surprising places.

SEEKING UNCOMMON PARTNERSHIPS

As we mentioned earlier, in Chapter 2 with the example of Pumps & Pipes, sometimes we seek out uncommon partnerships to learn, and sometimes we seek them out to form alliances that enable surprising business innovations. We're now in an age where it's crucial not only to watch what's happening within one's own industry but to look outside it. In a digital-delivery world, new developments can quickly jump the fence of one industry to influence another. As we've said before, competitors can come from anywhere. One of the primary concerns of a Detroit automaker, for example, used to be the threat of foreign cars infiltrating their territory—now it's self-driving cars from Google, ride-sharing from Uber and Lyft, urban scooters and bikes, and even ever-faster home delivery from Instacart and Amazon. Because disruption now comes from so many different angles, it is crucial to take in a wider view of what's happening around us and look for unexpected allies.

The upside is that it's not only possible to combine knowledge from disparate industries to deliver new value, but it's actually a very smart strategy to develop uncommon partnerships. Some unexpected examples:

- With no prior industry-specific experience, Amazon, Berkshire Hathaway, and JPMorgan Chase joined forces to create a new health insurance provider, called Haven, to better support their combined workforce of 1.2 million employees with lower healthcare costs.[21]

- Building-supply leader Lowe's partnered with Microsoft Hololens to create VR "Holorooms," where customers can envision what their remodels would look like as well as watch tutorials on how to

---

21 "Vision," *Haven*.

complete their projects. Lowe's Kyle Nel reports that customers who learned a skill in the Holoroom were 30 to 40 percent more likely to remember the steps than those who learned on YouTube.[22]

- In the pizza world, the holy grail is being able to deliver a piping hot pie to each door, but for driver safety reasons, one can't operate a working pizza oven in a moving vehicle. Pizza Hut has teamed with Toyota to test putting ovens in autonomous vehicles, so that a pizza can literally bake on its way to your house.[23]

- Martha Stewart has also leveraged uncommon partnerships throughout her career. As mentioned before, early introductions to technology visionaries gave her the confidence to radically shift the design and delivery process for her magazine. She has benefited not just from her curiosity about technology but also from her unexpected friendships—most notably her alliance with rapper Snoop Dogg. After inviting Snoop Dogg on her cooking show, the two struck up a lasting partnership. In 2016, they launched a new cooking show together on VH1, which spurred an entirely new, more diverse platform full of fans who adored their repartee. Who would have predicted that?

An additional thought on this topic: new possibilities can also spring from teaming up with competitors. While this might seem risky by old measures, it is increasingly becoming a pathway to bold innovation. In 2018, Honda announced a $2.75 billion investment in Cruise, the arm of General Motors developing autonomous cars. A conversation with the CIO of Insurer USAA

---

22 Jonathan Vanian, "Lowe's Wants People to Fix Their Bathrooms in Virtual Reality," *Fortune*, March 7, 2017.

23 "Pizza Hut Teams Up with Toyota to Unveil Pizza-Making Pickup Truck at Sema 2018," *HutLife*, October 30, 2018.

revealed they are partnering with State Farm Insurance on a blockchain initiative that would speed up the time it takes to resolve a customer's auto insurance claim between their two companies.

Consider: When does it make sense for a retail competitor of yours to become your innovation collaborator? And how can that make the fast-changing landscape less volatile?

REFRAMING AMBIGUITY

It's easy to get on board with the *concept* of embracing imperfection and constant iteration but much harder to put this into practice. It is encouraging, then, to see how an organization famous for its strict hierarchy and chain-of-command culture is addressing dynamic environments.

VUCA is an acronym that the U.S. military uses to assess new field environments that are increasingly Volatile, Uncertain, Complex, and Ambiguous. As detailed in the book *Team of Teams* by General Stanley McChrystal, while fighting in Afghanistan, the military discovered that the tactics of modern warfare operate in a decentralized way, making it no longer feasible for U.S. soldiers to run a solution through HQ before making a decision or rely on "best practices."[24] They needed to be able to act quickly to never-seen-before circumstances. In these field environments, soldiers were empowered to make more responsive decisions.

Similarly, without a shift in perspective and capacities, business leaders facing volatile and uncertain conditions will traditionally freeze instead of act. They will wait until they can get a handle on the unknowable: to see

---

24 Stanley McChrystal, *Team of Teams: New Rules of Engagement for a Complex World* (New York: Portfolio, 2015).

what the next killer app will be, or to gain certainty about the right time to invest in a new technology or process. As Ron Carucci noted in *Harvard Business Review*:

> *Too many leaders avoid making tough calls. In an effort not to upset oth-ers or lose status in the eyes of their followers, they concoct sophisticated justifications for putting off difficult decisions, and the delay often does far more damage than whatever fallout they were trying to avoid. In fact, hard decisions often get more complicated when they're deferred. And as a leader gets more senior, the need to make hard calls only intensifies. In our ten-year longitudinal study of more than 2,700 leaders, 57 percent of newly appointed executives said that decisions were more complicated and difficult than they expected.*[25]

Should a dental practice invest $300,000 in a new 3D printer now—or wait until the next model comes out? Should a company really trust a sales pre-diction algorithm they just invested in? Should a mobile phone manufac-turer abandon the keyboard that made them famous—or a DVD company transition to streaming? Rather than putting more at risk by delaying deci-sions to wait for ambiguity to clear—which in the new economy may never happen—we free ourselves to navigate.

When we navigate a future characterized by VUCA, it is important to focus on the *opportunities* that these ever-changing conditions present. As we shift our mindset to Leadering, we can reinterpret the VUCA acronym to reflect the capacities that enable us to help better navigate this dynamic environment: Vision, Understanding, Collaboration, and Agility.

25   Ron Carucci, "Leaders, Stop Avoiding Hard Decisions," *Harvard Business Review*, April 13, 2018.

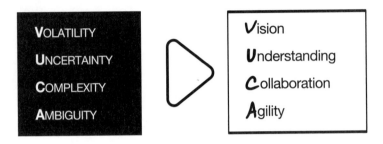

This means with a sense of wonder we can see new opportunities and approach them with greater empathy. We are able to enlist our network of partners and test/iterate quick solutions. We have a solid way to thrive in the swirl of change.

Even as the world is reeling from the COVID-19 pandemic, and as the social justice movement has hit a tipping point, there are moments of clarity and opportunities to pivot. Reddit founder Alexis Ohanian recently resigned his position on the board to make room for a Black board member and has pledged that a percentage of future earnings from his Reddit stock will be dedicated to funding Black causes, starting with $1 million donated to the Colin Kaepernick-funded Know Your Rights Camp.[26] In another example, Michael Tubbs, the twenty-nine-year-old mayor of Stockton, launched one of the first guaranteed income pilots in the U.S. last year.[27] It is now being tested with mayors in Los Angeles, Atlanta, and nine other U.S. cities.

For sure, we are facing a lot of ambiguity and complexity, but by developing the capacities to navigate constant change, and having the confidence to act, this concept can be reinterpreted into something more empowering—allowing

---

26 Kaya Yurieff, "Reddit Cofounder Alexis Ohanian Resigns from Board, Urges Seat to Be Filled by Black Candidate," *CNN Business*, June 5, 2020.

27 Rachel Sandler, "Mayors in 11 U.S. Cities Join Coalition to Launch Basic Income Pilot Programs in Their Cities," *Basic Income Today*, June 30, 2020.

you to find ways to use the shifting dynamics of an environment to your advantage—as well as for the advantage of your stakeholders.

CHAMPIONING CURIOSITY

In the last chapter, we discussed at length the value of wonder, but in order for this to penetrate an organization's culture, we need to consider how we are actively incentivizing it. In 2018, Francesca Gino published an article in *Harvard Business Review* on how leaders approach curiosity within their organizations.[28] She conducted a survey that found while leaders agree curiosity is a good thing, two misconceptions keep them from actively encouraging it in their companies.

The first misconception: curiosity is messy and costly. Leaders don't want their employees to get too curious, or they'll run amok, waste billable hours, and become difficult to contain. How do you even manage a process when you've allowed a bunch of wild ideas to be thrown out there? Leaders don't know how to channel unbridled curiosity, so they try to stamp it out. But channeled or redirected curiosity is the best kind of "messy" an organization can have; it's the fuel of innovative breakthroughs.

The second misconception: curiosity is an extravagance versus a necessity. Many leaders think *I'll get to it when I have time—or my team can pursue that when the real work is done.* In contrast, Francesca found that workforces that were more curious produced fewer decision-making errors, more creative innovations, more open communication, and better performance.

In my own experience, one of the most powerful ways to incentivize learning is to pay for it. Google was famous for its 20 percent time offer to employees

---

28 Francesca Gino, "The Business Case for Curiosity," *Harvard Business Review*, September 2018.

to work on anything they were passionate about. As I work with the artificial intelligence startup team at KUNGFU.AI, I watch how much time my colleagues spend sourcing and reading technical white papers, attending meetups, and developing demos that put the learning into practice—all necessary to keep up with and contribute to the latest thinking in the fast-moving AI / machine learning field. When I asked one of the most experienced technology leads how much time he invests in learning, I wasn't surprised when he estimated that learning accounts for roughly 20 percent of his work life.

You can't commit that kind of time to learn just on nights and weekends, so at KUNGFU.AI, the co-founder's billing rates—as for all the machine learning engineers—take into account the necessity for constant learning, not just producing. This ultimately maintains quality and competitive edge.

I discovered this for myself the hard way. Several years ago, I felt depleted in my energy and in my finances. So that December, I stepped back and asked myself what just happened and how could I sort this out so I could deliver better—and feel better? I did some calculating. Starting with a full year's upcoming calendar, I blacked out the weekends and vacations I wanted to spend with my fast-growing teens. Then I thought about how much time I spend designing TEDx events and other experiences. I quickly realized that in relation to what I charge clients, I had never accounted for time learning, be it through attending conferences, participating in thought leader groups, information sourcing, or curating events to find the best speakers available. I was trying to squeeze all this learning into the margins of a full life. And it wasn't working.

Rather than give up learning, I increased my consulting rates to more accurately reflect where and how I was spending my time—and the value of that to my clients. As a strategic futurist, I'm only useful if I, too, am keeping up to date with the ideas and the people architecting the future.

Actively cultivating and incentivizing curiosity is a growing issue that impacts not only how we learn individually but also how it influences every aspect of our organizations, including our procurement negotiations. Consider: What happens if, as we learn, the project we have been contracted to deliver needs to pivot or take an unscoped direction? What if the machine-learning algorithm a team is supervising raises new questions? Or we need more data?

Back in 1990, MIT professor Peter Senge coined a new term to explain what the future would need and expect from organizations:

> A *Learning Organization, he explained, is where people continue to expand their capacity to create the results they desire, where new and expansive patterns are nurtured, where collective aspiration is set free, and where people are continually learning to learn together.*[29]

Thirty years later, highly renowned corporate strategist John Hagel put it more simply: "We need to shift from cultures of efficiency to cultures of learning."

DIVING DEEPER
JOHN HAGEL ON SCALABLE LEARNING

John Hagel, co-chairman of Deloitte and co-founder of Center for the Edge, is a leading voice in the world of business transformation. He has laid the groundwork for understanding how big shifts in technology and culture are reshaping organizations

---

29 Peter Senge, *The Fifth Discipline: The Art and Practice of the Learning Organization* (New York: Currency, 2006).

and restructuring power. John believes that as institutions focus on meeting mounting financial performance pressure, their leaders are doubling down on driving efficiency at the expense of delivering innovative solutions to their stakeholders. To reduce the fear, distrust, and polarization this is contributing, John urges us to shift away from organizing for efficiency toward building cultures that enable scalable learning:

> *Our world is no longer stable. It's evolving at an accelerating rate with growing uncertainty. Customers are more powerful and less and less willing to settle for standardized, mass-market products and services. The combination of these two forces creates a paradox: scalable efficiency is becoming less and less efficient. So, what's the alternative? Scalable learning. In a rapidly changing world, the ability to learn faster at scale will increasingly determine success.*
>
> *By learning, I don't mean training programs or the sharing of existing knowledge. I'm talking about learning in the form of creating new knowledge by confronting situations that have never been seen before and developing new approaches to create value. That kind of learning occurs in the work environment on the front line. It's learning through action, not just sitting and reading books or thinking great new thoughts. And it will encourage us to come together into tightly knit workgroups rather than working in isolated cubicles.*
>
> —John Hagel

As an optimist, John believes this new decade will finally see the rise of opportunity-based narratives that can help all of us make the journey from fear to what he describes as "the passion of the explorer"; that as new solutions start to become attainable faster and with less effort, it will ignite in us the desire to embrace the opportunities ahead. And we will see that our fear is holding us back from acting more boldly. Through maturing digital infrastructures, small groups focused on impact will be connected into networks that can quickly spawn the movements that launch us into a decade of expanding opportunity for everyone.[30] As John reminds us, focusing on efficiency is more dangerous than investing in curiosity:

You need to spend time on the future even when there are more important things to do in the present, and even when there is no immediately apparent return to your efforts. In other words—and this is the hard part—if you want to be productive, you need to spend time doing things that feel ridiculously unproductive.

DEVELOPING YOUR ADAPTABILITY QUOTIENT

A compelling way to bundle all these approaches to navigating the twenty-first century is to think of them as improving your AQ: your *Adaptability Quotient*. Exponential economist and Singularity colleague Amin Toufani explains this as "a collection of capacities that improve our ability to make more confident decisions in circumstances that are less static

---

30 John Hagel, "On the Edge of a New Decade," *Edge Perspectives with John Hagel*, December 17, 2019.

and reliable—the new norm of our quickly shifting exponential world."[31] Moving beyond concepts of IQ (intelligence quotient) and EQ (emotional intelligence quotient), AQ is an answer to what the 1PR future needs of us.

IQ ▸ EQ ▸ AQ

We cannot possibly know it all anymore, so it's best to make peace with that straightaway.

Humility is a big component of our AQ—as is our openness to diverse collaborations. The more we learn from each other's toolboxes, the more adaptive and resilient we can be. We can drop the idea of having to know all the answers and develop the confidence to seek answers outside of our day-to-day experience.

This is a practice we must grow. With a higher AQ, as one line of business becomes more vulnerable, it is possible to seed new growth in another. Apple's iPhone sales are slowing, but they're making a tremendous amount of money on services—a new line of business for them—accelerating their growth from a $1 trillion (that's with a T) company to a $2 trillion valuation in the space of just *two* years.

As business management professor Leon C. Megginson wrote more than fifty years ago:

> *According to Darwin's* Origin of Species, *it is not the most intellectual of the species that survives; it is not the strongest that survives; but the species*

---

31   Natalie Fratto, "Screw Emotional Intelligence—Here's the Key to the Future of Work," *Fast Company*, January 29, 2018.

that survives is the one that is able best to adapt and adjust to the changing environment in which it finds itself.[32]

The point we often miss in our understanding of adaptation is that this is *not* about survival of the fittest individual, but rather it is about finding the best fit within an ecosystem in order to maintain a healthy equilibrium for the whole.

This means that for society to successfully navigate the changes ahead, we must ensure both individuals and the systems that support our lives—schools, government, industry—develop these "adaptive capacities" and that collectively we address imbalances in much more holistic, caring ways.

NAVIGATION IN ACTION

To be better prepared, Marriott has been cultivating its enterprise AQ with the Innovation Lab hotel rooms, which feature "Beta buttons" on the walls, tables, and iPads throughout the room to allow guests to give a quick thumbs up to pleasant experiences and a thumbs down to frustrating ones.[33] Marriott decided to purchase a property of their own to specifically collect this immediate feedback, giving their teams the ability to then advocate, act, and roll out changes more quickly and confidently throughout their network.

We have decades of training that taught us there was a way to do things—via "best practices" and "Six Sigma"—that created security, reduced risk, and ensured consistent, efficient delivery; we were trained to be highly skilled *replicators.*

---

32 Leon C. Megginson, "Lessons from Europe for American Business," *Southwestern Social Science Quarterly,* 1963, 44(1): 3-13.

33 Elizabeth Segran, "Marriott Is Preparing for Gen Z with an Innovation Lab Hotel," *Fast Company,* July 27, 2016.

In a fast-changing world, we need new practices that support us as fluid *navigators*. The 2020 pandemic response showed us how quickly we may have to adapt: in just one phenomenal example, a March 2020 headline incredulously reported that the New York City public school district worked to move 1.1 million children (the majority in low-income homes) to remote learning in a matter of *weeks*.[34] As semesters resumed in the fall, every superintendent had to continue making big decisions quickly with lots of input but very little consistent data or past practice to rely on. They and their teachers are each trying new experiments—from barriers around desks to hybrid schedules—one enterprising teacher is even using plastic inner tubes to keep kindergartners a safe distance from one another.[35] They are inventing, learning, and responding in real time.

Dynamic innovation, however, is iterative—so how do we know if we're doing it well? Booking.com has embraced a culture of experimentation and curiosity that allows employees to test anything, any time, without management's permission, which enables them to make decisions and accelerate innovations and improvements.[36] At any one moment, there might be multiple experiments being conducted to such an extent that no two landing pages are ever the same. Yet the website can be altered with little or no risk because changes are happening in real time. Results can be monitored to see if something is working or not within two hours without crashing the site. It's not just Booking.com; Mark Okerstrom, the CEO of Expedia Group, has described that "At any one time, we're running hundreds, if not thousands, of concurrent experiments, involving millions of visitors. Because of this, we don't have to guess what customers want; we have the

34 David W. Chen, "Teachers' Herculean Task: Moving 1.1 Million Children to Online School," *The New York Times*, March 29, 2020.

35 Hannah Wise, "Here's What America's Covid-Era Classrooms Look Like," *The New York Times*, August 27, 2020.

36 Stefan Thomke, "Building a Culture of Experimentation," *Harvard Business Review*, March 2020.

ability to run the most massive 'customer surveys' that exist, again and again, to have them tell us what they want."

The lesson is that it's not so important whether any one experiment succeeds or fails but how decisions are adjudicated under uncertainty. Organizations need to look at failures not as costly mistakes but as opportunities for learning.

Navigation takes *practice*. We can learn not to freeze in the face of change. We can cultivate our willingness to put new, creative ideas into action. We don't have to wait for a map. In the age of permanent ambiguity, you probably realize by now that a map isn't coming anyway.

Instead, Leadering means we become confident trailblazers. Able to sense the shifts, respond to the changes we see in real time, and competently explore the path we see before us. As we do, we will find our actions are all interrelated and we are much stronger working together than on our own.

CHAPTER FOUR

Connected (versus Alone)

"Being human is not about individual survival or escape. It's a team sport. Whatever future humans have, it will be together."

—Douglas Rushkoff, author, media theorist, and open-source advocate

Over four hundred international technology consultants gathered on Microsoft's Redmond, Washington, campus several years ago. That afternoon, they heard Bob Kelly, Microsoft's former head of cloud computing, speak excitedly about the significance of the digital cloud and how its evolving innovation was enabling the future of predictive analytics, augmented reality environments, AI-enabled solutions, and so many of the advances we can now envision. He spoke with such passion about the cloud's place as a major technology accelerant and what we could expect in years to come.

I was on this panel with Bob discussing the future of work. As he spoke, I began wondering how we, as human beings, could equally accelerate *our* capacities in order to stay aligned with all that the digital cloud would be ushering in. As he finished, I found myself spontaneously asking out loud to the room: "So then what is the equivalent for humans; the 'human cloud,' if you will?" How can we ensure we also thrive? Since then, I have given a lot of thought to how our human "technologies"—our ability to connect, coordinate, and care for one another, which I call our human cloud—are keeping up with these massive technological advancements (or not).

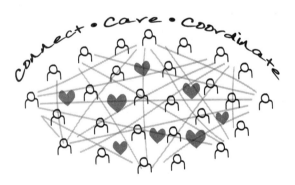

By many measures, society is better off now than at any time in history: lower infant mortality, higher literacy, less hunger, more freedoms. Prior to the pandemic, the World Bank's mission to halve the poverty rate around the world happened five years *ahead* of schedule, with the percentage living in extreme poverty down 36 percent between 1990 and 2015. These industrial advances have, however, come at a price. The health of a large portion of the U.S. population is declining due to increases in obesity, diabetes, cancer, heart disease, and addiction. There are alarming concerns about CO_2 emissions, waste, climate temperature rise, and biodiversity extinction. And for the third year in a row, life span in the U.S. is declining due to opioid death and suicide.[1] We are not taking good care of the whole.

While we can see how technology allows us to take tremendous steps forward in innovation, if those strides are taken with an extractive, short-term mindset that ignores our relationships and responsibilities to each other—they will come at the cost of our collective wellbeing. Just as the Industrial Revolution created environmental and health issues, the Digital Revolution is rapidly creating a new set of social concerns. Though prosperity and standards of living overall are up, we have become an increasingly anxious, addicted, inequitable, and separated culture. So how can we strengthen the social weave and avoid creating an increasingly lopsided and fragile society?

Research consistently points to the power of connection—connection to our colleagues, our business partners, our communities, and, vitally, even to ourselves—to improve our overall health, wellbeing, *and* productivity.

THE COST OF LONELINESS

Let's begin by acknowledging that although being connected to others keeps us thriving—especially during times of stress and change—we have

---

1   Lenny Bernstein, "U.S. Life Expectancy Declines Again, a Dismal Trend Not Seen Since World War I," *The Washington Post*, November 28, 2018.

become terrible at doing so. In study after study, we are reporting increasing rates of social isolation, with at least four in ten people feeling they have no one they could turn to for emotional support.[2] This is true across age groups, but of extraordinary concern are the rates of depression and suicide among teens.

Rashon Lane, a behavioral scientist at the Centers for Disease Control and Prevention, was an author of a recent study in which she discovered that symptoms of anxiety and depressive disorder had increased significantly relative to 2019. It illustrates a disproportionate impact on young adults who are between the ages of eighteen and twenty-four years old,[3] with 62.9 percent reportedly suffering from anxiety, depression, or both. The number of teens admitted to a hospital for a suicidal attempt or suicidal ideation also continues to grow, doubling since 2008 to roughly 1.1 million each year.[4] Think about it: over a million children a year are hospitalized for this. Something is definitely going wrong.

There are many factors contributing to the rise, but VR pioneer, tech philosopher, and outspoken critic of addictive social media practices, Jaron Lanier, made a very vivid point in a post he shared about his visit to a classroom of upscale teens; as they discussed the future, he was startled to hear them ask deep questions about the usefulness of being human in a world dominated and orchestrated by technology. "Why are we here?" they wanted to know. They worried their very existence had no value.[5] Heartbreaking.

---

2   Vivek Murthy, "Work and the Loneliness Epidemic," *Harvard Business Review*, September 2017.

3   Peri Klass, "Young Adults' Pandemic Mental Health Risks," *The New York Times*, August 24, 2020.

4   Dr. Edith Bracho-Sanchez, "Number of Children Going to ER with Suicidal Thoughts, Attempts Doubles, Study Finds," *CNN Health*, April 8, 2019.

5   New York Times Opinion, "Why Are We Here?" *Instagram*, Jaron Lanier, September 25, 2019.

Adults are in the same concerning boat. Former surgeon general Dr. Vivek Murthy was alarmed by findings that loneliness, in particular, is twice as deadly as obesity and as lethal as smoking fifteen cigarettes a day, fueling personal suffering and huge economic costs.[6] In an article in the *Harvard Business Review*, he further reported that lack of social support at work:

> *...can lead to mental sluggishness that impairs productivity, stifles creativity, and hinders decision-making. This directly impacts a company's revenue, spending, and organizational performance. The mental and physical effects of social isolation lead to higher costs for sick leave and health insurance claims. On the flip side, positive social relationships strengthen employee retention and productivity—positively impacting the bottom line.*

This is not something we can simply blame on social media or interoffice messaging apps.

As we continually pay attention to economic growth, we often turn a blind eye to its destructive costs. The purchases and corresponding healthcare expenses attached to alcoholism and addiction, for example, feed GDP while they drive the decline of our wellbeing. It begs the question, how well is this primary measure of growth really serving us?

Even during the pandemic, U.S. financial markets and stock prices continued to grow, while many of our historic community affiliations of support and connection have been eroding: as of 2016, single-person households in the U.S. outnumber married ones, while 110 million adults over eighteen years of age were unmarried. When we have them, our

---

6   Vivek Murthy, "Work and the Loneliness Epidemic," *Harvard Business Review*, September 2017.

families are smaller, and the percentage of households with no children at all has risen sharply.[7] Even the percentage of Americans who go to church has dropped.[8]

Loneliness persists in our work environments as we continue transitioning to gig, remote, solopreneur, and constantly varying shift work. Add to this picture the millions of people now WFH (working from home) expected to "figure it out" on our own, and we begin to appreciate how pervasive the problem is.

Professions that vary as widely as veterinarians, dentists, and military soldiers are all facing high rates of depression and suicide. It is even estimated over half of all CEOs feel lonely and isolated in their role.[9] Dr. Murthy describes the problem this way:

The world is suffering from an epidemic of loneliness. If we cannot rebuild strong, authentic social connections, we will continue to splinter apart—in the workplace and in society. Instead of coming together to take on the great challenges before us, we will retreat to our corners, angry, sick, and alone. We must take action now to build the connections that are the foundation of strong companies and strong communities—and that ensure greater health and wellbeing for all of us.

We are headed in the wrong direction. Our connections are actually ever more important as our work becomes more complex, variable, and

---

7   "The Majority of Children Live with Two Parents, Census Bureau Reports," *United States Census Bureau*, November 17, 2016.

8   Jeffrey M. Jones, "U.S. Church Membership Down Sharply in Past Two Decades," *Gallup*, April 18, 2019.

9   Vivek Murthy, "Work and the Loneliness Epidemic," *Harvard Business Review*, September 2017.

distributed. Simply put, we are better off as individuals and as organizations when we are *connected* than when we are alone. It is why building and leveraging connections is a core practice of Leadering.

THE IMPORTANCE OF COMMUNITY

Paradoxically, the need for connection and community has become acute as both the pandemic and the social justice movement create extraordinary levels of stress, isolation, and other pressures.

We long to feel a sense of affiliation as well as to feel useful. As we bravely march into new territories, we want to know we aren't alone; we need to believe there are people we can turn to who are vested in our success and growth. We want to feel secure as part of the human cloud.

Coworking has been on the rise for the past fifteen years. It makes sense, then, that global coworking megabrand WeWork grew so quickly around the world (management challenges notwithstanding) by promising to be the "analog social network" for entrepreneurs—another group hard hit by anxiety and loneliness. They started with one city in 2010 and by 2019, expanded to more than 111 cities with 528 offices. Entrepreneurial incubators have grown for a similar reason. Breaking out to start your own business is a high-risk venture, financially and socially. It's isolating to be out on the edge, constantly trying to galvanize others into investing in your dream. In the case of entrepreneurs, sharing physical space with others who are pursuing a business dream makes taking chances feel less daunting.

Meanwhile, back in our traditional offices, let's consider how loneliness affects the average office worker. Before we all moved into our shelter-in-place home office spaces, apparently, nearly 62 percent of American workers ate lunch at their office desks.[10] Alone. On social media site Tumblr, I once found a thread dedicated to posting solo lunch photos. The irony! As we collectively rethink where we physically work in the 2020s, it's important we also consider how we connect.

Turns out, the most important "technology" we have is simply to be human.

Prioritizing connection makes us healthier, less anxious, and more innovative. To not value our interconnectedness—to not leverage the "human cloud"—is to further contribute to our societal breakdowns. It can also lead to painful results if we make decisions that ignore our shared connectedness and humanity.

International consulting firm McKinsey was lambasted for helping institutions save money at the expense of human care. In one notable example, McKinsey advised Purdue Pharma on how to "turbocharge" opioid sales;[11] in another, the firm suggested that Immigration and Customs Enforcement reduce costs of caring for migrants and detainees by cutting back on food and medical care.[12] This corrosive, and honestly cruel, attitude has invaded the tech industry, too, as social media companies exploit our loneliness and anxiety to drive "engagement" in order to chase advertising revenue.

In his article "Survival of the Richest," media theorist, technology futurist, and prolific author Douglas Rushkoff described an especially disturbing disconnect in a private meeting he held with several billionaires whom he'd been led to believe wanted to better understand the transformative capacities of

---

10 "Failure to Lunch," *New York Times Magazine*, February 25, 2016.
11 Michael Forsyth and Walt Bogdanich, "McKinsey Advised Purdue Pharma How to 'Turbocharge' Opioid Sales, Lawsuit Says," *The New York Times*, February 1, 2019.
12 Ian MacDougall, "How McKinsey Helped the Trump Administration Carry Out Its Immigration Policies," *The New York Times*, December 3, 2019.

emerging technologies.[13] Instead, they wanted to learn how these technologies could serve not their companies or their stakeholders but *themselves.*

They asked how they might ensure their personal guards would keep their properties safe after an economic or environmental crash. Was there some kind of collar these billionaires could put on their security guards to monitor and control their actions, they wanted to know? Shocked, Douglas tried countering by asking them what might happen if—instead of seeking to *control* the people in their employ—these billionaires built meaningful relationships by, for example, inviting their guards to their sons' bar mitzvahs? A humanistic suggestion that was quickly dismissed.

That these captains of industry could envision a financial, societal, or environmental catastrophe, but felt no agency to either prevent or address these issues, shook Douglas. He has since founded a project called Team Human that explores how we ensure human interconnectedness remains central to our digital networks and technologies.

Clearly, when we don't feel connected to each other, we find it much easier to exploit and extract value from another.

DIVING DEEPER
DOUGLAS RUSHKOFF ON DECENTRALIZING POWER

Douglas Rushkoff, media theorist, author, and professor, is a social observer who for decades has focused on how technology is shaping the ways we connect and relate with one

---

13 Douglas Rushkoff, "Survival of the Richest," *Medium*, July 5, 2018.

another. In 2013, his book *Present Shock* helped us acknowledge the anxiety that accompanies a culture "when everything happens now" and better manage the implications of permanent ambiguity (and FOMO) that now shape our daily lives.

In *Throwing Rocks at the Google Bus*, Douglas exposes the ways shortsighted capital markets and short-term investors with a relentless drive for growth have shaped the toxic, extractive business models now fueling wealth inequality and threatening the long-term wellbeing of society. He reminds us that it hasn't always been this way: back when marketplaces began to emerge, people exchanged goods at markets and bazaars using currency designed only for that day, fostering a culture of interdependence and mutually beneficial win-win relationships. When feudal lords wanted in on the action, however, they created the kinds of rules and practices that effectively killed the natural, more equitable coordination between people…which are still shaping our business strategies today.

The digital economy has gone wrong. Everybody knows it, but no one knows quite how to fix it, or even how to explain the problem. This isn't the fault of digital technology at all, but the way we are deploying it: instead of building the distributed digital economy these new networks could foster, we are doubling down on the industrial age mandate for growth above all. This is more the legacy of early corporatism and central currency than a feature of digital technology. We are running a twenty-first century digital economy on a thirteenth century printing-press-era operating system.

—Douglas Rushkoff

His most recent book and growing podcast, *Team Human*, explores the desire to break apart calcified institutional systems that focus on centralized power at the expense of taking good care of individuals and society. Douglas encourages us to explore the ways digital technologies can be restructured to replace outdated hierarchies and foster strong connections— to each other and to the environments in which we operate—to build more fluid, responsive, and humane systems of collaborative benefit.

TELLING STORIES

The value of connection and community hasn't gone unnoticed in leadership and research circles either. Karen Tay, Smart Nation director for Singapore, lives in San Francisco and leads strategy and operations work across four time zones. As we all began working from home following the COVID-19 outbreak, she offered tips in a LinkedIn post for how to manage remote teams. For example, during her regular team video calls, she introduces a quick "social" question at the start, asking things like, "What's the song you listen to when you're having a bad day?" It only takes five minutes, and as Karen reports, often leads to a good laugh together before jumping into work. Several teammates mentioned that they look forward to this personal connection at the start of their calls. Research bears this value out too.

As reported in another *Harvard Business Review* story, several business school professors found a very effective tool that is as fun as it is simple:[14]

---

14 Leigh Thompson, "Research: For Better Brainstorming, Tell an Embarrassing Story," *Harvard Business Review*, October 2, 2017.

At your next team brainstorming session, how about you start with everyone sharing an embarrassing moment they've experienced in their lives? It could be a slip-up in sixth-grade gym class, a first-date disaster, or a time they uttered the wrong words giving a speech in a packed auditorium. Anything works. In this experiment, sharing simple, vulnerable moments and laughing together resulted in a 26 percent increase in the number of bold ideas created within the group.

Why does this work? Think about how these stories connect us: if I'm willing to share a personal or embarrassing event, and then you tell me your story, it creates an empathetic bridge between us. Suddenly I don't feel silly throwing out crazy ideas with the team, and we can all take more risks together. Researcher Amy Edmonson describes this more formally as creating "psychological safety."[15]

Parker Palmer, founder of the Center for Courage and Renewal, turned his focus on teams that have inherent tension, such as doctors and nurses, or sales and marketing units of large corporations. When day-to-day interactions involve a tug-of-war, Parker suggests starting meetings with a similar approach: invite each participant to tell a personal story. In the case of a contentious school board meeting, he opened by asking each participant to describe the best teacher they ever had. Doing so completely shifted the energy in the room. Instead of each person defending the point of view they walked in with, they became highly motivated to solve the problem, together. The point is to help people connect on a more human level and break down perceived barriers. With barriers down, a team can better relate to the human than the role—and therefore work more fluidly and respectfully together.

---

15 Amy Edmondson, "Creating Psychological Safety in the Workplace," interview with Chris Nickisch, *Harvard Business Review*, January 22, 2019.

Still need convincing? As he was forming his team, former surgeon general Vivek Murthy created a weekly "Inside Scoop" moment in which team members took turns creating a photo slideshow to share something about themselves during the first five minutes of the weekly staff meetings. Rather than seeing it as a waste of time, this quickly became people's favorite part of the week, and the results of this five-minute investment in each other were immediate. As Dr. Murthy shared:

> *People felt more valued by the team after seeing their colleagues' genuine reactions to their stories. Team members who had traditionally been quiet during discussions began speaking up. Many began taking on tasks outside their traditional roles. They appeared less stressed at work. And most of them told me how much more connected they felt to their colleagues and the mission they served.[16]*

While it's common for managers to worry about taking these few "unproductive" minutes away from the specific agenda, Leading understands that doing so vastly improves performance across many measures. Google's Project Aristotle, which studied hundreds of teams over the course of a few years to understand what factors lead to more effective output, found that *vulnerability, camaraderie,* and *social connection* led to better collaboration and team performance.[17]

The learning here is clear: having that sense of psychological safety within a community inspires us to engage more together and contribute more boldly. When we trust we are seen and appreciated, we give more. Most importantly, in a fast-moving VUCA environment filled with ambiguity

---

16 Vivek Murthy, "Work and the Loneliness Epidemic," *Harvard Business Review*, September 2017.

17 Charles Duhigg, "What Google Learned from Its Quest to Build the Perfect Team," *The New York Times*, February 25, 2016.

and the demand for constant learning, this fundamental appreciation of our shared humanness is *the* key to confidently conceiving, prototyping, and accepting feedback on radically new ideas.

CONNECTING TO OURSELVES

As the future demands bigger ideas and greater adaptiveness from us, we will need to reinforce our human cloud with not only rich opportunities to connect, but also the willingness to expose ourselves more fully and build even deeper levels of trust. We must acquire greater personal resilience and a more compassionate understanding of ourselves. This will enable us to more confidently open up to new thinking, respectfully challenge ideas, and receive feedback from a growing constellation of peers and partners. With strong support, each of these practices can be cultivated; we just haven't been asked to before.

WELCOMING THE DARK SIDE

In many business cultures, employees don't show up entirely as they are or expose how they are feeling. Nor are they encouraged to. As such, they spend energy posturing, wanting to make sure it's clear that "everything is great" and they're on top of their game. In a culture like that, people hide mistakes and vulnerabilities. And they certainly stay away from anything new that could challenge their sense of security. Not surprisingly, this echoes the old Industrial Revolution-based economy where people were taught that mistakes were costly disruptions to the maximum efficiency of honed replication, as opposed to opportunities for growth and breakthroughs. Transparency suffers in this kind of environment. So do communication, collaboration, learning, and the opportunity to build trust.

We need to embrace, rather than deny, our vulnerabilities. In *An Everyone Culture: Becoming a Deliberately Developmental Organization*, Robert Keegan and his research team at Harvard coach organizations to recognize employees' blind spots and leverage mistakes as opportunities for personal and professional growth.[18] Robert and his team found that the encouragement to be fully themselves and walk through the perceived risks improved people's ability to navigate ambiguous environments, thereby contributing to impressive growth for the companies they studied.

Mike Robbins, author of *Bring Your Whole Self to Work*, also described this need for vulnerability in the workplace:

> *When we don't bring our whole selves to work, we suffer—engagement, productivity, and our wellbeing is diminished. We aren't able to do our best, most innovative work, and we waste too much time trying to look good, fit in, and do or say the "right" thing. For teams and organizations, this lack of psychological safety makes it difficult for the group or company to thrive and perform at their highest level because people are holding back some of who they really are.[19]*

This, of course, is a practice; it takes time and skill to build trust and learn to do this comfortably.

However, it matters, because when we feel safe and respected for bringing our whole selves (and full lives) into our work environment, we build the honest and robust connections that allow us to weather challenges more effectively. We are then more engaged and willing to proactively contribute.

---

18 Robert Keegan, Lisa Lahey, Andy Fleming, and Matthew Miller, *An Everyone Culture: Becoming a Deliberately Developmental Organization* (Brighton: Harvard Business Review Press, 2016).

19 Henna Inam, "Bring Your Whole Self to Work," *Forbes*, May 10, 2018.

DEVELOPING EMOTIONAL RESILIENCE

This new era demands more creative risk-taking, shared thinking and building, and questioning of conventional, often extractive or biased, approaches. To avoid dangerous myopia, we must be challenged to see our blind spots. This requires us to be more personally visible, to openly examine our values, and to be authentic and vulnerable about how unfamiliar ideas and perspectives make us feel. But doing so can put us in a very uncomfortable place at times—especially in a highly homogenous team or industry. Being the outlier who questions an idea or challenges an approach is not easy (believe me, I know).

Being real in a fast-changing environment takes courage and support. Being able to openly listen to and appreciate someone else's point of view, receive candid feedback on our thinking, or accept a challenge to one of our long-held beliefs requires an evolved kind of inner fortitude. At the core, we must believe that we are enough and that our value is less tied to what we have to prove and more to our willingness to learn.

Let's also get real here and admit that learning *itself* can cause its own waves of self-doubt and frustration, making us occasionally question in a dark moment how we even got this far. This is so very human. Taking the time for self-care and reflection allows us to become more conscious of what we are feeling (and why). With deeper emotional grounding and resilience, we can strengthen our AQ and respond to new or challenging ideas with greater openness and understanding.

SELF-AWARENESS FOR COOPERATIVE ADVANTAGE

"When we take care of our center, we can handle the chaos on the edge."
—Shaku Selvakumar, technology CMO and founder of ActivaTeen

"Know thyself" has never been better business advice.

When interviewing American swimmer and Olympian Michael Phelps for a large corporate event, I was, of course, inspired to hear his stories of victory and perseverance, but it was his open sharing of seeking help for extreme depression that earned my deepest respect. Following a disappointing experience at the 2012 London Olympic Games, he found himself spiraling into four scary days of suicidal ideation and pain. Bravely, Michael checked himself into a treatment center. During the first several counseling sessions, he was asked simply to focus on one thing: his counselor asked him to look at a wall of emoji-type faces and point to the one that most expressed his feelings at the moment. "Seriously?!" he barked. "How ridiculous!" But soon after, he was able to connect his anger to a deep well of unexpressed rage stemming from childhood and his complex feelings with his father. From there, the healing and learning began, allowing him to return to the Olympic arena stronger, healthier, and clearer. Swimming for himself rather than to live up to the perceived expectations of others, Michael earned six medals in the 2016 Rio games , including five golds, and became the oldest individual gold medalist in Olympic swimming history, as well as the first swimmer to win four consecutive golds in the same event.

Greater self-awareness allows us to *respond*, rather than *react*, intentionally from a place of centeredness and as an expression of our values. When we take care of ourselves and nurture our "center," we are freer to meet the challenges of the future without fear and to interact more openly with others from a place of internal integrity and calm.

As the loneliness epidemic has taken hold, a whole "anxiety economy" has sprung up to help people calm down and connect more meaningfully to themselves and others. Recreational marijuana and CBD sales[20] have boomed in recent years alongside gravity blankets and houseplants to help us improve our focus, sleep, and neurological health. Michael Phelps has become a spokesperson for Talkspace, the fast-growing online, on-demand counseling service he uses. Meditation apps ping us a few times a day to remind us to take deep breaths for one minute; Calm has become a billion-dollar business on the Apple app store. Mindfulness is now often included as part of executive training at large corporations, and in our children's schools, SEL (social and emotional learning) has become an integral part of their classrooms. Even military leaders are employing mindfulness tools to help them be more effective in the field. And as first responders around the U.S. have begun learning mindfulness techniques, these front-line professionals have found that meditation helps them ease stress and bring more compassion to their work, improving community relationships while on the job.[21]

Mindfulness practices are not only becoming accepted—from Chili's restaurant leadership to the United Way's transformative CEO (photographed in *Harvard Business Review* meditating at his desk[22])—but they could be considered essential to manage the volatile environments we find ourselves in. Recognizing the importance of this practice in reducing stress and feelings of isolation as the boundaries between our private lives and our work continue to erode, Microsoft is now collaborating with meditation app Headspace to integrate mindfulness features into their Teams

---

20 "Martha Launches a New Line of CBD Products, Created with Canopy Growth," *Martha Stewart*, September 10, 2020.

21 Barry Yeoman, "Mindful Policing: The Future of Force," *Mindful*, June 14, 2017.

22 Brian Gallagher, "United Way's CEO on Shifting a Century-Old Business Model," *Harvard Business Review*, October 2018.

workflow offerings, potentially replacing our daily commutes with a daily reflection practice instead.

The cornerstone of researcher and author Brené Brown's powerful work on team dynamics and success is recognizing our own vulnerability, resilience, and self-awareness.

DIVING DEEPER
BRENÉ BROWN ON LEVERAGING VULNERABILITY

Brené Brown is a shame and empathy researcher and five-time number one *New York Times* bestselling author who speaks to our need for vulnerability, compassion, and courage in both our personal and professional lives. Brené urges us to recognize people as whole individuals rather than facades that simply show up to get work done. She argues there needs to be congruence: if you're asking your employees to be vulnerable, but then you criticize them for speaking up, your actions have defeated the purpose of your request. How do you celebrate accomplishments and encourage people to learn?

To me, a leader is someone who holds her or himself accountable for finding potential in people and processes. A critical mass of brave leaders is the foundation of an intentionally courageous culture. Every time we are brave with our lives, we make the people around us a little braver and our organizations bolder and stronger.

—Brené Brown

> When we reflect on who we are and bring a greater sense of self-awareness to our work, we can put practices and structures in place that fully leverage our strengths for collaboration. Brené has pushed the conversation of vulnerability and wholeheartedness to the forefront of Leadering and increased our capacity to celebrate diversity and change.

UNLOCKING THE HUMAN CLOUD

As we become more accepting and compassionate with ourselves, we become that much more comfortable (and less threatened) learning and building with others, allowing us to unlock entirely new possibilities for business growth and innovation.

During the Oslo Business Forum last year, I strapped on a pair of VR goggles and was taken on a digital journey through the back-end processing and logistics needed to enable me to not only design my very own custom pair of Adidas sneakers but have them delivered within days. Imagine all the players that need to come together to deliver on this promise of future retail: from the AI-powered online site that guides my choices and maybe takes my Bitcoin payment, to the materials partners alerted in real time of the colors and textures I've chosen, to the 3D printer or robot seamstresses nearest me waiting to assemble and sustainably package my shoes, to the scheduling of drone pick-up, to the transport to a secure delivery site. Executing something like this requires a well-coordinated and synchronized collection of many partners and systems.

In the old economy, we were taught autonomy was a strength. We believed it decreased dependency (and therefore risk) and gave an organization a proprietary advantage. A client once even asked me to sign a non-disclosure agreement so that I would not be able to share their newly defined values with anyone. Contrast this to the behavior of new-economy companies emerging at the same time, who would instead want to spray-paint their values on the roof of their headquarters (if they could), for *every* airline passenger to see. This way, they would be better able to draw talent and resources to them. The old economy incentivized us to keep our beliefs secret and rely on just ourselves. But in the 1PR, to meet complex market needs and wants with even greater speed, we have to collaborate with a collection of partners to manifest our vision.

GATHERING YOUR PYNKRS

When we actively grow our personal communities, we not only find new partners and collaborators, but we create a rich network of minds to explore the possibilities of the future. Joining "share groups" in which peers learn together is one avenue. In fact, it has never been easier to reach out and connect with anyone around the world. In just two days within my own network, I heard from a design school in India, a like-minded AI entrepreneur in California who was galvanized by one of my online webinars and wants to build an AI app with me, an IoT startup in Ukraine asking for input, and a cryptocurrency advocate who offered to champion my work. LinkedIn, as another common starting point, is a treasure trove of people you can follow and converse with on any range of business, leadership, and technology topics. Taking the time to actively build relationships with thought leaders and innovators gives us resources we can turn to when taking on a new assignment or trying to vet a new approach.

A former collaborator of mine, Lynne Casey, and I described this network of thinkers and supporters we had each built as our PYNKrs—People You

Need to Know. Making time for deep conversations with these people, asking and answering questions, sorting through new ideas and potential applications, and exploring the horizon together is what gives me the confidence to exchange ideas with C-suite executives, accept a global foresight assignment, or stand on stage sharing my perspectives in front of several thousand people. I know I am never alone.

Does all of this seem obvious to you? Well, interestingly, each time my teams and I dive into a new consulting assignment, we see how isolated leaders in most organizations are.

Very few executives have connections outside of their business circles, with almost no portal for new information or outside perspectives to flow into. This gap inspired us to make our collection of PYNKrs and their work more visible to others. It also led us to launch the Femme Futurists Society,[23] in which we introduce those that are curious to the world-shaping ideas of leading futurists from across the globe. You've been meeting some of these inspiring thinkers along the way as you've been reading this book.

Two masters of this practice are Jerry Michalski, founder of REX, the Relationship Economy Expedition, which connects tech, business, and education leaders together; and Yarrow Kraner, founder of HATCH: a gathering of artists, technologists, and business innovators who want to hatch a better world. They have each formed thoughtfully curated communities of "change-agents, mavericks, and explorers," who very few others know are out there. They've each designed their community in ways that nourish every person and encourage all of us to share. Neither is a "networking group." Neither is focused on efficiency or a transactional outcome. They are giving those who work on the edge—and who, like the CEOs

---

23 www.femmefuturists.com

mentioned earlier, often feel isolated—an opportunity to give and take openly and generously. Being a part of both REX and HATCH has allowed me to expand, enrich, and tap into my human cloud.

The most important feature of these communities is that they're not homogenous. These are not groups of peers, but rather diverse collections of makers and builders who, when they exchange ideas, give each other entirely new input. To truly innovate, we have to find and connect with the interesting people outside our day-to-day work—we have to get out and meet people who can help us change the whole game.

LEVERAGING ECOSYSTEMS

TATA Consultancy Services (TCS), India's largest IT consultancy, with a market capitalization of over $100 billion, has identified the need to cultivate and leverage ecosystem partners as one of the key imperatives for delivering what they describe as "Business 4.0." While they acknowledge many organizations are struggling to dynamically configure and manage a growing list of ecosystem partners, in their 2019 report, they point out the

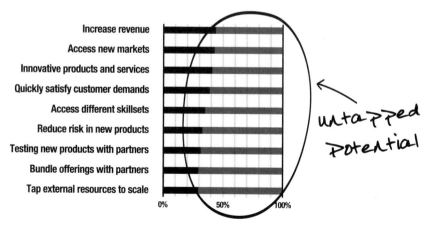

Credit: TCS Business 4.0 Framework

benefits of developing these capacities. At the top: higher revenues, access to new markets and different skills, and the ability to more quickly and relevantly satisfy customer demands.[24]

These benefits apply not only to companies producing products and managing supply chains but to entire industries as well. Healthcare is transforming from a bloated, ineffective, clinical-based model to a community-centric one that integrates a wide range of human, ground-level support services with very advanced technological solutions. It now includes things like home DNA testing kits, data from wearables, and retail health clinics that also offer mental health services. The list continues to expand.

As an outgrowth of Defense Secretary Ash Carter's military innovation plan, in 2018, the U.S. Army established its Futures Command center in Austin, Texas, to foster collaborations with civilian innovators and university labs working in AI, VR, 3D printing, and robotics. This opened in the glass-walled offices of Austin's entrepreneurial tech hub, Capital Factory, with only twelve people, and just a year later the program has grown to twenty-four thousand people around the world, helping direct a $30 billion modernization effort that is reportedly fueling the Army's "largest reorganization effort in more than forty years."[25]

THE DEATH OF SILOS

The Futures Command center's success is especially impressive when you consider what it takes to truly foster this level of shared learning and collaboration at scale. From my observations, software and machine-learning

---

24 "Business 4.0," *Tata Consultancy Services Limited*, 2018.
25 Sean Kimmons, "In First Year, Futures Command Grows from 12 to 24,000 Personnel," *Army News Service*, July 19, 2019.

engineers work differently from the operations-centric world that raised me. Peer coding to reduce mistakes, fluid roles within project teams (meaning: sometimes you're the lead, sometimes the support), shared learning, geographically distributed locations united by scrum sessions, and clearly defined sprints that allow for new input rather than detailed project roadmaps—this was all new to me when I joined my first AI startup company. How eye-opening! Part of it is ethos: *building* versus *optimizing* requires a different way of working. Part of it is having collaborative tools that reduce friction: Github. Jira. Confluence. Slack. Project rooms... and Zoom, Microsoft Teams, and Google Meetings. The list of new platforms or concepts we experiment with grows each year and enables us to flatten hierarchy and steadily improve our abilities to sense and respond. Even Facebook announced big advances in virtual reality as they unveiled "Infinite Office," a new feature for business collaboration that will allow users to enter a virtual office from any place they choose to work.

But we cannot rely solely on software to unleash the potential in our new relationships; we must open our thinking to up our "connectional intelligence."[26] This is a term coined by Erica Dhawan, co-author of *Get Big Things Done* and a global expert on connecting humans inside and outside of traditional organizational structures. She demonstrates the power of connectional intelligence with a story about a law firm's incoming associates who, in 2012, had created an internal, modified version of Twitter to discuss the details of their cases with each other, openly asking for advice and exchanging helpful information. They were working far more efficiently and quickly—so much so that they were reporting fewer billing hours. A traditional firm guided by an old-economy mindset would have prioritized billing over all else and shut down the associates' messaging network. Instead, this firm recognized the value of what these associates

---

26 EricaDhawan.com

had created and opted to raise awareness of the network among all their employees, inviting the younger associates to mentor the older generation.

By actively cultivating and harvesting the shared learning of their human cloud, the firm was not only delivering better as a collective, but it was also able to take on more meaningful work with the same staff, presumably delivering greater value to their clients and more satisfaction for associates. While the new technology was the enabler, these productivity advances were only possible because the people—the young associates who took the initiative to create the discussion tool and the leadership that expanded it company-wide—valued and prioritized connectedness.

In her influential work, Erica shares many stories of how organizations can actively break down silos, embrace crowdsourcing insights—even for highly scientific or technical questions—and intentionally design physical spaces for more organic interactions.[27] Google, for example, has studied the optimal time each person should spend in line in their company cafeterias in order to give coworkers time to connect without frustrating them (four minutes seems optimal). But one of the biggest AQ-related advantages in a future of increasingly independent and distributed talent will be the ability to create compelling ways to draw folks to each other in service of the big tasks that need to get done. As Erica puts it, "Connectional intelligence is about the ability to structure problems in such a way that many people will want to pitch in to solve them."

We continue to advocate that as traditional hierarchies and organization structures become flatter, as the safety of silos disintegrates, as the role of middle-management gets closer scrutiny, and as we shift to more self-organized work and teams, the ability to use new tools and work in ways

---

27 CotentialGroup.com

that foster human connection ensures we transition to a digital economy and more sustainable, transformative business models with less anxiety and turbulence.

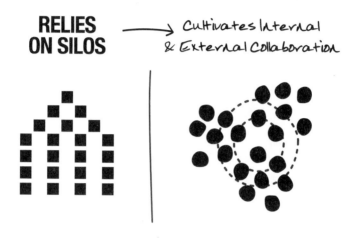

RELIES ON SILOS ⟶ Cultivates Internal & External Collaboration

GETTING IT DONE: INTEGRATED PROJECT DELIVERY

While there are so many encouraging reasons to cultivate the human cloud, it is always helpful to see how this actually works in practice. When speaking at an architecture conference, I perked up when I heard a team of Canadian practitioners describe how they have successfully transitioned from a traditional "waterfall" approach—in which one team or company hands their work off sequentially to the next team in the building process—to a much more integrated one that challenges many best-practice assumptions.

Architecting something from the ground up—literally, in the case of a building—takes a great deal of effort, focus, and faith. It requires the talents of a large number of design and construction experts, who traditionally operate under separate contractual agreements. This siloed arrangement inhibits collaboration and encourages the tendency to blame "the other guy" when best-laid plans don't come to fruition. Collaboration doesn't always come naturally to us, and as a result, we organize with the goal of "not failing" versus organizing in a way that embraces possibility and allows us to respond dynamically to changes. Leadering flips this and sees collaboration as a way of mitigating risk versus creating it.

In most construction projects, it is nearly impossible to make any design modifications along the way without going backward and incurring large costs, but these architects committed to an Integrated Project Delivery (IPD) approach to ensure all players have input throughout the design and construction processes. Meaning all professionals are on board at the start of the design phase and can give input on concepts and blueprints; and although there are still handoffs of active work throughout the building process, any who have "finished" their chief phase remain involved to advise and have skin in the game until completion. Working this way creates greater engagement and learning among all participants, as they tangibly see how their work connects to others' and can experience their input being valued. In contrast to initial expectations, having all players involved throughout the IPD process in many cases *saves* costs for everyone involved.

The key to fostering smooth collaboration with a large number of partners is establishing a shared intention and approach. At the outset, IPD participants agree to the values they will be governed by. They then use these values to guide all major decisions, which incentivizes more holistic solutions and innovative thinking.

Take the example of a handrail installation in a new school building: when insight came in about student needs, this integrated team agreed to pilot a custom design—one geared to optimizing the material they chose for construction *and* better serving the client's needs. They built charging outlets into each handrail to support student devices (like their tablets, phones,

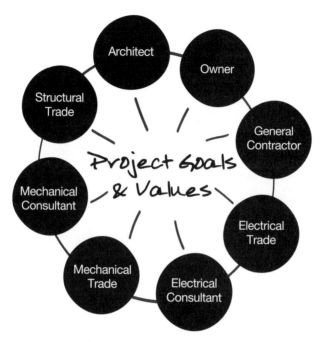

Credit: Integrated Project Delivery Alliance

and earbuds), as students often wait for others around staircases, landings, and patios. They designed and 3D printed this custom staircase for the new school rather than going with the premanufactured option originally recommended and budgeted, because ultimately, this responsive, higher-quality solution resulted in a significant 7 percent savings. Confident they were focused on the same goals from the outset and checking in with each other along the way, this integrated team was able to shift gears halfway through the project.

Most encouragingly, however, the IPD process is built to confidently address when things go wrong versus trying to control for each variable from the starting line. In this fast-changing world, we can only take risks if we feel we are held safely when things don't go as planned; building trust, sharing insights, and creating a faster, less expensive way to recover from mistakes encourages bolder thinking and more responsive problem-solving.

Refining and codifying this approach over the past ten years, a community of architects, designers, and builders in Canada has created a workbook, simply titled *Integrated Project Delivery: An Action Guide for Leaders.*[28] As I flip through it, I wonder: How can this approach to collaboration—in expensive, high-stakes environments, no less—be applied to other industries? As all businesses confront the mandate to design and build new solutions (versus replicate and deliver flawlessly), what can we learn from this architectural community and their experience with IPD? And I wonder if the members of the Integrated Project Delivery Alliance can see any value in training leaders outside their industry, maybe even creating a new consulting revenue stream?

As we seek to learn with each other, guide, and validate new ideas, we grow a kind of social brain. And that becomes another game-changer.

THE NEW SHAPE OF POWER

At this moment in time there is an incredible volume of traffic every single minute of the day on social networks: 527,760 Snapchat photos shared, 120 professionals join LinkedIn, 4,146,600 users watch YouTube videos (four million per minute), 456,000 tweets are sent, and 46,740 photos are posted on Instagram.[29] Within all this activity are tremendous opportunities for connection—both good and bad.

---

28 James Pease et al., *Integrated Project Delivery: An Action Guide for Leaders*, 2019.

29 Michael Einstein, "Some Amazing Statistics about Online Data Creation and Growth Rates," *Information Overload Research Group*, April 17, 2019.

Jeremy Heimans and Henry Timms were each early pioneers in leveraging technologies and tendencies, encouraging us to connect and coordinate with strangers. Henry created #GivingTuesday, the international generosity movement centered on charitable giving on the Tuesday after Thanksgiving. And Jeremy co-founded a global civic organization called Avaaz.org that claims over forty million members in 194 countries,[30] as well as an agency called Purpose, which is focused on building social movements. Together, they authored a *Harvard Business Review* article in 2014[31] and a subsequent book in 2018 calling us to understand "New Power." They were motivated by how the new hyperconnected landscape was enabling "movements to build, businesses to thrive, and ideas to catch fire" as they saw the big shift taking place between old power and new:

- **Old power works like a currency. It is held by few.** Once gained, it is jealously guarded, and the powerful have a substantial store of it to spend. It is closed, inaccessible, and leader-driven. It downloads, and it captures.

- **New power operates differently, like a current. It is made by many.** It is open, participatory, and peer-driven. It uploads, and it distributes. Like water or electricity, it's most forceful when it surges. The goal with new power is not to hoard it but to channel it.

- Old power models ask only that we comply or consume (e.g., doctors). New power models demand and allow for more: that we share ideas, create content or assets, or even shape a community (e.g., *patientslikeme.org*).

---

30 Avaaz.org, 2020.

31 Jeremy Heimans and Henry Timms, "Understanding 'New Power,'" *Harvard Business Review*, December 2014.

OLD POWER VALUES	NEW POWER VALUES
CURRENCY	Current
HELD BY FEW	Made by Many
DOWNLOADS	Uploads
COMMANDS	Shares
LEADER-DRIVEN	Peer-Driven
CLOSED	Open
CONTROL	*Agency*

Credit: Jeremy Heimans and Henry Timms

TEDx is a prime example of new power in action. In 2009, TED—the highly curated global gathering of thought leaders and speakers across the domains of technology, entertainment, design, and so much more— decided to embrace their mission of "ideas worth sharing" and start an initiative to offer regional TEDsters the chance to create an event in their local community. These curators would follow a set of shared guidelines and best practices but act without direct supervision or centralized control from "big TED." I was thrilled to be one of the first licensed organizers who pledged to uphold the ethos but in my own way. There was a clear frame, but within that, we were each free to curate the content we believed worked best for our unique locales—from the Sydney Opera House to a low-caste school in India, to a prison in San Diego—and a new state-of-the-art motor racing compound in Austin. *We* had the power. And it unleashed extraordinary creativity and commitment that challenged old-power business models. Though no local organizer has been paid, over the past ten years, more than 100,000 TEDx events have been produced, and the movement continues to roar forward, launching many extraordinary ideas and leaders into our lives.

As powerful as community gathering is, however, it is not our only seat of power. We also each hold it in the palm of our hand—literally—feeding our social streams with constant expectations and feedback to companies, candidates, and each other. Which begs an additional compass question: Have you cultivated a community that cares and given them the tools to advocate for and create with you?

We are also now holding companies and public figures accountable to greater standards of care for their stakeholders. We need to believe and see that through a company's actions, they *authentically* care. In the old economy, we valued companies for perfect production and delivery of their products; in the new economy, we value companies we can trust to build ever-changing solutions for our wellbeing. When we feel a company has our backs, we're more likely to trust them even when they stumble—and indeed, come to defend them if necessary.

This shift to new power does not, however, mean all is polite, respectful, or true. And the rise of conspiracy theories, name-calling, and trolling is further amplified by algorithms that prey on agitation and demonize our differences. It is helpful to remember that social media channels also connect those who feel isolated to communities of support, validation, and, when needed, care. Comedian Sarah Silverman shows us how it's done.

THE BEAUTY OF CONNECTION

It started with one word. Specifically, a different "C" word, which a Twitter user hurled at performer Sarah Silverman in response to one of her posts. Understandably, she could have ignored the guy or lashed out with her own salvo, but Sarah made a more heart-centered choice. She looked through his Twitter stream, read a string of prior posts, and learned that he was experiencing back pain and expressing a lot of anger in response.

Rather than send him a private message, Sarah posted a public response to him: "*I believe in you. I read ur timeline & I see what ur doing & your rage is thinly veiled pain. But u know that. I know this feeling. Ps My back [F] sux too. see what happens when u choose love. I see it in you.*"[32]

The tweets went back and forth from there. He described how he'd been out of work for a long period of time and had no resources for the medical care he needed. He quickly apologized to Sarah for what he had called her—all of this in the open for anyone interested to read. Sarah then reached out to the Twitterverse to help raise money for his medical costs and find physicians in his local area who could help. When he finally received an MRI, it turns out this "troll" had five cracked vertebrae, had no income, had suffered serious trauma at age eight, had no health insurance, and had no one he could turn to. With this insight, it becomes clearer to see what would make someone hurl their pain (inside and out) onto the rest of the world. A psychologist might say this man wanted to ease his isolation by making everyone else feel hurt too.

Sarah had learned this years earlier in an experience with what she called "the most honest heckler ever"; after doing his heckling thing at one of her

---

32 Bill Murphy Jr., "People Can't Stop Talking about How Sarah Silverman Handled a Twitter Troll. (It's a Master Class in Emotional Intelligence)," *Inc.*, January 7, 2018.

comedy shows, this guy got quiet, and she heard him say under his breath, "I exist." She realized then that was the whole point of heckling (and trolling): an unhappy or struggling person is acting out to be seen and heard.

Her Twitter story is not only heartening, but it also illustrates in multiple ways how critical compassionate response is in our shift to a more connected mindset.

Sarah's ability to act from a caring and nonjudgmental place rather than react from anger demonstrates a personal resilience and healthy sense of self; she didn't feel provoked to defend herself because she quickly recognized these ugly remarks had nothing actually to do with her. Similarly, in our professional lives, it is important that in moments of confusion or stress brought on by change or ambiguity, we don't get hijacked by the stories in our heads that turn something that simply *happens* into something that personally impacts our sense of self. Also, Sarah's recognition of her own vulnerability when she experienced severe back pain enabled her to more quickly recognize the man's situation and empathize. In our work relationships, even just being able to identify how we are feeling (or have felt) is crucial to our ability to connect and collaborate effectively in high-stress environments.

During the pandemic, we have witnessed so many acts of corporate compassion. Luxury conglomerate LVMH was one of the first to convert their perfume manufacturing to fill bottles of badly needed hand sanitizer, joined then by vacuum maker Dyson committing to making ventilators and Hanes hosiery producing face masks. Silicon Valley tech giants pledged to keep paying those whose on-site work was temporarily furloughed, and huge financial giants such as Visa and JPMorgan Chase pledged no pandemic-related layoffs.

But there is another story we've been inspired by for years: Have you heard of Gravity Payments? The credit card processing and financial services company was founded in Seattle in 2004 by young entrepreneur Dan Price. Dan had an epiphany as he was hiking and listening to a close friend reveal how financially stressful her life was, even though she was working fifty hours a week and making $40,000 a year. By then, Dan was a successful CEO, and he reflected that a third of his employees at the time were paid even less. So, in 2015, he made the decision to reduce his compensation by $1 million and establish a minimum "living wage" for all employees of $70,000. Contrary to what many may have anticipated, business tripled and profits have continued to improve.

What Dan discovered is that "If we make sure to partner with [employees] so that they have everything that they need, then they have increased capacity and they're not distracted trying to figure out how to make ends meet." He connected the dots and recognized, "We need people to solve problems and act quickly and decisively and take care of our customers. Because when you're being paid a living wage, then you feel valued as an employee, and you feel like, wow, this company respects my intellect and my ability, and they want me to make the decisions and not just pass the buck." Dan's decision was acknowledged by *Fast Company* as a World Changing Idea in 2020, employee turnover has dropped, personal 401(k) contributions have doubled, some employees have been able to buy their first homes, and more than 70 percent of employees with debt have been able to pay it down. Some employees say that they've been able to afford to buy healthier food or move closer to the office.

As we have seen, embracing connection as a Leadering strategy opens up many new opportunities for learning, innovation, and success in delivery. Most importantly, it prevents leaders from segregating business performance from their humanity. Leadering believes in the tremendous long-term value created when these drives are united.

CONNECTION IN ACTION

Several years ago, we bridged the worlds of creators and executives for an unusually enriching and wide-ranging project. Dubbed "The Wonder Project," it was initiated by a visionary vice president of marketing for a global consumer products company that was curious to meet the people, ideas, and communities building the future; he was excited to make a significant strategic investment in expanding the organization's human cloud.

Together with the global head of advertising, the global head of research and insights, and two top executives from their global ad agency, we spent several months hosting custom salons and dinners in cities around the United States in which we gathered tech entrepreneurs, high-powered professionals, entertainment producers, political leaders, and other corporate executives for rich conversations on where things were headed. These discussions led to profound new insights. We looked at the factors that drove the old economy—including centralized power and a growing middle class—and compared them to what we saw taking shape in the new, digitally powered economy—a growing rift between rich and poor, weakened mass brands, a deep political divide, and increasing decentralization.

In crafting The Wonder Project together with these executives, I was struck by how nervous they initially were to meet new people and reach out to communities outside of their peers. The key is to structure these experiences so all sides are giving and receiving mutual learning and relational benefits (versus financial payment). It is also important to give the value of these experiences enough time to play out.

Undirected exploration is seen as a huge risk—and, admittedly, two of the execs on board had a difficult time waiting to see what we would learn. But as they experienced, our most valuable insights were revealed when we simply brought an open-minded curiosity to the conversations. Often, executives are focused on extracting information, but that doesn't work in these kinds of settings; this is a conversation, not an interrogation. The key is to learn, question, and wonder together. To connect.

There are natural explorers inside every organization—I estimate 10 to 20 percent are curious and active learners eager to share new ideas with their peers. While current structures inhibit them, actively empowering these bridge-builders to connect to one another and to the rest of the organization is a potent way to bring a wider lens on your business, your industry, and the world. PwC (formerly PricewaterhouseCoopers), for example, is giving self-identified young "Digital Accelerators" room to run, making them a big part of a $3 billion commitment to upskilling the entire organization.

Unfortunately, when organizations are not open to or ready for fostering connection and community, opportunities can be lost.

Several years ago, my team and I were invited to help the leadership of one of the world's largest dining chains define the core of their growth strategy: their North Star. Such an extraordinary opportunity! Up until then, a lot of time had been spent deciding what to change about the dining room environment or which items to add to an already full menu. My team and I believed we had uncovered a bigger, more relevant way to connect. Literally.

Research had revealed that most customers go to this chain restaurant to connect; with family, coworkers, and friends. Using our two-question compass, "What does the future need and expect of us?" and "What are we in a unique position to create and contribute?" we saw society's growing wave of loneliness and polarization as an important opportunity. Strategically, it seemed a natural move to try initiatives that would enhance community-building. We could invite local nonprofit groups to host meetings in the restaurants before they opened for business. We could enhance the on-premises dining experience by hosting a "community table" in each restaurant, giving customers the chance to connect with one another (especially attractive as the incidence of dining, working, and living alone grows). Yet another opportunity appeared in the shape of a big, empty building on the company HQ campus, which for those who worked there had become a depressing sight. To us, this seemed the ideal spot to create an incubator for restaurant startups, offering exchanges of mentoring wisdom and energy between the seasoned corporate executives and insightful but less experienced entrepreneurs. To my team, it seemed like such a great way to build goodwill within the community while gaining emergent perspectives. And if one of these entrepreneurs' efforts ever started getting *too* successful, the chain would be in the pole position to acquire it.

Disappointing to us at the time, the company decided not to employ any of these ideas; they couldn't imagine how a community-centric purpose would be able to drive immediate revenue. Six months later, however, one of their largest competitors started offering community tables, specifically reaching out to millennials. And entrepreneurial incubators specializing in food startups are growing. While our recommendations may have not been the right solution for this organization (or recognizably relevant at the right time), I still firmly believe there is huge opportunity to build a dining brand authentically focused on fostering community. Even in a post-COVID world.

Restaurants aren't the only examples of an industry using physical spaces to build community and connectedness. Prior to the pandemic, Walgreens was collaborating with Humana[33] to create neighborhood health destina-

---

33 Bruce Jepsen, "Walgreens Partnership Boosts Humana's Medicare Enrollment," *Forbes*, February 7, 2019.

tions for seniors, who appreciate not just the high quality of clinical care but also the social interactions, the personal attention, the convenience, and the enhanced coordination between their pharmacist, physician, and the health guides offered on-site.[34]

In a particularly empathetic effort, German grocer Lidl created pop-up bakeries throughout Ireland to encourage teens to speak openly about mental health. The spaces offered a range of activities in the evenings, including meditation, acoustic sessions, laughter yoga, and sing-along socials. "Youth mental health is something I am hugely passionate about," said a Lidl bakery ambassador, "and we all have a role to play in this."[35] Right on!

How the ongoing impact of the pandemic will alter our interactions in physical locations will need to play out, but, as we are growing to appreciate, meaningful connection goes much deeper. It means investing in the degree and quality of our relationships—right now.

Even as work demands seem to grow larger every day, we need to prioritize time to connect. Do you pack your meeting agendas full of discussion items, with no free-form time for people to share stories with each other? Have you been checking in on your clients and customers? How are you encouraging them to connect with each other? Do you make time to cultivate relationships with those outside of your immediate circle? Have you built the psychological capacity and infrastructure to nurture partnerships and broad ecosystems? Is there tolerance of dissenting opinions and space for new ideas? Can you and your teams bring your full humanity to work? And how are you connecting to *your* center?

---

34 "Humana and Walgreens to Open Additional In-Store Partners in Primary Care Centers," *Walgreens Newsroom*, July 30, 2019.

35 Gurjit Degun, "Lidl Creates Bakery Pop-Up for Youths to Discuss Mental Health," *Campaign*, August 23, 2018.

Bottom line: in our ever-evolving digital age, the time we spend connecting with each other (and ourselves) is an important investment in running a thriving, innovative organization. And it is so important that we do better.

CHAPTER FIVE

Contribute (versus Extract)

"Make the world work for 100 percent of humanity, in the shortest amount of time, through spontaneous cooperation, without ecological offense or the disadvantage of anyone."

—R. Buckminster Fuller, architect, inventor, and author

Gail Evans was a custodian at Kodak in the 1980s. She was a full-time employee with vacation time, tuition reimbursement, and sick leave. With that level of financial security and support, she decided to take computer science classes, in which she excelled. Her Kodak colleagues recognized her efforts and even encouraged her to teach her computer science skills to fellow employees.

Due to this and other opportunities, Gail moved out of janitorial services and into Kodak's then-emerging computer science division. She went on to become the chief technology officer of Kodak, with subsequent posts at Microsoft and Hewlett-Packard. Today, she is chief digital officer for Mercer Global Investments.

In a 2017 *New York Times* article, journalist Neil Irwin compared Gail's career opportunities with Marta Ramos, a present-day janitor at Apple's Cupertino headquarters thirty-five years later.[1] Like many other companies, in a strategic move to focus on its core competencies and reduce inefficiencies, Apple had outsourced custodial services to an external supplier. And like many of these kinds of staffing businesses, this company only hires contract employees. As a result, in contrast to Gail, Marta has no job security, benefits, tuition reimbursement, or sick leave—which means she has far less ability to genuinely invest in her future and move beyond this low-paying role, a growing class divide that became even more visible when the COVID-19 pandemic hit.

The issue here is not so much that we should keep every single person on as full-time employees like we did "in the old days." The new question we should be asking is how can we ensure that outsourced labor has a way

---

1   Neil Irwin, "To Understand Rising Inequality, Consider the Janitors at Two Top Companies, Then and Now," *The New York Times*, September 3, 2017.

of receiving similar privileges and workforce protections as those working full-time—whether they are a janitor or a software developer? Having lost our connection to one another, our human cloud has taken a hit. Looking ahead, what additional societal responsibilities will corporations need to address as this new digital economy takes form...and how could these reshape the role of business in society?

THE PRESSURE TO ACCOUNT FOR EXTERNALITIES

I'm not sure when the concept of "externalities" (as described in Chapter 1) entered the business lexicon, but in a controversial *Harvard Business Review* article back in 2010, the concept was defined and thoughtfully explored, opening the debate on how much responsibility a company holds for the impact their actions have on the wellbeing of the community they serve, on the environment, and on overall societal cohesion...both now and over time.[2]

Not surprisingly, then, as we see breakdowns increase in severity, the choices every business makes—and the responsibility it takes (or doesn't) as a member of society—receive greater scrutiny. Deservedly. We celebrate those advocating for healthy practices because we can now see that when companies push negative externalities outside their sphere of responsibility, the hidden costs are passed along for others to shoulder.

For decades, we saw profits rise for big food and beverage companies, benefiting their investors or shareholders, while taxpayers had to foot the bill for rising healthcare costs related to escalating rates of obesity, diabetes, heart disease, and associated illnesses. This frustration led lawmakers to

---

2   Michael Schrage, "Embracing Externalities Is the Road to Hell," *Harvard Business Review*, April 21, 2010.

push for ingredient, sodium, sugar, and calorie labeling on packages and in restaurants. Similarly, the public called for a ban on using trans fats in our foods to stem a rise in diet-related cancers. These pressures also drove then-NYC mayor Michael Bloomberg to propose a tax on Big Gulp-size sodas (64 oz. or more), which has since been shut down in the courts as unconstitutional.[3] But while beverage companies are incentivized to drive sales of high-fructose-laden soda syrup by seducing customers to buy cheap upgrades to this size, researchers at Harvard's T.H. Chan School of Public Health have concluded that Cook County's public health system has had to absorb more than $200 million in costs to treat sugar consumption-related diseases like diabetes, heart disease, and tooth decay.[4]

Expressing a similar frustration, the coastal city of Charleston, South Carolina, recently became the first in the country to file a $2 billion lawsuit against major oil companies who hid research linking the growth of their products to rising sea levels. Their mayor sees it this way:

> As this lawsuit shows, these companies have known for more than fifty years that their products were going to cause the worst flooding the world has seen since Noah built the Ark...and instead of warning us, they covered up the truth and turned our flooding problems into their profits.

The emerging digital era also raises new questions about how to either absorb or deter a whole new set of externalities from data privacy breaches, labor trafficking and, as we just demonstrated, avoiding fair pay and benefit status for independent contractors.

---

3   John Kell, "Michael Bloomberg Drops $18M for His Crusade against Sugary Sodas," *Fortune*, November 3, 2016.

4   "Harvard Researcher: Cook County Soda Tax Would Reduce Diabetes, Extend Lives, and Avert $222 Million in Heath Costs over 10 Years," *Healthy Food America*, 2019.

As we look ahead to what the future needs and expects from each of us, we face an imperative to actively and intentionally address four areas of urgent need:

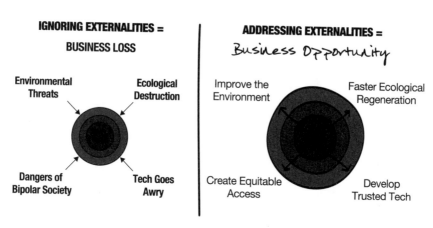

The eye-popping statistics around each of these areas demand our attention.

STABILIZING THE ENVIRONMENT

A report by Thomson Reuters highlights that the world's 250 biggest listed companies account for a third of all human-made greenhouse gas emissions,[5] but few have concrete goals to limit rising temperatures.[6] We are now at the point where the climate change crisis, rising sea levels, and species extinction have become shockingly real.

IPBES (Intergovernmental Science-Policy Platform on Biodiversity and Ecosystem Services) Chair Sir Robert Watson states, "The health of ecosystems on which we and all other species depend is deteriorating more

---

5   Alister Doyle, "World's Biggest 250 Companies Responsible for One Third of All Greenhouse Emissions, Finds Report," *Independent*, October 31, 2017.

6   "The Story of Silent Spring," *NRDC*, August 13, 2015.

rapidly than ever. We are eroding the very foundations of our economies, livelihoods, food security, health, and quality of life worldwide." Also identified as a key element of more sustainable future policies is the "evolution of global financial and economic systems to build a global sustainable economy, steering away from the currently limited paradigm of economic growth." What is the cost of doing nothing? Consider just a few statistics from the Global Commission on Adaptation report:[7]

- Without adaptation, climate change may depress growth in global agriculture yields up to 30 percent by 2050. The five hundred million small farms around the world that currently supply 80 percent of the world's food supply will be most affected.

- The number of people who may lack sufficient water at least one month per year will soar from 3.6 billion today to more than five billion by 2050.

- Rising seas and greater storm surges could force hundreds of millions of people in coastal cities from their homes, with a total cost to coastal urban areas of more than $1 trillion each year by 2050.

- Climate change could push more than one hundred million people within developing countries below the poverty line by 2030.

As the report concludes, "The costs of climate change on people and the economy are clear. The toll on human life is irrefutable. The question is, how will the world respond: Will we delay and pay more or plan ahead and prosper?"

---

7   "Adapt Now: A Global Call for Leadership on Climate Resilience," *Global Commission on Adaptation*, 2019.

REDUCING IMPACT ON OUR ECOSYSTEMS

Beyond climate change, we are putting additional pressure on our environment through our thoughtless ecological habits. As far back as 1962, environmentalist Rachel Carson began warning us of the "Silent Spring" we might have to face if our escalating actions killed off the birds who sing to us. And yet, a landmark report made headlines all around the world in May 2019 announcing that "one million species are at risk for extinction and humans are screwed."[8] Conducted by the Intergovernmental Science-Policy Platform on Biodiversity and Ecosystem Services, and years in the making, the report was prepared by 150 leading international experts from fifty countries. Here's the takeaway:

Human activity has significantly altered three-quarters of the Earth's land and around two-thirds of the marine environment. More than a third of marine mammals and more than 40 percent of amphibian species are threatened. By 2050, plastic in the oceans will outweigh fish. Hundreds of billions of dollars' worth of crops are at risk from the loss of bees and other pollinators. As many as three hundred million people face a higher risk of floods and hurricanes because of the loss of coastal ecosystems. And as forests disappear, we're losing one of the most powerful tools we have to combat climate change.

Reinforcing these findings, the Global Commission on Adaptation has reported that more than five hundred species of land animals are on the brink of extinction and likely to be lost within twenty years. A number that would normally take thousands of years.

---

8 "Global Assessment Report on Biodiversity and Ecosystem Services," *Intergovernmental Science-Policy Platform on Biodiversity and Ecosystem Services*, May 2019.

For about 3.85 billion years, nature sustained the planet through a symbiotic interdependence between its biological systems and physical infrastructure. Then along came humans. According to the United Nations Population Fund, it took hundreds of thousands of years for the world population to grow to one billion, and in just another two hundred years or so, it grew sevenfold.[9] It may possibly climb to over nine billion by 2050.

Along with the rise in population is an equal rise in waste and pollution.[10] Shockingly, electronic waste reached a record 53.6 million tons globally in 2019—the weight of 350 cruise ships the size of the *Queen Mary II*—with $57 billion in gold and other components discarded, mostly dumped or burned.[11] This makes e-waste the fastest-growing domestic waste stream, and it's set to double in numbers by 2030. Even tourism is not immune. There are over 1.4 billion tourists arriving at their destination every year.[12] That's forty-five arrivals every single second. Increased pressure on resources, destruction to habitat and wildlife, loss of cultural identity, vehicle and human congestion/pollution, destruction of monuments, and more are shaking up the tourism industry, putting the need for more sustainable travel front and center.

The impacts of overconsumption, toxic manufacturing, and dirty industries have all taken their toll on what was once a finely crafted ecosystem, creating a scarcity of resources for future generations unless we collectively shift course as quickly as possible.

---

9   United Nations Population Fund, 2019.
10 Rebecca Harrington, "By 2050, the Oceans Could Have More Plastic than Fish," *Business Insider*, January 26, 2017.
11 "The Global E-Waste Monitor 2020," *International Solid Waste Association*, July 2, 2020.
12 "Number of Tourist Arrivals Somewhere on Earth This Year," *The World Counts*, 2020.

ADDRESSING INEQUITY IN A
BIPOLAR SOCIETY

As we were all trying to adapt to shelter-in-place restrictions, a friend in another city shared that the school district there sent an email to all families asking who had access to internet connectivity. A well-meaning gesture, which ironically failed to recognize that a portion of the intended respondents would not *actually* receive the survey without it.

The third area of externalities causing urgent concern is the increasing inequities stemming from our bipolar economy. The COVID-19 crisis has made the gaps in our social, economic, and emotional wellbeing abundantly clear. We have witnessed who can easily transition to remote work, distance learning, and telemedicine; who has access to reliable healthcare, sick leave, and enough savings to pay the rent when furloughed; who has the means to invest in a record-low stock market or interest rates; and who doesn't and can't.

While the move to a digital economy creates many jobs and opportunities for different types of work lifestyles, the shift away from steady manufacturing or industrial trades—often union-protected work—has contributed to a hollowing out of the U.S. economy. GDP has enjoyed a sharp rise, but the gains of this growth in productivity have not correlated with an equal rise in median income. Instead, income, education access, healthcare availability, and even life span have pulled to the extremes of high and low. This issue is becoming more visible and urgent as the gap grows, with the most vulnerable populations hardest hit.

In 2018, it was reported that the twenty-six richest people on Earth had the same net worth of the poorest half of the world's population (meaning some 3.8 billion people combined).[13] While there are always questions about the way this specific math is done, we are all seeing the impacts.

In 2019, a report by the Federal Reserve Board showed that roughly 40 percent of the American population could not cover a $400 emergency expense without charging it on a credit card or borrowing from a friend.[14] Some 39.7 million Americans lived in poverty[15] and one in five children lived in families with incomes below the federal poverty line.[16] Exacerbating this condition, in the competitive bid to hire the best technology talent, salaries for hard-to-find software engineers and data scientists continue to climb, fueling the market for luxury lifestyles. This has pushed the cost of living so high that in some counties with a concentration of tech business, such as the Bay Area surrounding San Francisco, residents with six-figure incomes can qualify as "low income."[17]

Income volatility has also been rising. The Pew Research Center estimates that 34 percent of all American households (nearly a third) suffer up to a 25 percent fluctuation in income from one year to the next—due in part to the growth of the gig economy, the transition to service sector shift work, more people taking on side hustles to supplement earnings, and full-time work shifting to contracts.[18]

---

13   Larry Elliot, "World's 26 Richest People Own as Much as Poorest 50 Percent, Says Oxfam," *The Guardian*, January 21, 2019.

14   Anna Bahney, "40 Percent of Americans Can't Cover a $400 Emergency Expense," *CNN*, May 22, 2018.

15   "What Is the Current Poverty Rate in the United States?" *Center for Poverty Research*, October 15, 2018.

16   "Children in Poverty," *Child Trends*, January 28, 2019.

17   Michelle Robertson, "A Six-Figure Salary Is Considered 'Low Income' in San Francisco, and the Threshold Is Rising," *SFGate*, June 26, 2018.

18   "How Income Volatility Interacts with American Families' Financial Security," *PEW*, March 9, 2017.

In cities like Seattle, San Francisco, and Austin, there have been robust legislative debates on how to address dual issues of rising housing costs and the growing percentage of citizens experiencing homelessness. Proposed solutions include new corporate taxes, as were passed in San Francisco in 2019.[19] Feeling the heat, that same year Google announced plans to invest $1 billion to construct affordable housing in the Bay Area over the next decade.[20] A consortium of Bay Area philanthropists, including Facebook CEO Mark Zuckerberg, announced a $500 million donation to preserve and produce more affordable housing in the region.[21] Microsoft committed $500 million in tax incentives and loans to generate housing in Seattle, where there are similar strains—and similar calls for taxation.[22] As the economic gulf widens, businesses are feeling the pressure to consider and care for the talent that sustains them and the global communities of which they are a part.

As we pull out of this pandemic-induced economic landslide, how will we address these glaring imbalances to ensure all have the opportunity, education, and support to get back on a secure track—in the U.S. and around the world?

KEEPING EXPONENTIAL TECHNOLOGIES SAFE

The fourth area that we as leaders, innovators, and members of society must consider is our responsibilities for the externalities of each technological marvel we bring into existence, acquire, or use.

---

19 Trisha Thadani, "Here Comes Another: Third Tax on SF's Business, Tech Industry Headed to November Ballot," *San Francisco Chronicle*, June 13, 2019.
20 Sundar Pichai, "$1 Billion for 20,000 Bay Area Homes," *Google Company Announcements*, 2019.
21 Nour Malas, "Facebook CEO's Foundation, Firms to Raise $500 Million for San Francisco Area Housing," *The Wall Street Journal*, January 24, 2019.
22 Vernal Coleman and Mike Rosenberg, "Microsoft Pledges $500 Million to Tackle Housing Crisis in Seattle, Eastside," *The Seattle Times*, January 16, 2019.

If the twentieth century produced a wide range of environmental and health externalities, then it is realistic to expect this next era could have its own—even more dire—impacts. As social media manipulation, cybersecurity threats, the looming fear of AI bias, facial recognition abuses, privacy threats, and deepfake technologies grows, our faith in the political process, the integrity of elections and judicial process, and our ability to trust any general news source or story—or each other—deteriorates. Collectively, these fears, plus mounting concerns about the safety of advances such as bioengineered food and 5G cell towers, are slowing technology adoption. And sometimes even provoking a backlash.

The implications for companies failing to account for the impact of their actions are playing out in real time, with greater visibility and speed than in the past. In 2019, we saw nearly four thousand Google employees voicing ethical concerns over the use of artificial intelligence in drone warfare and expressing frustrations about Google's political decisions amid a growing lack of transparency.[23] In response to the overwhelming sentiment expressed by their employees, including the resignation of key talent, Google backed out of the deal with the Pentagon to make military applications and is now focused (domestically) on non-weapons-related technologies.[24]

Also in 2019, AI researchers from industry and academia signed an open letter calling on Amazon to stop selling its facial recognition technology to law enforcement[25] after Amazon pitched its Rekognition system to

---

23 Kate Conger, "Google Employees Resign in Protest against Pentagon Contract," *Gizmodo*, May 14, 2018.

24 Gopal Ratnam, "Google Looks Past Project Maven to Work Anew with the Pentagon," *Roll Call*, November 12, 2019.

25 Concerned Researchers, "On Recent Research Auditing Commercial Facial Analysis Technology," *Medium*, March 26, 2019.

ICE, triggering a widespread backlash from human rights advocates and its own employees.[26] More broadly, the many flaws still present in facial recognition technology, including racial bias and lack of accuracy, have some concerned whether the technology can be deployed ethically in the hands of law enforcement. San Francisco, California, and Somerville, Massachusetts, have banned municipal use of face recognition, and a similar measure is being considered in Cambridge, Massachusetts. Portland has taken it one step further with the most restrictive initiative in the country, banning all facial recognition technologies not just by law enforcement but also in private organizations (such as retailers). More broadly, Joy Buolamwini, the founder of the Algorithmic Justice League, has launched the Safe Face Pledge, encouraging all organizations to make public commitments to prevent the abuse of facial analysis technology.

This kind of citizen oversight is becoming the norm.

The internet was originally imagined by its founders to be a democratizing platform. There were no guidelines; instead, there was an assumption that people would do the right thing in using it. But as companies made the worldwide internet accessible and often free, the functionality of the internet has grown largely unchecked and unregulated, exerting enormous influence on our lives. According to the latest research, 49 percent of the world's population use social media, with an average of two hours and 22 minutes per day spent engaging—an almost 50 percent increase since 2012.[27] We happily give up our data and time in return for "free" access, but it is becoming clearer that this kind of access carries hidden costs: one privacy scandal after another has rocked the world of social media; we're

---

26 Ali Breland, "Amazon Employees Protest Sale of Facial Recognition Tech to Law Enforcement," *The Hill*, June 21, 2018.

27 J. Clement, "Daily Social Media Usage Worldwide 2012-2019," *Statista*, February 26, 2020.

constantly followed with personalized advertising; the social pressure to accumulate likes and paint our lives as perfect is causing real-world harm, and fake news has become pervasive. As the adage goes, if you aren't paying for the product, then you *are* the product. Extractive business models that create addictive habits and then harvest our data by exploiting our desire to connect need to be replaced.

For years, Facebook has been under significant scrutiny, mired in one issue after another since news broke of the Cambridge Analytica scandal—if you recall, they're the political consulting firm that did work for the Trump campaign and harvested raw data from up to eighty-seven million Facebook profiles, influencing the outcome of the U.S. 2016 elections, as well as the Brexit vote in the U.K.—these incidents have provoked serious questions around what exactly Facebook does with users' data and how safe the platform really is.

At this moment, Facebook is being called out yet again. Software engineer Timothy Aveni resigned publicly from the company, accusing them of being "complicit in the propagation of weaponized hatred," garnering sixty-three thousand responses of support on Twitter—and prompting Talkspace CEO Oren Frank to state that "We at Talkspace discontinued our partnership discussions with Facebook today. We will not support a platform that incites violence, racism, and lies."[28]

In fact, in the latest *Digital Trust Report* by Business Insider, Facebook performed worse across every pillar after another damaging year for its public image.[29] Nearly half (47 percent) of respondents believe Facebook

---

28 Christina Farr, "Talkspace CEO Says He's Pulling Out of Six-Figure Deal with Facebook, Won't Support a Platform That Incites 'Racism, Violence and Lies,'" *CNBC*, June 1, 2020.

29 Audrey Schomer, "Digital Trust Report 2019: Popular Social Media Platforms Ranked by Consumer Trust Metrics," *Business Insider*, October 15, 2019.

is extremely likely to show them deceptive content like fake news, and more than four in five (81 percent) said they were only slightly or not at all confident in the platform to protect their privacy and data. Conversely, LinkedIn—which operates quite differently and encourages a very different social etiquette—is the most trusted of all social media.

As technology becomes ever more prominent in our lives, who can we trust? And whose responsibility is it ultimately to protect users when the internet and social media have been monetized and incentivized to become platforms that stalk and exploit versus serve and empower? Bill Duvall, scientist and a founding father of the internet, believes:

> *Only the people who helped build and advance the internet—technologists—can truly understand the complexity of its problems. It's up to tech companies, not governments, to find and apply the technologies and policies that will fix the problems. To do that properly may require tech companies to put the interests of shareholders aside for a time, and do right by the societies in which they make their profits.*[30]

I argue the same is true for the advertisers that prop up these addictive models. According to Statista, in 2019, about 98.5 percent of Facebook's global revenue was generated from advertising, whereas only around 2 percent was generated by payments and other fees.[31] Facebook ad revenue stood at close to $69.7 billion in 2019, a new record for the company. This is up from $11.5 billion just five years prior, as the average revenue per user (AVPR) in the U.S. alone rose from $6.81 in 2013 to $24.96 in 2019.

---

30 Mark Sullivan, "50 Years Later, the Internet's Inventors Are Horrified by What It's Become," *Fast Company*, November 21, 2019.

31 J. Clement, "Facebook: Advertising Revenue Worldwide 2009-2019," *Statista*, February 28, 2020.

You can imagine, then, the impact when 750 major Facebook advertisers boycotted the platform in July 2020, in protest to what they viewed as Mark Zuckerberg's reluctance to take responsibility for divisive and hate-fueled rhetoric.

As users, we must also adopt healthier digital hygiene habits or remain at the mercy of advertisers exploiting our presence and data to meet the aggressive, short-term revenue expectations investors increasingly demand. And we must have more empathy for our tech-hungry kids who are the targets of the best software engineers in the world—paid well to ensure that kids are never satiated.

At least until we push back.

We are developing technological innovations we never even dared imagine before now, so how will we ensure social responsibility is built in to avoid importing—and amplifying—extractive mistakes of the past? Apple started alerting us to how much time we have spent on our devices, comparing our behavior week to week. Twitter, in an attempt to dampen the spread of fake news and intentional disinformation, is not only working on ways to limit how quickly we can reshare potentially inflammatory content, but in 2020 CEO and founder Jack Dorsey actively stepped in to flag misleading content from the outset. Even that which is posted by government leaders.

Quantitative futurist Amy Webb, author of *The Big Nine*,[32] joins the Center for Humane Technology,[33] founded by Tristan Harris and other early

---

32 Amy Webb, *The Big Nine: How the Tech Titans and Their Thinking Machines Could Warp Humanity* (New York: PublicAffairs, 2019).
33 John Brandon, "Why 'The Social Dilemma' on Netflix Is Such an Important Film," *Forbes*, September 17, 2020.

executives of Google and Facebook, in warning us to pay much closer attention to the business models fueling these tech titans and the impact these in turn have on our human cloud as we advance deeper into the digital economy.

Others are developing ways to wipe out these concerns altogether: DuckDuckGo, for example, is a Google search alternative that protects users' privacy by not profiling them and by serving up the same search results to everyone, avoiding the filter bubble of personalized search results.[34] The growth of the distributed internet hopes to bring privacy, agency, and true freedom of expression back to social networks, making it possible for a Facebook alternative such as Junto (built on Holochain) to emerge.[35]

As I sat recently with one of the principal machine learning engineers at our AI startup, working together to articulate our small but growing company's mission, his earnest description struck me: "We want to be proud of what we build." Remembering we are only 1 percent in, it was such an elegant way to sum up that our work and our choices *matter*. Especially in this coming era of exponential impact.

SHIFTING EXPECTATIONS FOR THE BOTTOM LINE

As old-economy productivity slows and the bill for unintended externalities comes due, we are experiencing the diminishing returns of industrial culture and economy rooted in *extraction*. A myopic focus on consumption, comparable year-over-year (or quarter-after-quarter) ROI growth, and a continuously rising GDP are stunting long-term success, stifling innovation, and increasing distrust.

---

34 DuckDuckGo.com, 2019.
35 Junto.com, 2019.

Alternatively, and very encouragingly, we can also see the thrust and velocity generated by those who believe the role of business is to create value for all stakeholders and who, driven by a bigger mission to contribute to society, have the commitment and engaged talent to innovate boldly. While we could argue this is a trendy shift in mindset, in reality, this is *the* twenty-first-century mandate and the path to building strong, healthy, inclusive, environmentally and financially sustainable organizations.

To succeed in the future, we have to appreciate that we are no longer in a *transaction* economy, in which companies operate strictly for profit at any cost. We're now in a *relationship* economy, in which we recognize that business is part of a complex web of relationships—with its customers, partners, vendors, employees, stakeholders, and community.

To solve the world's biggest problems and create a safe and thriving future will require a shift from thinking the world is bigger than us (so we can just keep extracting without consequence) to waking up to the reality that, instead, we are bigger than the world. Thus, we need very different strategies for how we operate.

We need our mindset to shift from one where our businesses are oriented to only extract value to one where they focus on contributing value as they build.

The growth of companies that have made this their practice all along—such as U.S. retailer Costco, whose $40 billion in sales is a testament to their pro-people profitability model—demonstrates it is possible to take care of people and please growth-oriented shareholders simultaneously. In the future, this will not only be considered *possible*; it will become the *mandate*.

Economist Kate Raworth agrees; as she puts it, twentieth-century business was dominated by one narrow mindset that asked one overriding question:

"How much financial value can we extract?" Whereas today, visionary corporate and civic leaders have shifted to asking, "How many benefits can we generate by the way we design things? What else can it give back to the system of which we are a part?"

FROM CSR TO SLO

These two powerful acronyms represent where we've come from and where we're headed, as the implicit agreement business has with society is shifting from a focus on Corporate Social Responsibility to a Social License to Operate.

Corporate philanthropy and concern for correcting industrial hazards have been widely discussed since the beginning of the labor movement at the turn of the twentieth century. As the impacts of the Industrial Revolution became visible, citizens became increasingly concerned with the growth of air pollution, slums, child labor, hazardous factory conditions, sweatshop demands, and so on. This thinking took a big leap in the 1960s and '70s as the concept of corporate social responsibility (CSR) took hold as a self-regulating way for business to honor its social contract with society.

While CSR has continued to evolve and become standardized business practice, I describe this as a form of "value transfer" in which we extract value over *here* and then transfer a bit of it over *there* to help improve conditions in some way for those not directly related to the business. For example, one can picture a corporation with business practices that saturate the globe with unhealthy but high-margin products in heavy-duty plastic containers to keep share prices high—which then, in turn, offers a tiny percentage of billion-dollar profits to a collection of small NGOs in an undeveloped country or to local efforts to keep parks clean.

In our strategy work, we advocate for a more integrated and long-term approach that aims to minimize externalities with *every* action a business takes—from sourcing, to waste production, to employee wellbeing, to how a product or service is used and disposed of when it's finished. Indra Nooyi, former PepsiCo CEO, phrased it so well as she described the company's "Performance with Purpose" mission:

> *Every aspect of business as we know it is being disrupted because of technology, geopolitics, the democratization of media, and so on. Some people see this as an opportunity. Others are scared to death...When we articulated this notion of performance with purpose, people said, "Oh, this is corporate social responsibility." Wrong. This is not about how we spend the money we make. The focus needs to be on how we make the money.*[36]

Thinking longer-term, PepsiCo has responded to this call by launching a sustainability initiative to positively impact areas in which they operate, encompassing agriculture, water issues, packaging, products, climate, and people—including the health of the products they sell.

Earlier, we mentioned Larry Fink, CEO of BlackRock, the world's largest investment firm, as his annual letters to investee CEOs ricocheted to others. In his 2018 letter, he contended that each company is given a "social license to operate" that is contingent upon that company providing something of value in exchange for a community's resources: including raw materials, labor, time, and attention. In other words, increasingly the community will decide if they support the decisions you are making and grant permission to carry on.

---

36 Robert Safian, "Generation Flux's Secret Weapon," *Fast Company*, October 14, 2014.

CORPORATE SOCIAL RESPONSIBILITY	SOCIAL LICENSE TO OPERATE
VALUE TRANSFER A focus on value extraction in which a small percentage of value is transferred to altruistic endeavors that may or may not be linked to the impact of the business itself	**Value Creation** A structural approach to business in which societal value is prioritized and intentionally created with every action, including sourcing, development, distribution, hiring, allocation of profitability
HOW WE SPEND THE MONEY WE MAKE	How we make Money

It is encouraging to hear a highly successful investor whose firm is compensated on financial performance call for such a big shift in focus and responsibility, given these two needs actually support rather than conflict with each other.

RECALIBRATING BUSINESS SUCCESS

In a scathing 2019 Medium post and follow-up *New York Times* article, Jamie Gamble described that the global crises we face today are a result, in part, of the actions of executives. A former attorney, Jamie represented businesses from Facebook and Google to General Motors and JPMorgan Chase—the "corporate persons," he said, who were "the most powerful people in the world."

In his experience, these corporations are so beholden to shareholder expectations that shareholders can sue a company that places stakeholder value—and the investment in healthy, sustainable products and services—above maximizing profit. Gamble notes that this power dynamic means that corporate leaders are "legally obligated to act like sociopaths."[37]

Read that again: our current system can hold business leaders liable if they choose to put value to stakeholders (the people upon whom the success of an enterprise depends) above maximum short-term profit. It means the concerns of one group of stakeholders are effectively hijacking the needs of all others.

What if, in the same way that shareholders have the power to sue a company for not acting in their financial best interest, a stakeholder could legally hold a company accountable for not delivering on their purpose?

For most businesses—even large corporations—there is no current legal obligation to consider these five layers of impact that Jamie Gamble identifies: the relationship with employees, the relationship with customers, the relationship with the communities in which the business both operates and serves, their effects on the environment, and their effects on future generations. With a balance between purpose and profit, signing up to be a certified B-corporation (for benefit corporation) stands for exactly that.[38] They are legally required to consider the impact of their decisions on their workers, customers, suppliers, community, and the environment. Companies such as Eileen Fisher, Ben & Jerry's, Dannon, and 3,333 others across seventy-one countries operate with the unified goal of using business as a force for good.

---

37 Andrew Ross Sorkin, "Ex-Corporate Lawyer's Idea: Rein in 'Sociopaths' in the Boardroom," *The New York Times*, July 29, 2019.

38 BCorporation.net

While legal air cover helps, corporate profitability is not inconsistent with strong environmental, social, and governance practices (ESG). Many of the world's biggest and best-known brands were on the 2019 list of Best ESG Companies, including Microsoft, Hasbro, Owens Corning, Home Depot, and Salesforce—a list put together to encourage socially responsible investing.

Again, this isn't brand-new thinking. Paypal's CEO, Dan Schulman, has been championing what he calls "moral leadership" for decades, and Whole Foods founder John Mackey was similarly an early champion for "conscious (stakeholder) capitalism."

It is increasingly paramount for leaders to address the ways they do business and consider their company's contribution to each of these five stakeholders. How do you plan to contribute to each of them? And have you begun factoring in the mandate for social equity as well?

THE DEMAND FOR BETTER BUSINESS

Recent studies show that "more than nine in ten millennials would switch brands to one associated with a cause" and that millennials are "prepared to make personal sacrifices to make an impact on issues they care about, whether that's paying more for a product, sharing products rather than buying, or taking a pay cut to work for a responsible company."[39] Nine in ten. This is the generation that will be driving the majority of purchases for decades to come.

Compelled by headlines of increasing corporate earnings next to those raising awareness of growing environmental and social equity concerns, a

---

39 "Three-Quarters of Millennials Would Take a Pay Cut to Work for a Socially Responsible Company, According to the Research from Cone Communications," *Cone Communications*, November 2, 2016.

report by global media agency Havas found that a massive 77 percent of consumers prefer to buy from companies who share their values and are intent on making the world a better place.[40] This is because, as hyperbolic as it sounds, we're beginning to see how connected our actions and decisions are to the greater wellbeing of our entire human ecosystem. Here are some ways this ripple effect is playing out right now.

The weed killer Roundup has been classified as a "probable carcinogen," linked directly to several forms of cancer by the World Health Organization,[41] and worryingly, the chemical compound was found in boxes of Cheerios and Nature Valley products.[42] Meanwhile, Hugh Grant, CEO of Monsanto, the company that developed Roundup, once admitted in an interview: "We were so far removed from the supermarket shelf, that was never something we gave a lot of thought to. We never thought about our place in the food chain."[43]

How does a seed and pesticide company not actively consider its role in the food chain? And how many other industry leaders are still oblivious to their place in society's overall wellbeing—from petrochemical-laden cosmetics to antibiotic-dependent farmers? These behaviors catch up with us, as Monsanto was ordered to pay a $2 billion judgment in 2019 to a couple who claimed their dual cancer diagnoses were caused by thirty-year use of Roundup.[44]

---

40   "Building Meaningful Is Good for Business: 77% of Consumers Buy Brands Who Share Their Values," *Havas Media*, February 21, 2019.

41   Tracy Loew, "Roundup a 'Probable Carcinogen,' WHO Report Says," *USA Today*, March 20, 2015.

42   Aria Bendix, "An Environmental Watchdog Found Traces of Weed-Killer in Cheerios and Nature Valley Products. Here's How Worried You Should Be," *Business Insider France*, June 13, 2019.

43   Oliver Wright, "Monsanto Chief Admits 'Hubris' Is to Blame for Public Fears over GM," *Independent*, March 23, 2015.

44   April Siese, "Jury Awards Couple $2 Billion in Monsanto Roundup Cancer Lawsuit Trial," *CBS News*, May 13, 2019.

Flipping this around, paying attention to externalities can also pay dividends in very positive ways. Patagonia, for example, is a nearly $1 billion clothing company with activism built into its strategy. As CEO Rose Marcario put it, "You can serve the interests of your employees and do what's right for the planet and still make great margins."[45]

The degree to which an organization takes society (or externalities) into account in its choices will take on even greater importance in a future where traceability and transparency become the norm.

Technology and data have traditionally been used to sell consumers more, but with everything becoming increasingly connected and "intelligent," brands that are ahead of the curve are using data to help us buy smarter and potentially even consume less. In the future, access to our own aggregated personal data will allow us to develop a very real understanding of our levels of consumption—what we're using, where it's from, how much we're consuming, and the impacts on the world around us. All of which will frame our buying habits and investment decisions.

Slaveryfootprint.org uses algorithms and public data to calculate how many labor-trafficked humans are likely making the products your household owns and consumes. This is a sobering exercise. And given how frightened today's youth is about the looming threat of climate change, we can expect to see a rise in products and brands that help us make more environmentally responsible choices too. A credit card issued by a Swedish fintech company, Doconomy, lets customers set a carbon emission budget each month, then calculates the impact of each purchase put on the card and stops working altogether if the limit is hit.

---

45 Rhymer Rigby, "The Profitable Company That Cares about the Planet," *Financial Times*, May 16, 2018.

It would be easy to focus on a world in peril and a planet in crisis, yet there are others for whom these shifting societal concerns represent boundless opportunities. Confronting these problems empowers their businesses to be part of the solution.

THE BUSINESS UPSIDE OF SUSTAINABILITY

As of now, only 15 percent of the world's land and 7 percent of the world's oceans are protected.[46] However, as fast as we're witnessing the decline of our environment, we're also seeing counteractions not just by businesses but by countries, citizens, and communities all over the world.

Concern for the planet has been galvanizing public figures and celebrities to do more than lend their names to a cause; they are actively investing in solutions in order to influence outcomes. Robert Downey Jr., for instance, announced plans at Amazon's re:MARS conference in Las Vegas in 2019 to start a foundation led by scientific experts that will explore robotics and nanotechnology as a means to clean up the planet.[47] The resulting Footprint Coalition has a goal of significantly impacting climate change within ten years.[48] And the Leonardo DiCaprio Foundation has surpassed the $100 million mark in grants to protect and restore the environment and its ecosystems.[49]

Unilever has committed to the sustainable cultivation and use of palm oil in order to eliminate the impacts of rain forest deforestation.[50] Other

---

46 "Increased Growth of Protected Areas in 2017," *Protected Planet*, 2018.
47 Jillian D'Onfro, "Robert Downey Jr. Announces Project to Clean Up the Environment Using Robotics at Amazon's AI Conference," *Forbes*, June 5, 2019.
48 FootprintCoalition.com, 2019.
49 LeonardoDiCaprio.org, 2019.
50 "Transforming the Palm Oil Industry," *Unilever*, 2020.

innovative for-profits, such as beverage company Rebbl, are leveraging an opportunity to contribute to a social need via their core business. Founded by a collaboration between entrepreneurs Palo Hawken and David Batstone, head of the nonprofit Not for Sale, Rebbl's mission was to create sustainable income for communities at risk of human trafficking and exploitation.[51] One of these communities is the Peruvian Amazon, where Rebbl worked with remote villages to set up a supply chain for one of their key ingredients, Brazil nuts. It took the company eight years to develop a steady source for the nuts. And in a testament to the value of building product partnerships, the brand has taken off, selling over twenty million bottles of product.

Sustainability isn't just an altruistic goal—it's an important facet of building trust and loyalty among stakeholders. And an increasingly critical driver of innovation.

RETHINKING FOOD

While the U.S. middle class is shrinking, in 2017, the Brookings Institute reported that globally, "We are witnessing the most rapid growth of the middle class the world has ever seen," expanding by 160 million each year for the next five years and potentially reaching 5.2 billion people by 2028.[52] Fueled primarily by growth in emerging markets, they anticipated the global middle class would swell consumption by $29 trillion more per year over the next ten years, accounting for roughly a third of projected GDP growth. While the global recession induced by the pandemic will adjust this timeline, unless we can find ways to rethink manufacturing—and

---

51 Nithin Coca, "Rebbl Documentary a Case Study on Benefits of Ethical Supply Chains," *Sustainable Brands*, September 2019.

52 Homi Kharas, "The Unprecedented Expansion of the Global Middle Class," *Brookings*, February 28, 2017.

our consumption—the constraints on resources and the environmental impacts will potentially cause the collapse of multiple ecosystems as well as human suffering to communities that rely on them.

As we consider what it will take to feed a fast-growing population, we will face some challenging choices. On the one hand, says the United Nations' Food and Agriculture Organization (FAO), "If you look at [farming] growth in the last fifteen years, about 70 percent came from new land cultivation. When you go from six to nine billion [in population] over the next thirty to forty years, there is no new land. Can you do it without biotech?"[53] Highly unlikely.

On the other hand, many would say there is much land currently underutilized that if put to use could ease some of the food burden. But it's not just an issue of food production; it's also the problem of food waste, which, in a landmark move in 2015, France declared illegal.[54] And which now nearly two hundred major food suppliers, retailers, and manufacturers (including Nestlé and PepsiCo) have pledged to cut in half by 2030.[55]

This global food challenge is driving a shift to plant-based proteins and plant-based milk, as animal agriculture is reportedly responsible for 14.5 percent of global greenhouse emissions, according to the FAO,[56] with 65 percent of those emissions coming from beef and dairy cattle. Conversely, a study commissioned by the fast-growing beef alternative company

---

53 "The State of the World's Land and Water Resources for Food and Agriculture," *Food and Agriculture Organization of the United Nations*, 2011.

54 Roberto A. Ferdman, "France Is Making It Illegal for Supermarkets to Throw Away Edible Food," *The Washington Post*, May 22, 2015.

55 Jessi Devenyns, "Nearly 200 Companies Pledge to Halve Food Waste by 2030," *Food Dive*, September 28, 2020.

56 Emma Newburger, "Beyond Meat Uses Climate Change to Market Fake Meat Substitutes. Scientists Are Cautious," *CNBC*, September 2, 2019.

Beyond Meat found that, from cradle to distribution, their plant-based Beyond Burger generates 90 percent fewer greenhouse gas emissions and requires 46 percent less energy, 99 percent less water, and 93 percent less land compared to a quarter pound of U.S. beef. The nut milk and alternative milk industries are also growing rapidly, and some are predicting they will outstrip the cow dairy market.[57] Plummeting sales continue to plague this once household staple,[58] recently evidenced by the 163-year-old dairy company Borden filing for bankruptcy in January 2020,[59] while Beyond Meat was the most successful IPO of 2019. Seeing the wave swelling, even food titans Hormel and Tyson are getting in the game with investments in a variety of meat alternatives.

Cities across the world are integrating vertical farming in novel ways. In North Chungcheong, South Korea, a vertical farm was built in an abandoned highway tunnel. In use until 2002, the tunnel had a sharp curve that proved too dangerous for traffic. A safer road was built nearby, and the closed tunnel was filled with plants and a watering and lighting system that makes it possible to grow crops year-round.[60] In such conditions, seasonal volatility is negligible; if a season of crops is lost, it takes far less time to get back into production than conventional farming. As renewable energy costs continue to decline, and robotics and AI are used to optimize both yield and nutrition, food production will be completely revamped as new ways of farming—both on land and indoors—continue to expand in size and sophistication. This is a key example of what is possible in the 1PR.

---

57 Brian Kateman, "Non-Dairy Milk Alternatives Are Experiencing a 'Holy Cow!' Moment," *Forbes*, August 19, 2019.

58 Rina Raphael, "Don't Cry, but Milk Sales Plummeted by $1.1 Billion Last Year," *Fast Company*, March 25, 2019.

59 Becky Yerak, "Borden Dairy Files for Bankruptcy," *The Wall Street Journal*, January 6, 2020.

60 Temujin Doran and Katie Pisa, "This Farm Is Growing Food Deep beneath South Korean Mountains," *CNN World*, December 9, 2019.

BUILDING CIRCULAR SUPPLY CHAINS

Apparel is the second-largest consumer industry after packaged foods. The rise of "fast fashion," globalization, and manic overproduction of ever-cheaper clothes and ever-changing styles has led to vast levels of over-consumption, with more than eighty billion pieces of clothing produced worldwide per year. The waste, cost, and human impacts are considerable. As the Global Wellness Summit described in its trends overview:

> *Every second, the equivalent of one garbage truck of textiles is landfilled or burned. Three in five garments bought end up in a landfill/burned within a year. Less than 1 percent of clothing material is ever recycled. This "take-make-dispose" model creates a staggering 1.2 billion tons of greenhouse gas emissions annually and dumps 20 percent of all global wastewater, and if nothing changes, the fashion industry will use up more than 25 percent of the world's entire carbon budget by 2050.[61]*

Patagonia created a stir in 2011 when they ran a Black Friday ad encouraging shoppers not to buy a new jacket.[62] They are so committed to reuse, they have several services that either fix your broken zippers, torn wetsuits, and ripped gear directly or teach you how to do it yourself. Garments that can't be saved can be traded in and become a part of Patagonia's recrafted Worn Wear line. Since 2014, Patagonia has seen its revenue and profit quadruple, and in 2019 *Inc.* magazine acknowledged them as Company of the Year.[63]

Alternatively, one of many businesses that have since begun showing the strain of this backlash against rampant consumerism and disposable

61 "2019 Global Wellness Trends," *Global Wellness Summit*, 2019.
62 "Don't Buy This Jacket, Black Friday and the New York Times," *Patagonia*, November 25, 2011.
63 Lindsay Blakely, "Patagonia's Unapologetically Political Strategy and the Massive Business It Has Built," *Inc.*, August 10, 2020.

fashion is H&M. With a decrease in sales (the first in two decades) and low share price, H&M has declared that by 2030 it aims to use only recycled or other sustainably sourced materials, and by 2040 it wants to be 100 percent climate positive.[64] The second-largest clothing retailer in the world, they currently source 35 percent of their materials from sustainable or recycled sources.

IKEA, the world's largest furniture manufacturer, set a similarly ambitious goal to use only renewable and recycled material in its products, as well as cut the climate impact of its stores and operations by 100 percent by 2030.[65] IKEA's CEO Torbjörn Lööf said of their commitment:

> *Through our size and reach, we have the opportunity to inspire and enable more than one billion people to live better lives, within the limits of the planet. We are committed to taking the lead, working together with everyone—from raw material suppliers all the way to our customers and partners.*

Adidas has announced they will create eleven million new shoes using recycled plastic that has been pulled from our planet's oceans.[66] The initiative is part of Adidas's efforts to embrace the circular economy, which focuses on restorative and regenerative practices in the design and production of new products in order to simultaneously benefit businesses, society, and the environment.[67] Dharan Kirupanantham, who is an eco-innovation program leader at the sportswear brand, says, "The circular economy is the

64 "Sustainability Report 2018," *H&M Group*, 2018.

65 "IKEA Takes Sustainable Living to a New Level, with New Commitments to Become People and Planet Positive by 2030," *IKEA*, June 7, 2018.

66 Jessica Stewart, "Adidas Vows to Make 11 Million Pairs of Shoes Using Ocean Plastic," *My Modern Met*, March 26, 2019.

67 Ellen MacArthur, "What Is the Circular Economy?" *Ellen MacArthur Foundation*, 2017.

solution. We don't see it any other way. This is not just good for the planet; this is good for business."

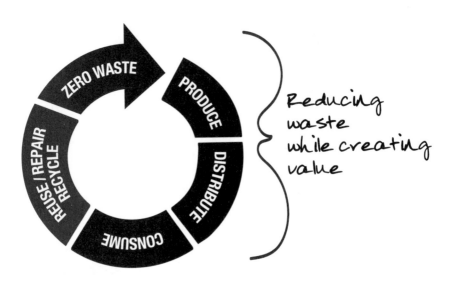

In addition to environmental sustainability, there is another important shift happening that businesses must pay attention to: how we prioritize and take care of the talent advancing the 1PR with their ideas and energy.

REDEFINING THE NATURE OF WORK

As automation shifts not only the work we do (calling for massive investments in reskilling and upskilling) but also changes how we assign and support the ways it gets done, our industrial-era mindsets and our drives for efficiency over humanity are beginning to backfire. This 1PR is bringing a whole new slew of questions our way on how we navigate in the changing world. To get a better look ahead it is helpful to differentiate between the "Future of Work" (FOW) and the "Future of Working" (FOWing), as each raises different issues and opportunities for innovation.

WHAT IS "WORK"?

Beyond the questions of whether remote work increases productivity or how to integrate augmenting technologies, the Future of Work asks questions about the nature of work itself. It digs into the nature of what we do and how these roles are created, valued, and impact society. We have come to define *work* as energy expended for the benefit of and compensation by others, but there are many things we do that contribute indirect value as well, including parent, mentor, content contributor, volunteer, learner, artist, inventor, caregiver...the list goes on. While only a few of these activities usually receive direct monetary compensation and are therefore labeled as "work," I'd offer they all contribute to societal wealth and will be recognized as such in the decades ahead. This feeds into the growing conversations around offering a guaranteed basic income or universal basic housing and education.

Trying to project the future of employment is not a straightforward economics modeling exercise; there are many variables that will shape how, where, and even how much we will be willing to work. Second, so much of the data is contradictory. We are reading headline after headline about how the latest developments in AI and robotics will cause machines to replace workers in unprecedented numbers, while, prior to the pandemic, there were 6.6 million jobs open across the country and a historically low unemployment rate.[68]

Which narrative should we believe? And importantly, which should we build toward? The fact is, we'll have to make peace with paradox. A big part of what makes this shift to the future challenging is that the path is not only unknown; it is also full of juxtapositions.

---

68 "The U.S. Now Has a Record 6.6 Million Job Openings," *The Washington Post*, May 8, 2018.

FOUR FUTURES FOR WORK?

A 2019 survey by Northeastern University and Gallup found that a majority of Americans anticipate that AI will eliminate more jobs than it creates.[69] And in 2018, a fear of robot replacement led fifty thousand workers to threaten a city-wide strike in Las Vegas if new contracts didn't include a measure of job security.[70] Is this just fear? No. The automotive industry is already shedding jobs, with more than eighty thousand expected to disappear as electric vehicles, self-driving technology, and ride-sharing services continue to radically transform the transportation industry.[71] And we have already discussed the great shift that cattle and dairy farmers are facing. So given this conflicting information, it is really hard to get a clear picture of the present, let alone projections for the future. Will jobs be *more* or *less* plentiful in an exponential economy?

Because this is such an important issue with compelling arguments for both hypotheses, a thorough study was done in 2016, called the Shift Commission on Work, Workers, and Technology. It tackled this question by narrowing forty-six variables down to the two that a hundred futurists believe matter most: *Will we have more work or less? And will this work be more full-time or more "gig" work?* From these two variables, the authors created a matrix of four distinct, equally plausible scenarios, ranging from more work in the future—with more of that work fulfilled through gigs—to the prospect of *less* work in the future, with fewer gigs.

69 Shelly Hagan, "Americans Surveyed See Artificial Intelligence as Jobs Killer," *Bloomberg*, July 9, 2019.

70 Heather Wilde, "50,000 Las Vegas Workers Called a Strike to Keep Their Jobs Safe from Robots," *Inc.*, May 30, 2018.

71 Christoph Rauwald, David Welch, and Anurag Kotoky, "Carmakers Shed 80,000 Jobs as Electric Shift Upends Industry," *Bloomberg*, December 3, 2019.

FOUR FUTURES FOR WORK?

Each of these scenarios could work out well or poorly for both people and society, depending on how we prepare:

LESS WORK

Rock-Paper-Scissors Economy

Available work is reconfigured to task-based format; many people piece together their income (and benefits?) through digital platforms / algorithmic matchmakers

King of the Castle Economy

A corporate-centered economy in which economic life is organized around large profitable organizations and the few they employ

MORE WORK

Jump Rope Economy

A flexible portfolio approach in which people build reputational rankings with each task / role they complete, combining multiple income streams that vary constantly

Go Economy

A technology-driven economy in which people embrace connectivity as machines take over routine tasks, freeing workers to focus on creative, strategic assignments / needs

MOSTLY TASKS   **MOSTLY JOBS**

Credit: SHIFT Commission, New America and Bloomberg

Importantly, the authors of this study did not narrow this learning down to one single answer or recommendation. Instead, the commission advocated we prepare for *all* these scenarios simultaneously.[72]

---

72 "The Commission on Work, Workers, and Technology," *Shift*, 2016.

Only time will tell if advancements in technology will create more employment or less, and how this will reshape how we work. But rather than ignoring this issue, how can we move forward without knowing that fact definitively...yet? Rather than go all in on one uncertain future, Leadering asks us to simultaneously commit resources to a range of likely possibilities.

SUPPORTING TALENT IN A SHIFTING SOCIETY

At the moment, however, we are very focused on the "Future of Working," concerned with *how are we getting things done?* Meaning: Who is working full-time or not? Who is an employee or not? Which technologies do we / should we use? Is anyone creating intellectual property; if so, who owns it? Where is it best to work? Do we all feel safe? Do we feel good about what we create/produce? How much autonomy and privacy do we have/give? Should talent be surveilled? And so on.

Van Ton-Quinlivan, former chancellor of the California Community Colleges and Future of Work resident for the Institute for the Future, gave a commencement speech in 2018,[73] which she closed by asking graduating students to consider this list of "what if's":

- What if your colleagues are humans, robots, or avatars?
- What if technology platforms and their algorithms become the new middle management to assign and match work?
- What if you identify yourself through a personalized learning record not tied to any education institution or employer?

73 Van Ton-Quinlivan, "Golden Gate University Graduate Commencement Address," *Golden Gate University*, YouTube, May 1, 2019.

There will be many questions to resolve and new initiatives to create as enterprise, civic, and government leaders deepen their understanding of the Future of Work and the Future of Working. Here are the issues many are tackling at the moment.

WORKER WELLBEING

The contrast in the conditions mentioned earlier in which janitors Gail and Marta worked at Kodak and Apple, respectively, illuminates the ways in which worker wellbeing has somehow been removed from the balance sheet of many thriving businesses. This shift clearly creates a whole slew of externalities, including the multigenerational health conditions caused by increased stress and chronic poverty. This disregard for workers as humans has manifested in practices such as "clopening," in which retail shift workers are expected to close a store late at night and then return a few short hours later to open it again. It seems stunning to me that a law was necessary to prevent this practice.[74] Federal legislators such as Elizabeth Warren are sounding the alarm about the ways in which unpredictable schedules assigned by algorithms are making it nearly impossible to schedule childcare, work out safe transportation options, or take classes.

The pressure to classify jobs as "essential" during the pandemic—from meat-packers to teachers—has raised many concerns. The flip side is: Who is considered expendable?

This conversation extends from on-demand drivers to the professional ranks, including those who code or design but are not full-time employees. As of today, the estimated percentage of Google's talent force who are "TVCs"

---

74 Julia Wolfe, Janelle Jones, and David Cooper, "'Fair Workweek' Laws Help More than 1.8 Million Workers," *Economic Policy Institute*, July 19, 2018.

(temporary workers, contract employees, or vendors) has grown to 54 percent, none of whom receive the same benefits and perks, including vacation time, as the remaining 46 percent doing similar work as full-time employees.[75] Uber has been on this same battleground, as they fought to continue classifying the drivers working for their platform as independent contractors or freelancers rather than as employees and therefore avoiding Social Security payments, health insurance coverage, and other mandated benefits of full employment.[76] The company's CEO, Dara Khosrowshahi, recently advocated for what he describes as "the third way" in a recent *New York Times* op-ed titled "Gig Workers Deserve Better."[77] He suggests companies that rely on gig work should, collectively, be required by law to create benefits funds that can be used by workers for anything from health insurance to paid time off, thereby still providing the flexibility both talent and employers desire while ensuring there is enough to support their broader wellbeing.

Microsoft provides an encouraging example of how to change things; in a decisive move by their general counsel, Dev Stahlkopf, Microsoft now requires all vendors to provide contract employees who do "substantial work"—from shuttle drivers to food service workers to receptionists—with twelve weeks of parental leave at two-thirds of their wages, up to $1,000 per week. As mentioned, they are also experimenting with a four-day workweek and seeing 40 percent productivity gains.

This isn't just an issue for low-paid, part-time employees or contractors. The continuous debate on parental leave and accessible, affordable, quality

---

75 Johan Moreno, "Google Follows a Growing Workplace Trend: Hiring More Contractors than Employees," *Forbes*, May 31, 2019.

76 Andrew J. Hawkins, "Uber Drivers Are Freelancers, Not Employees, Federal Labor Law Says," *The Verge*, May 14, 2019.

77 Dara Khosrowshahi, "I Am the CEO of Uber. Gig Workers Deserve Better," *The New York Times*, August 10, 2020.

childcare rages on, as it has become abundantly clear how challenging it is to balance paid work with unpaid caregiving—a figure Oxfam estimates to be equivalent to $10.8 trillion in economic value (nearly three times larger than the entire tech industry).[78]

And the 24/7 nature of knowledge work means there is rarely an "off button." Even the move to offer unlimited vacation days is somehow psychologically disincentivizing folks from taking them. And the high stores of energy that constant learning, experimenting, and collaborating require make it relevant to question whether a traditional industrial-era office schedule holds any more. Provocatively, many of the world's most innovative thinkers and prolific creators, such as Charles Darwin, may have only "worked" five hours a day. They spent more time learning and synthesizing than they spent producing. And yet, many of our traditional corporate structures are built to incentivize production rather than nurture innovative thinking.

Changes brought on by the Industrial Revolution more than 150 years ago resulted in hard-fought new "rules" and new precedents for what was deemed worker care back then. The rise of labor movements and unions together with caring businesses instituted things like the five-day workweek, paid holidays, and the idea of pensions and employer contribution to healthcare. More than a century later, we're strangely still tied to that model—without much reassessment of how needs and work itself have changed. Given we are only "1 percent in" to this 1PR, we have not yet had the corresponding societal reassessment of what worker care means today and for the future. But it *is* coming. Jacinda Ardern, New Zealand's prime minister, is curious to implement nationally the four-day workweek that Microsoft and others have piloted. A trust management company in her country, Perpetual Guardian, has already made permanent a four-day

---

78 "Not All Gaps Are Created Equal: The True Value of Care Work," *Oxfam International*, 2020.

workweek—at regular employee five-day salaries—reporting a 20 percent gain in employee productivity and a 45 percent increase in work/life balance.

It is time to explore a new talent model shaped for the phenomenal century ahead.

INVESTING IN RESKILLING

We raised the question earlier about the need to prepare an entire population for reskilling, but we have a long way to go. According to research conducted by McKinsey, as many as 375 million workers globally might have to change occupations in the next decade, and nearly nine in ten executives and managers say their organizations either face skill gaps already or expect gaps to develop in the next ten years.[79] Though many companies are beginning to think about reskilling, only one in three is actually doing something about it, which reveals a glaring gap organizations are struggling to close. We are at an important inflection point that raises pressing new questions, such as: How do we find the time to learn new skills while managing current workloads? Who should pay for this education? And what happens to those who fall behind? The way companies demonstrate they care says a lot about their preparedness for the future.

Retail giant Walmart created a pilot to offer college education for a dollar a day, subsidizing the cost of tuition, books, and fees for their associates, in a program that has since been enormously successful and continues to expand.[80] Starbucks, meanwhile, offers full tuition reimbursement to

---

79 "Beyond Hiring: How Companies Are Reskilling to Address Talent Gaps," *McKinsey & Company*, February 12, 2020.

80 "Walmart's New Education Benefit Puts Cap and Gown within Reach for Associates," *Walmart*, May 30, 2018.

employees who pursue a bachelor's degree.[81] Similar to PwC, Amazon announced plans to spend $700 million to retrain one hundred thousand employees—around a third of its U.S. workforce—by 2025.[82] The program includes paid intensive classroom training and in-house apprenticeships.

AT&T is another corporate heavy hitter focusing on reskilling upwards of 275,000 employees by partnering with educational think tank Udacity; together, they are discovering innovative ways to provide accessible learning that will help people be productive in the new economy. The impact of this reskilling goes beyond AT&T's own benefit, as the company estimates it will need a smaller workforce in the future. But even employees who decide not to stay with AT&T will be better prepared for being productive participants in the demands and expectations of the new economy.

Spurred by the same intention, in 2016, Nick Dalton, executive VP of HR business transformation for Unilever, launched Unilever's Future of Work initiative—an overarching plan to prepare the workforce for a digitalized and highly automated era based on this vision described by Chief HR Officer Leena Nair:

> The digital revolution is a human revolution. Ultimately, it is people who will bring it to life in businesses. We need to lead our organizations to a new future of work—one that has the potential to be more inclusive, more purposeful, and one which can deliver more positive impact to our people, our consumers, and the competitive growth of our business.

---

81 "Starbucks Offers Full Tuition Reimbursement for Employees to Complete a Bachelor's Degree," *Starbucks*, June 15, 2014.
82 Jordan Valinsky, "Amazon Plans to Retrain 100,000 Employees," *CNN Business*, July 11, 2019.

First, they decided they needed to *change the way they change*, recognizing that this transformation required new ways of thinking about the company, operations, and workplace. Then, believing that if you change the workforce, you can change the world, they developed a plan focused on accelerating the speed of change, reskilling staff through instilling a culture of lifelong learning and by adopting flexible work practices. Unilever's goal was to ensure that 80 to 100 percent of the workforce displaced by automation would ultimately get a new internal job, get a comparable external position, or opt for an appropriate early retirement. As a *Harvard Business Review* case study shared, a key priority for Unilever was to include workers in the debates, discussions, and decisions that would shape their future; as such, most managers and employees agreed that this strategy was the right way forward.

Guided by a strong purpose and a pledge that no one is left behind, Unilever found that employees were 35 percent less likely to quit if they had access to lifelong learning and upskilling, representing a potential savings of around $8 million per year in hiring costs for every seven hundred employees trained. The training ensured that employees could take their credentials with them even after they left Unilever. And in particularly tight talent markets such as China, Unilever conducts talent swaps that temporarily assign high-potential employees to another firm like Alibaba, Tencent, or JD. The idea is for these employees to develop a specific skillset during a short term that would then allow them to bring that learning, agility, and thinking back into Unilever. Though a global company, they are also sensitive to local context, as their changes depend on the geography, governmental leadership, trade unions, and other economic prospects in each country. In Brazil, for example, Unilever trained entire families—not just the employee—on the digital tools necessary to start their own business after a restructuring.

All focused on insightful and empathetic ways of thinking about workforce development, these companies are not solely focused on what they can extract from the top 10 percent of our high-potential people; they are seeking to help *everyone* develop capacities to contribute to the future—whether they ultimately stay with the company or not. Rather than promising jobs for life, they want to help everyone develop the skills for life.

WINNING TALENT THROUGH VALUES

The tide is shifting. Historically, we chased loyalty. But trust, advocacy, and talent have become the new currencies in our changing global economy. The 2019 Edelman Trust Barometer revealed that trust had changed profoundly in the past year, with people shifting their trust to more close, local relationships within their control, most notably their employers:[83]

- Only one in five feels that the system is working for them, with nearly half of the mass population believing that the system is failing them.

- In contrast, globally, 75 percent of people trust "my employer" to do what is right.

- Employees are ready and willing to trust their employers, but the trust must be earned through more than "business as usual." Seventy-one percent of employees believe it's critically important for "my CEO" to respond to challenging times. More than 76 percent of the general population concur.

- Employees who have trust in their employer are far more likely to engage in beneficial actions on the employer's behalf—they will

---

83 "19th Annual Edelman Trust Barometer," *Edelman*, 2019.

advocate for the organization, are more engaged, and remain far more loyal and committed.

Being clear about a company's values—right from the recruitment and hiring stage—serves both the organization and the talent they need to attract and retain. The more aligned those two are, the better. PepsiCo's Indra Nooyi recognized the importance of these factors in a tight labor market; as a result, her company positioned their purpose front and center in their operations and encouraged employees to bring their whole selves to work.

When there is a disconnect between a company's values and its actions, we are increasingly seeing employees emboldened to speak up and challenge the gap. After an unsuccessful attempt to get shareholder approval of a climate-oriented resolution, more than eight thousand Amazon employees signed an open letter to Jeff Bezos and the company's board of directors stating their dissatisfaction with Amazon's stance on climate action. The stakes have been raised for corporations and local governments to step in and lead the charge toward a future of prosperity. This effort led Amazon to create an aggressive Climate Pledge that includes a commitment to run fully on renewable energy by 2030.

In light of the Black Lives Matter movement and social justice issues we're now seeing, many other companies are pivoting to reform work environments, transform retail experiences, and address economic disparities, all in response to similar employee backlash. Accused of a racist company culture, Yael Aflalo, founder of sustainable womenswear brand Reformation, resigned after accusations by employees.[84] Hit by a shareholder lawsuit for

---

84 Jemima McEvoy, "Every CEO and Leader That Stepped Down Since Black Lives Matter Protests Began," *Forbes*, July 1, 2020.

lack of diversity due to no Black board members or executive leaders, Cisco has since invested over $100 million into diversity initiatives committed to adding 75 percent more Black executives by 2023.[85]

In a new-power world, public opinion of a particular company can turn quickly. In April 2019, Airbnb was lauded for its very caring approach to laying off full-time company employees—providing at least fourteen weeks of severance pay, four months of mental health support, and health insurance coverage for one year for U.S. employees—only then to be lambasted in a long *Wired* article for how poorly independent contractors (even those who worked for them full time for over a year) were treated by comparison because they had been hired through an agency.

In a highly competitive talent future, the social contract between talent—whether on staff or via contract—will shift, putting ever-increasing visibility on company practices and how congruently they are actually expressed.

LISTENING TO COMMUNITY NEEDS

Finally, it is also important to recognize the expectations communities have for the businesses they support. Historically, the primary metrics of concern were the number of jobs created and taxes generated—and chambers of commerce and local legislators dangled large financial incentives to lure these to their town or city over another. This social contract, however, is starting to shift, as there is now a broader set of considerations that make a company a welcome addition to communities.

---

85 Allison Levitsky, "Cisco, Sued over Lack of Diversity, Commits to Hiring 75 Percent More Black Executives," *Silicon Valley Business Journal*, September 24, 2020.

In 2018, Seattle's city council voted unanimously to apply a per-employee tax on its largest employers—including Amazon, Starbucks, and Microsoft—to help cover the city's affordable housing efforts. Microsoft and Amazon pushed back, and within six weeks, the vote was overturned.[86] Local government and corporations butted heads again in San Francisco when the CEOs of Salesforce and Twitter squared off against policymakers over legislation regarding a housing referendum and businesses being held accountable.

Communities are now beginning to consider these implications more heavily in their decision to bring a new employer to town—or not. When Amazon wanted to build its second headquarters in New York, they faced big pushback because citizens didn't feel enough of the city's population would benefit from Amazon's presence. Surprised by the response, the company reversed their decision and pulled out of town.[87] After all, they had invested in this highly public search; another alternative, however, could have been for Amazon to take a step back to better understand where the backlash was coming from, empathetically engage the community (Sarah Silverman-style), and see if a compromise was possible.

These examples show how growing awareness and lower tolerance of extractive behaviors are slowly shaping the decisions of major corporations, putting new pressure on business leaders to listen. The CEO of Starbucks, Howard Schultz, spoke to the imperative companies are now facing after years of extraction when he said:

In the last few years, we have seen the fracturing of the American Dream. There's no doubt, the inequality within the country has created a situation

---

86 Sarah Holder, "Who Should Pay for a City's Homelessness Crisis?" *Citylab*, July 25, 2018.

87 J. David Goodman and Karen Weise, "Why the Amazon Deal Collapsed: A Tech Giant Stumbles in NY's Raucous Political Arena," *The New York Times*, February 15, 2019.

where many Americans are being left behind. The question for all of us is, should we accept that, or should we try and do something about it?[88]

The businesses that can answer this question in ways that resonate with their stakeholders and benefit the society and ecosystems in which they operate are the ones poised to succeed in this new economy.

CONTRIBUTION IN ACTION

"One of the things great companies do is consciously design their culture, and those that do start with a purpose. They have principles and values, and they are the best performing ones. They understand success is built by great teams and they share their success with their teams."

—Ann Rhoades, president of People Ink and
culture champion of Southwest Airlines

Leading calls for a shift from a mindset of corporate philanthropy or CSR to more fully accepting one's social license to operate (SLO) and striving to create value with *every* step of our work. As we consider how to run companies that thrive in the future, there is incredible opportunity to connect to a deep sense of purpose; to fulfill needs for a wide range of stakeholders who, in turn, will support our organizations; and to think big about how we can use our businesses to care for our communities, our local environment, and even the world. We can be inspired today by the tangible actions of others already putting this into practice.

As discussed earlier, clothing production has doubled over the last fifteen years, and simultaneously, customers are wearing their clothes fewer times

---

88 "Starbucks to Offer Employees Free Tuition to Complete Online Bachelor's Degree," *The Washington Post*, June 15, 2014.

before throwing them out.[89] With this statistic in mind, fashion giant Zara announced that 100 percent of the linen, cotton, and polyester used in their clothing will be sustainable, organic, or recycled by 2025. During their 2019 shareholders' meeting, Zara's parent company and the world's largest fashion retailer, Inditex, pledged to boost sustainability across all its brands.

In yet another green approach to fashion retail, the apparel resale market is expected to exceed $51 billion in five years, prompting brands such as Eileen Fisher and Patagonia to reconsider traditional product offerings. They are taking back their own brand's secondhand clothing to resell themselves. To date, the Eileen Fisher Renew initiative has taken back more than a million pieces of clothing and resold them online or in stores.[90] Hailed as a benchmark for a sustainable approach in an industry that accounts for a monumental amount of waste, this model opens up a significant new revenue stream for the apparel makers versus allowing secondhand stores such as ThredUp or Poshmark to reap the benefits. In an article for *Forbes*, *New York Times* fashion director Vanessa Friedman ponders, "Given the growth of resale, you have to wonder why every brand doesn't do [this], instead of letting another retailer profit from their brand name."[91]

In 2014, with an eye to the expanded role they are working to have in their industry, CVS, the leader in pharmacy retail and healthcare services, made the values-based choice to stop selling tobacco products in its stores. In the first eight months since pulling the products, studies showed that overall cigarette sales dropped by 1 percent in the U.S. (which translates into almost one hundred million fewer packs of cigarettes being sold across the

---

89 Elizabeth Segran, "Zara built a $20B Empire on Fast Fashion. Now It Needs to Slow Down," *Fast Company*, July 24, 2019.
90 "We'd Still Like Our Clothes Back," *Eileen Fisher Renew*, 2019.
91 Pamela Danziger, "How Patagonia, REI and Eileen Fisher Are Using Secondhand Sales to Get More New Customers," *Forbes*, June 10, 2019.

country).[92] Recognizing the responsibilities of being a healthcare company, CVS made headlines again in 2018 when they banned the use of retouched, photo-manipulated images to sell their CVS-branded beauty products. By convincing the largest beauty and cosmetic brands, such as CoverGirl, to join the Beauty Mark effort (as it is called), within a year, 70 percent of all beauty imagery in stores was compliant with the no-manipulation standard.[93] The company aims to have transparent labeling on all beauty imagery in their aisles; images that have not been retouched will have a watermark to verify they haven't been altered.[94] Since taking these two purpose-driven actions, total sales have increased and CVS has seen a significant "fan base" of people looking to work for them.

Empathy also fuels innovation. Austin-based financial firm Kasasa built a new product to help community banks and credit unions (their customers) stay competitive with the mega-banks in their industry. In 2018, they rolled out the Kasasa Loan, a "takeback loan" model allowing customers to overpay toward their overall loan amount, yet still have their overpayment funds available to them if needed.

Kasasa recognized that while most of us strive to pay down our debt as quickly as possible, we live in an environment rife with income volatility with far less financial security today than in the past. They addressed this problem by allowing customers to pay ahead of their amortization schedule, while holding that money in reserve. If the customer needs the money, they have access to it; if not, the funds are applied to the loan to speed up the final payoff. This became a lifesaver for those suffering during the pandemic.

---

92 "We Quit Tobacco, Here's What Happened Next," *CVS*, September 1, 2015.

93 Rina Raphael, "Big Beauty Brands Eagerly Join the CVS Photoshop Ban," *Fast Company*, January 24, 2019.

94 Julia Horowitz, "CVS Will Stop Airbrushing Photos It Uses to Sell Beauty Products," *CNN Business*, January 15, 2018.

You can imagine the level of trust and loyalty this product engenders in customers. Kasasa's program is just one example of how companies are thinking of the value they deliver differently—with a goal to contribute rather than extract.

As we approach the future with a Leadering mindset of contribution over extraction and see changes as opportunities, we are able to not only choose the future we want but commit to creating long-term sustainable value for all stakeholders as we steward our resources and influence with much more care.

CHAPTER SIX

Be Audacious (versus Incremental)

"The new challenge isn't so much a technological one but rather our capacity to forget everything we know about a given field to have the audacity to invent the future."

—Amin Toufani, chair of finance and economics, Singularity University

Steve, a fifty-four-year-old with multiple sclerosis, cerebral palsy, heart disease, and diabetes, was homeless. As part of a pilot program called MyConnections in Phoenix, Arizona, he was given a safe apartment in which to live—an apartment funded by UnitedHealthcare. The medical insurance company had recently committed to paying for housing and support services for roughly sixty formerly homeless recipients of Medicaid. As reported, in the twelve months prior to moving in, Steve went to the emergency room eighty-one times, spent seventeen days hospitalized, and had medical costs, on average, of $12,945 per month.[1] These costs were humanely but unsustainably absorbed by some combination of the insurer, the hospital, and the taxpayers. However, in the nine months since Steve has gotten a roof over his head and health coaching, his average monthly medical expenses dropped more than 80 percent to $2,073. The success of this audacious, non-traditional pilot has made this medical care program a business imperative for UnitedHealthcare, which it plans to expand into thirty markets.

Leadering moves from thinking myopically to solving *systemically*. By looking at the influences shaping healthcare costs, UnitedHealthcare understood they could step outside of their traditional services to invest in affordable housing, while at the same time lowering their costs. As we take a closer look at the role of business in a shifting society, we have to ask bigger questions.

To date, we as leaders haven't been encouraged to ask ourselves or our organizations: Where is it we can really add the most value or drive a truly transformative solution? *What is the biggest and boldest we can play?*

Instead, we have been incentivized to stay in our lane, take small steps, and repeat the success of the past, even in the face of so many new

---

1   John Tozzi, "America's Largest Health Insurer Is Giving Apartments to Homeless People," *Bloomberg*, November 5, 2019.

challenges. As we are beginning to see, however, these challenges are also opportunities. And, honestly, if leaders like you and I don't take them on, then who will?

THE POWER OF A MASSIVE TRANSFORMATIVE PURPOSE

As our awareness of our mutual reliance on each other grows and our connection to our own sense of self strengthens, we are called to reach for something bigger. Imagine the potential in orienting toward a shared, expansive *direction* versus a finite list of *directives* someone handed you.

How do we know we are headed in the right direction? In the absence of a map, the thing that ensures our new compass guides us safely is our North Star—a sense of individual and collective purpose that we can confidently navigate toward. As such, thinking too small and too short term puts us at risk. Whereas in the past, we believed small steps kept us safe, now this approach puts us in real danger of missing the big opportunity waiting to be fulfilled; the twenty-first century demands that we define a bold purpose and pursue it with audacious action.

What does the future need and expect from us?

What are we each in a unique position to contribute to it?

A BOLD COMMITMENT TO VALUE CREATION THAT HAS TRANSFORMATIVE EXTERNAL IMPACTS

Embracing the future requires a holistic understanding of purpose, people, and planet. To fully harvest this emerging business potential, we need to see beyond our current limits and reframe our mission. Singularity University, a Silicon Valley-based global learning and innovation community, challenges all leaders to define and deliver their "massive transformative purpose" (MTP). It is not a goal; rather, an MTP is widely defined as a bold and audacious aspirational statement that has transformative external impacts across society, industries, and the world. The point is to deploy exponentially powerful new tools to improve as many lives as possible for the greater good. Singularity University describes the power of an MTP this way:

> *Social movements, rapidly growing organizations, and remarkable breakthroughs in science and technology have something in common—they're often byproducts of a deeply unifying purpose. There's a name for this breed of motivation. It's called massive transformative purpose, or MTP. Setting out to solve big problems brings purpose and meaning to work—it gives us a compelling reason to get out of bed in the morning and face another day.*[2]

It gives us motivation to cross the liminal gap.

Singularity University encourages all leaders to think beyond a new social media app or business improvement feature. In this vein, PwC's $3 billion commitment to upskill both employees and civic leaders is fueled by their purpose to "build trust in society and solve important problems." And while TED took a risk launching the global community-led TEDx program, the thirty-four thousand global events created since has given them enough

---

2   Allison E. Berman, "The Motivating Power of a Massive Transformative Purpose," *Singularity Hub*, November 8, 2016.

content to expand into publishing, podcasts, radio, and more—allowing them to advance their MTP to widely "share ideas worth spreading."

Purpose pulls us toward each other. It is through an audacious shared vision of the future that people can unlock their wonder and creativity to push past the known. And in my view, being audacious is about being compassionate and transformative at the same time. The future demands that our MTPs take into account our wider stakeholders, not just current customers—which together can present us huge opportunities.

We have highlighted Unilever several times, as their corporate purpose infuses decisions made at every level of the organization, all around the world. They believe, "To succeed requires the highest standards of corporate behavior towards everyone we work with, the communities we touch, and the environment on which we have an impact." And Unilever CEO Alan Jope believes that "More than ever, the world needs purposeful, multi-stakeholder businesses if we are to leave a more sustainable and fairer world to future generations."[3] With a vision to demonstrate unequivocally that sustainable business delivers superior returns for all stakeholders, this commitment was positively reinforced when they announced in 2018 that their purpose-led twenty-eight "Sustainable Living Brands" (including Dove, Knorr, and Ben & Jerry's) were growing 69 percent faster than the rest of the business...and delivering 75 percent of the company's growth.[4]

Purpose is profitable. Even when tackling the most daunting problem.

As part of Bill Gates's mission to reverse climate danger, he partnered with UN Secretary General Ban Ki-moon and Kristalina Georgieva (on leave as

---

3 "Our Values and Principles," *Unilever*, 2020.
4 "Unilever's Purpose-Led Brands Outperform," *Unilever*, November 6, 2019.

CEO of the World Bank) on a global commission in 2019. The commission released a new report calling on global leadership—specifically banks and governments, but we would contend why not business leaders as well?—to better adapt to and shape climate resilience, with the warning that prospects are grim if we don't.[5] Rather than only sound another alarm, the report calculates that an investment of $1.8 trillion now in key developments—clean drinking water, better preparing coastal cities, and addressing poverty, to name just a few examples—could generate $7.1 trillion in total net *benefits* over the next ten years.

The report also states that "While there's a clear case for adaptation, it isn't happening quickly enough, or at a great enough scale." It's clear that such initiatives are lucrative, so it seems astonishing that more companies are not investing in developments from which they could be reaping enormous benefits.

We must *all* become more bold.

WHY PLAY BIG NOW?

The issues begging for our attention now make the need to play bigger very clear. Just this morning, two headlines crossed my desk that deserve our attention. First, a team of theoretical physicists specializing in complex systems has concluded that global deforestation due to human activities is on track to trigger the "irreversible collapse" of human civilization within the next two to four decades (let that sink in).[6] Meanwhile, another warned of the "feminist recession" caused by the pandemic, as U.S. women are

---

5   "Adapt Now: A Global Call for Leadership on Climate Resilience," *Global Commission on Adaptation*, 2019.
6   Nafeez Ahmed, "Theoretical Physicists Say 90% Chance of Societal Collapse within Several Decades," *Vice*, July 28, 2020.

experiencing double-digit unemployment—a higher increase than men and the highest level since this statistic began being tracked in 1948.[7] And the job loss is greatest for women of color. As visionary leaders are increasingly demonstrating, these are the kinds of problems we can actively solve through changes in policies and practice once we make the commitment.

Spurred into action in the aftermath of the Parkland school shooting, Dick's Sporting Goods removed assault-style weapons from their inventory and raised the age to purchase any gun to twenty-one years old. It didn't stop there. CEO Ed Stack then requested that the $5 million worth of guns they removed from the store shelves be melted down and made into scrap metal. After the announcement, customers boycotted the company, more than sixty employees quit, and they've estimated the policy cost them around $250 million. But in an interesting turn of events, Dick's Sporting Goods posted a 3.2 percent boost in sales for the third quarter of 2019—their biggest in three years—and long-term forecasts look good for continued growth (COVID-19 pandemic notwithstanding). As of the writing of this book, they've also removed all guns from around 20 percent of their urban stores, more effectively aligning the availability of hunting rifles with the communities that actually hunt.

Playing big means you don't shift course away from your North Star when a hard decision has to be made—like going against a traditional business practice or leaving some profit on the table. Playing safe in this new era mires you in the incremental and ultimately won't position you well as people become more emotionally connected to the choices they make— as shoppers, investors, and talent. Making clear what your organization believes in and acting congruently sets you up for much bigger success in the 1PR.

---

7   Julia Reihs, "America's First Female Recession," *The 19th*, August 2, 2020.

Admittedly, this is a difficult mindset shift for established, hundred-plus-year-old businesses that saw success in the Industrial Revolution. But as many of these companies begin to stagnate or even flounder, the pressure on their leaders to embrace bold thinking will increase. Consider the audacity demonstrated by traditional companies that are willing to make the leap.

Erick Thürmer's family tool company dates back to 1898 when his great-grandfather patented the design of the fastener thread, otherwise known as the common screw. After completing a business leaders' retreat in the jungle and the desert, as well as an executive program at Singularity University, Erick had some fairly major life epiphanies. As the current CEO and owner of the Danish company, he returned back to Denmark and set about making some dramatic changes, including letting go about a quarter of his workforce and installing an all-female board of directors.

He and his wife adjusted their compensation to be the lowest in the company and adopted a purpose-driven rather than profit-first mindset. It became clear that their commitment to purpose was more than just lip service when the development team presented a patent for a new gun silencer to the all-female board. Rather than profit on something they were concerned would make society less safe, the board immediately decided to shelve releasing the silencer and put the patent away in a drawer, most likely never to be seen again. It's not that the board didn't care about the financial success of the company; it just wasn't their primary motivation anymore. Erick has this to say about his decisions:

> *Thürmer is famous for designing the fasteners in the Eiffel Tower, but also infamous for supplying the fasteners in the Titanic. People often overlook the daring it takes to be a visionary. You have to do things that are unpopular, and you won't always win. But the alternative—a company, or even*

a life of stagnation—keeps me motivated to take those risks necessary to become a visionary.[8]

While there are issues unique to each business, enterprise, and nation, there are several concerns that require a global response. The United Nations has created a worldwide call to action for the most pressing ones.

A GLOBAL BENCHMARK

Just five years ago, the United Nations General Assembly launched the Sustainable Development Goals (aka SDGs): a "blueprint to achieve a better, more sustainable future for all."

This thinking is seeping in. A survey by the United Nations and business consultancy Accenture found that CEOs now see a mandate to solve societal challenges as a core element in the search for competitive advantage. Even prior to the pandemic, 87 percent believed that the SDGs, as a global benchmark, represent an opportunity to rethink approaches to sustainable value creation: 63 percent of executives believe that sustainability will cause major changes in their businesses in the next five years; 78 percent already see opportunities to contribute through their core business; and an overwhelming 97 percent believe that sustainability is important to the future success of their business.[9] According to the UN Global Compact:

CEOs are demonstrating a growing understanding of sustainable development, making deeper commitments, and innovating solutions to global challenges. To accelerate progress and to play their part in delivering the

---

8   Erick Thürmer, "Exponential Innovation Is Risky and Spiritual," *Singularity University,* November 11, 2019.

9   "The UN Global Compact-Accenture Strategy CEO Study 2016," *United Nations Global Compact,* 2016.

SDGs (Sustainable Development Goals), businesses must partner with governments, consumers, and investors to raise the bar.

The Sustainable Development Goals call attention to seventeen of what the UN sees as the world's greatest challenges over the next fifteen years, with all 193 member states making a shared commitment to:

SUSTAINABLE DEVELOPMENT GOALS

1. End poverty
2. End hunger
3. Improve health and wellbeing
4. Provide quality education
5. Ensure gender equality
6. Provide clean water and sanitation
7. Deliver affordable and clean energy
8. Improve working conditions and spur economic growth
9. Enhance innovation and infrastructure
10. Reduce inequalities
11. Create sustainable cities and communities
12. Promote responsible consumption and production
13. Reduce climate impact
14. Care for life below water
15. Care for life on land
16. Promote peace and justice
17. Create partnerships to address sustainable goals

Credit: United Nations Global Compact, 2016

Understanding how much leverage investors and capital markets play in determining our priorities, one clear part of the puzzle is to encourage shareholders and investors to jump on board the sustainability bandwagon. The most direct way to incentivize corporations to address these challenges and growing pressures is to make doing so an integral part of how top executives earn their living.

Harvard Business Review suggests tying executive compensation to sustainability and an incentive structure in which bonuses depend largely, or solely, on executives' success in tapping big strategic opportunities related to sustainability.[10] Royal Dutch Shell CEO Ben van Beurden more than doubled his salary in 2018, partly due to the mandate for aligning with the Paris Agreement that aims for net-zero carbon emissions by the second half of the century,[11] and outlining plans to reduce its net carbon footprint 20 percent by 2035.[12] Pushing top executives to go strategically on the offense moves the work of advancing sustainability from the periphery of the business to its heart.

THE FUTURE IS MOBILIZING

While many adults are still wondering what to do or whether to take action, teens today aren't waiting for our leaders to get their act together. They are a generation with an empowered social brain coming of age in an era of disruption, reinvention, and huge responsibility. Fueled by an enormous fear for their own wellbeing, youth around the world are taking tangible action. And for good reasons. As described by *Time* magazine, we are headed for a "Youthquake."[13]

Put yourself in the shoes of a teenager today. Previous generations each had their own clearly defined existential threat: for the Greatest Generation, it

---

10 Seymour Burchman, "How to Tie Executive Compensation to Sustainability," *Harvard Business Review*, November 12, 2018.

11 Jasper Jolly, "Shell CEO's Pay More than Doubles to £17.2M," *The Guardian*, March 14, 2019.

12 Adam Vaughan, "Shell Says It Wants to Double Green Energy Investment," *The Guardian*, December 26, 2018.

13 Charlotte Alter, "How Millennial Leaders Will Change America," *Time*, January 23, 2020.

was the risk of another world war. For those who came of age during the Cold War, it was the threat of nuclear holocaust. For teens today, one of the biggest threats they feel is the current environmental crisis.

In one powerful illustration, Greta Thunberg's unflinching willingness to call out the inaction of government has inspired a swelling global movement. A Swedish high school student, Greta took time off school every Friday to stage a sit-in at Swedish parliament, in an effort to hold them accountable for not making bold enough decisions related to climate change. Fast-forward twelve months, and her initiative caught on with Climate Change Action Day, where it's estimated that as many as six million young people from 150 countries around the globe took time off from school to march or gather in support of the environment. New York City schools even granted this an excused absence. Greta was invited to visit the White House, a trip for which she refused to fly, due to the high emissions of burning jet fuel. She became *Time*'s 2019 Person of the Year, the youngest ever.

Less famously, but just as audaciously, in the U.S. a group of twenty-one students and (now) young adults has tenaciously been challenging the federal government from within by filing the lawsuit *Juliana, et al. v. United States*. For the past five years, these young plaintiffs, ranging in age from twelve to twenty-three, have been working their way through the complex court system, asserting that the government violated their rights to life and liberty by encouraging activities that damaged the environment. Two presidential administrations have tried to have the suit thrown out on the basis, actually, of its sheer audacity, but in 2016 Judge Ann Aiken of the U.S. District Court of Oregon pushed the case forward by acknowledging that access to a clean environment was a fundamental right. The government appealed Judge Aiken's ruling, and the trial has now been thrown out because of the sheer vastness of redressing this claim.

From demanding action on climate change around the world, to vocally advocating for gun safety in the States, to marching for greater racial and gender equality and economic inclusion in every nation, Generation Z (as they are known in the Western world) feels incredibly empowered to be part of the solution to the crises they face. We need to pay attention.

When you consider that, as of 2017, 42 percent of the global population is under twenty-five, their worries, outrage, and agency will impact everything from elections to policies and spending habits in the not-too-distant future.

BUILDING A BETTER NEXT

During the pandemic, the prime minister of New Zealand, Jacinda Ardern, has been lauded for her quick, empathetic yet clear actions to not just contain the COVID-19 virus but to actually eliminate it from her country. Contributing to her successful Leading was the trust she had built prior by boldly announcing in 2019 that the government will no longer measure the health of the country using GDP but instead will use a new wellbeing budget to assess the long-term impacts of policy on the quality of people's lives. Jacinda has stated, "We need to address the societal wellbeing of our nation, not just the economic wellbeing," arguing for a shift beyond short-term economic performance and for seeing politics through a lens of "kindness, empathy, and wellbeing."[14]

As quickly as we are being required to evolve and contribute, there is also an increasing recognition and sense of urgency in society to develop new metrics to measure "success." Just as businesses are

---

14 Ceri Parker, "New Zealand Will Have a New 'Wellbeing Budget,' Says Jacinda Ardern," *World Economic Forum*, January 23, 2019.

recalibrating beyond shareholder capitalism, the public sector is seeking a new economic measure beyond GDP, as it no longer represents an accurate account of global wealth, nor supports the prosperity of people and the planet.

MEASURE WHAT WE VALUE, VALUE WHAT WE MEASURE

The man behind GDP, Simon Kuznets, warned when he conceived this back in the 1930s, that, "It counts the things that we're buying and selling. It is not a measure of how well we are all doing." But even so, for seventy-five years, the world has marched to the drum of Gross Domestic Product (GDP)—a narrow, distorted, and short-term measure focusing on new goods and services, without accounting for whether it helps or harms our natural environment.[15] As Chief Economist for the World Economic Forum (WEF) Jennifer Blanke points out, "It's easy to forget that it was not initially intended for this purpose; it merely provides a measure of the final goods and services produced in an economy over a given period, without any attention to what is produced, how it's produced, or who is producing it."

Why does this matter? Because as Nobel Prize-winning economist Joseph Stiglitz described at the WEF gathering in Davos in 2019:

What we measure informs what we do. And if we measure the wrong thing, we're going to do the wrong thing. GDP in the U.S. has gone up every year except 2009, but most Americans are worse off than they were a third of a century ago. The benefits have gone to the very top. At the bottom, real

---

15   Ross Chainey, "Beyond GDP—Is It Time to Rethink the Way We Measure Growth?" *World Economic Forum*, April 13, 2016.

wages adjusted for today are lower than they were sixty years ago. So this is an economic system that is not working for most people.[16]

True.

With its specific focus on production and consumption, currently GDP incentivizes things like cigarette manufacturing, opioid sales, and growing incarceration rates, while it excludes practices that are circular, regenerative, or highly valuable but without any direct compensation attached. Nor does it account for the extractive practices that have put our environment in jeopardy. As MIT professor Erik Brynjolfsson stated clearly at the Davos event, "We need a new model for growth. Just as we're reinventing business, we need to reinvent the way we measure the economy."

Fifty years ago, Milton Friedman helped usher in an era of "short-termism," myopic capitalism in which extractive growth and various forms of labor slavery and unpaid caregiving have played vital yet totally invisible roles. While he declared the only purpose of business is to create profits for shareholders, given the breakdowns in planetary, personal, and societal health, it is time we are guided by a healthier narrative—one in which we encourage leaders to stay focused on their business by understanding that rather than transferring a tiny amount of value via CSR, they have a responsibility to create societal, systemic value with *every* decision made, from cradle to grave.

Put simply, shifts brought on by the digitally led 1PR will render GDP even less of a reflection of the things that really matter.

---

16 "Beyond GDP," *World Economic Forum*, 2020.

BEYOND GDP TO SWI?

Riane Eisler is an internationally renowned social systems scientist, author, and attorney who, for more than forty years, has been developing a collection of Social Wealth Economic Indicators (SWEI) that measure a range of economic, social, and environmental activities and instruments. Since 2019, a task force composed of economists, businesspeople, social activists, and other leaders has been forming to develop a Social Wealth Index (SWI), which will condense and update SWEI into two easily accessible numbers. The SWI measure not only accounts for where we are (outputs) but also the investments (inputs) needed to develop a healthy, sustainable economy and society. It structures and makes visible the tremendous amount of activity and investment needed—plus the enormous returns we all experience when caring for people and nature. Importantly, the SWI also points out the huge costs of not doing so, not only in human and environmental terms but also in purely economic terms. It also shows the value of caring business and government policies, such as de-privatizing prisons.

While SWI is a more robust *accounting* of a flourishing economy, the concept of "Partnerism," also put forth by Riane, is the huge *mindset shift* needed to reframe the social and economic models we aim to measure. While we remain in a tiring tug-of-war between the merits of capitalism versus socialism, the truth is that both are rooted in domination systems that, for thousands of years, have shaped society through hierarchy and ranking. This distorted domination framing has created vast wealth and lifted billions out of poverty globally while simultaneously accelerating unprecedented harm to our physical, emotional, and planetary health. Partnerism represents a shift to power *with* versus power *over*, restoring the missing balance. It incentivizes a much more inclusive, equitable, and complete economic model that was actually present in many ancient and flourishing societies way back when.

DIVING DEEPER

RIANE EISLER ON THE CARING ECONOMY

Riane Eisler is a social systems scientist who is opening the conversation around how we measure the economic value of "invisible roles."

The work of caregiving for children, the elderly, the sick, and even the environment is currently discounted. This labor entails an invisible, unaccounted but enormous amount of expended energy. Why have we deemed it unworthy of our measurements of work and productivity?

As well as invisible labor, Riane's work is helping us understand hidden costs to the way we do business. Traditionally in business, we value the job over the person. In a stark example, an estimated 40.3 million men, women, and children were trafficked in slavery in 2016,[17] while that year a half-million people were paid pennies to train Amazon's AI.[18]

But we're seeing shifts in this mentality around the world. Sweden provides a stunning example of valuing unpaid labor: Swedish parents receive eighteen months of paid parental leave per child, with job security guaranteed for when they return to work. Perhaps not coincidentally, Swedish workers

---

17 "Measurement, Action, Freedom: An Independent Assessment of Government Progress Towards Achieving UN Sustainable Development Goal 8.7," *Global Slavery Index*, 2019.

18 Hope Reese and Nick Heath, "Inside Amazon's Clickworker Platform: How Half a Million People Are Being Paid Pennies to Train AI," *Tech Republic*, December 16, 2016.

are far less concerned than Americans about the potential of robotics to take over their jobs; they feel well held in the system.

Some countries, such as New Zealand, Bhutan, Iceland, Finland, and Costa Rica, are now including measures of well-being as an economic indicator alongside their GDP.

Riane is diving into the valuation arena and studying metrics involved with the cost of the way we've built business—and the value missed along the way. In fact, wellness initiatives are becoming commonplace in communities and companies around the world, a testament to Riane's efforts to bring care-giving and related work out from the shadows and give it the value it deserves.

> This notion that man can, and should, have abso-lute dominion over the 'chaotic' powers of nature and woman...is what ultimately lies behind man's famous 'conquest of nature'—a conquest that is today punctur-ing holes in the earth's ozone layer, destroying our forests, polluting our air and water, and increasingly threatening the welfare, and even survival, of thousands of living spe-cies, including our own.
>
> —Riane Eisler

Her work should be considered scaffolding for how we can better value individual contributions and needs in our society and how we subsequently build a more sustainable and equi-table structure.

THE EVOLVING SHAPE OF BUSINESS

During a podcast interview recently, I was asked about the role of business in advancing something as sensitive as brain-computing interfaces (BCI). My reply was that unlike government, nonprofits, or the private sector, business is best designed to drive and distribute innovation. That is what capital and market systems incentivize. But how we put those pieces together in an exponential economy matters given how much power these kinds of technologies put in their hands...and their boardrooms.

Business leaders and entrepreneurs will increasingly face a fast torrent of new questions as they consider how to shape their businesses ahead: which technologies to bet on and how they will impact the delivery of products and services (or actually, how they could turn our products *into* services), the new paths of value they create, the unintended negative and positive impacts they could have, and how to ensure the organization is financially sustainable as it addresses and anticipates the needs of a growing set of stakeholders.

There is so much opportunity; consider again how companies like Microsoft and Apple have adapted their organizations, culture, and talent rapidly enough to harness the benefits of radically scalable yet infinitely personal digital offerings. Not surprisingly, they are two of the seven most valuable companies globally, along with Google, Amazon, Facebook, and Tencent, based on a platform model that supports the creation of digital communities and marketplaces that allow different groups to interact and transact.[19]

As we look around the corner, what will the models of success be? What will the value propositions, contributions, and delivery models of the

---

19 Jennifer L. Schenker, "The Platform Economy," *Medium*, January 19, 2019.

future look like? Will brands create their own branded ecosystems or fluidly plug into existing ones? How will they seamlessly integrate digital technologies onto physical experiences (e.g., AR games and stats continuously available at a live sporting event), and what behaviors will we choose to incentivize and monetize (e.g., if someone positively rates or comments on a digital billboard or simply notices a branded product embedded in a VR game)?

In the growing swarm of ethical issues around privacy, attention, and "stalking versus serving" business models, will companies be guarded or transparent with how they do business and provide customer value? How will other technologies track and hold them accountable? And how will value exchange be handled? As today's evolution to contactless embedded virtual wallets grows, will they continue to erode traditional bank relationships and how "money" flows? Most important of all, how do we ensure we don't replicate industrial-era thinking in this new digital-first customer engagement age? I am fascinated by what an era of constant data flow, dynamic algorithmic decision-making, increasingly fluid microtransactions, and our desire to hold each other well makes possible.

As we try to imagine what comes next, I find it intriguing to revisit the genesis of Wikipedia. Would you have guessed just nineteen years ago that it would have been possible to do away with hardcovers of the *Encyclopedia Britannica* and instead crowdsource a whole hive of planetary information made centrally available for anyone in the world to access with a few simple keystrokes? Would you have imagined that a resource tool that anyone can edit would ever be able to become a trusted (enough) source of information? And furthermore, could you conceive of any way that such a robust information database would be given away for free without contributors being paid or this information being owned by any one entity?

As the internet emerged, developers tried to apply an analog model to this new digital environment and created Encarta (Microsoft)—essentially a digital version of a traditional encyclopedia—and, naturally, made the assumption that people would first pay a subscription fee for the service and then later accept free with advertisements. These original assumptions completely missed that the internet (and later the "selfie") would dramatically change behaviors and expectations. Our new ability to connect, create, and coordinate in real time with one another made it possible for Wikipedia to become the world's ninth-most-popular website in terms of global internet engagement, with worldwide monthly readership of approximately 495 million and as many as 15.5 billion monthly page views as of September 2018 (according to Wikipedia). Not surprisingly, Wikipedia has become the preferred resource for everyday, on-demand information and is a visible testament to communal trust, while helping establish a new mindset and collective consumer influence over access, data, and informative content.

Just as Spotify, Uber, Airbnb, and Snapchat showed us, new technologies will empower new forms of value creation and exchange. This is the kind of completely different thinking that will allow us to thrive in a future in which Peter Diamandis, entrepreneur and co-founder of Singularity University and the X Prize, believes these six "Ds" of exponential technological development and growth will lead to both great upheaval and new opportunity: Digitization, Deception, Disruption, Demonetization, Dematerialization, and Democratization. We are in for a fascinating ride ahead.

We could end this subject here for now, but it feels incomplete to have a discussion on the future of business without stepping back for a moment to consider the role that both money and debt play in where we are now. In 2010, anthropologist David Graeber wrote the book *Debt: The First 5,000 Years*, in which he shared a peek into the subject. He concluded:

Throughout its five-thousand-year history, debt has always involved institutions—whether Mesopotamian sacred kingship, Mosaic jubilees, Sharia, or Canon Law—that place controls on debt's potentially catastrophic social consequences. It is only in the current era that we have begun to see the creation of the first effective planetary administrative system, operating through the IMF, World Bank, corporations, and other financial institutions, largely to protect the interests of creditors.[20]

This issue of a debt-dependent economic system will receive a lot of attention ahead. And seemingly audacious alternatives will arise. David closed his essay on debt by offering us this provocative question: "In a society in which the foundation of violence had finally been yanked away, what exactly would free men and women owe each other? What sorts of promises and commitments should they make to each other?"

The pandemic has forced us to take a closer look at our twentieth-century choices. As we enter the first percent of this fast-evolving future, we have the opportunity to reshape the ways we coordinate with each other to ensure greater flourishing and fairness. Charles Eisenstadt, author of *Sacred Economics*, invites us to think of it this way:

After years of confinement to the road of our predecessors, we finally have a choice. We are right to stop, stunned at the newness of our situation. Of the hundred paths that radiate out in front of us, some lead in the same direction we've already been headed. Some lead to hell on earth. And some lead to a world more healed and more beautiful than we ever dared believe to be possible.[21]

---

20 David Graeber, *Debt: The First 5,000 Years* (New York: Melville House, 2012).
21 Charles Eisenstadt, *Sacred Economics: Money, Gift, and Society in the Age of Transition* (Berkeley: North Atlantic Books, 2011).

REBUILDING THE INTERNET

In the same way that we need to rethink how we value labor and consumption as indicators of economic prosperity, we are called to rethink access to another system that has become fundamental to our lives: the internet.

"What If Mother Nature Rebuilt the Internet?" was the title of a talk I gave in 2018 at the SXSW conference along with my close friend and visionary colleague Matthew Schutte. To a small audience, we introduced Holochain, a way of redesigning how we access information and coordinate action via the World Wide Web, using the organic patterns of nature as the designing principle. We were in a small room of only fifty or sixty attendees, most of whom admittedly left both more curious and more confused than when they had entered. It is not easy to wrap your brain around a huge paradigm shift. But a small number of those listening intently had a major epiphany. They recognized that what we were sharing was a game-changing idea that could profoundly shift the way the internet works. By providing an entirely different way of patterning or structuring the framework and tech upon which it runs, the internet could better serve us, its constituents.

The way the internet has currently taken shape has created huge amounts of economic value, opened access, and changed the way we now do almost every task, from banking to buying to falling in love. But its centralized design has also taken some dark turns that a different approach could correct for—such as unauthorized surveillance, cybercrime, incentives to spread misinformation and hate, abuse of personal data, and very real fears the whole thing could go down. Alternatively, can you envision turning the internet inside out by putting the individual (and our data) at the center, rather than the application itself? Such an "agent-centric" approach means you would no longer have to go to a centralized application to make something happen, therefore making things safer, more resilient, and open to whole new levels of participation and coordination.

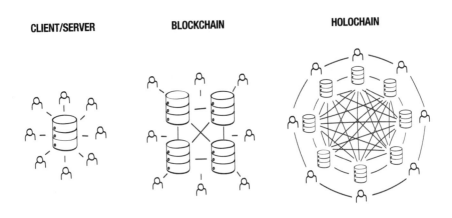

Holochain offers a path to a distributed internet designed to solve these problems. While often compared to blockchain technologies, Holochain is actually built from a completely different ethos and engineering approach, as it enables individual authority over data sharing, access, and storage. Imagine an internet with no central servers collecting, analyzing, and exploiting our data. Imagine a decentralized solution with no bottlenecks, ledgers, or gated access. What would be possible then? What problems does this solve for—and what opportunities does it open up?

This isn't just about shifting the ways we communicate online or the ways we exchange money or assign value via tokens. Something like Holochain (and there are others working on alternative distributed internet protocols) could enable us to create things such as our own distributed renewable energy exchanges. Or car-sharing communities. Or safer, less manipulatable social networks. Even our own cloud hosting platforms in which individuals are incentivized to host applications versus going through corporate web servers.

It is a long path with many technicalities to absorb. While digging into the coding intricacies is helpful for some, I invite you to see the bigger picture and wonder, "What if?" Here is a metaphor I use to help me: while I still can't fully explain the physics of how planes fly, I fully appreciate the value of being able to get from here to there much faster; similarly, I'm also able to see the infrastructure needed—such as a ticketing system, route maps, and safety inspections. Excitedly, I can imagine the new opportunities that being able to fly people and goods in a plane opens for global business exchange and value.

We are just starting to see some early infrastructure bridges that will make a distributed internet work, such as smartphones with built-in cryptocurrency wallets and external distributed hosting ports. But here is the exciting question: How will individuals and communities be able to more directly benefit economically from a growing digital future as centralized structures are replaced with cooperative networks in which *we* hold (and can choose to share and/or monetize) the data we each create?

DIVING DEEPER
ARTHUR BROCK AND RADICAL COLLABORATION

Arthur Brock is the founder of Holochain and the Metacurrency Project, and with his developments in cryptocurrency, he's challenging old models of capital. Many of our exchange models are based on a certain way of thinking about capital, land, and labor in an industrial context. Now that we've shifted to an information economy, there are whole new levels of resources that change the paradigm and alter how we exchange and relate to one another.

Arthur's projects are giving birth to a distributed, self-regulated social system, which enables a new form of social coordination with the abilities to see, create, and exchange value directly with each other.

One of the results of this work is Holochain, an innovation that moves beyond blockchain technology. Simply defined, Holochain is a pattern of building distributed applications. Of all the applications built on the web today, very few, if any, are distributed; they are produced and delivered through a central server. When you use Uber or Airbnb or Facebook, your browsing and usage data go through enormous servers. Holochain is built to be agent-centric rather than data-centric, which puts the user and their needs at the heart of each interaction. Through Holochain, you can decide how you want to be connected to people and whom to share data with by exchanging information directly with each other; that data doesn't travel through servers.

For example, if I have solar power capabilities and you have wind ones, and we want to create our own energy exchange, we can easily build our own system that doesn't go through a central server or current regulatory authority. We decide how to measure and account for our energy trade through microtransactions. Think how these direct interpersonal interactions could shape the future at scale: we'll be able to self-regulate and value information in much more fluid, dynamic, and resilient ways.

Why is it so imperative to pursue audacious, status-quo-breaking ideas?

Humankind has built a global, electronic, communications network, which enables us to collaborate on scales like never before. However, the gap between theory and practice is immense. Technical barriers constrain access and make it difficult for applications to interface with each other. We have weak tools for working on large-scale collaboration and decision-making, and the power dynamics of who controls shared data and communications keeps it out of reach...But what if we could elegantly transcend all of these technical barriers at once? After all, shouldn't our technology actually help us work together?[22]

—Arthur Brock

REIMAGINING ORGANIZATIONS

Challenging orthodoxies is necessary if we are to boldly architect the future. This doesn't only apply to the business models or technological tools we adopt; it's worth also considering what radical change in our own organizational models could look like.

Ricardo Semler is a business visionary in Brazil, who, in the 1980s, took over his father's company and set about modernizing management practices to form a new kind of industrialized democracy. The company has since grown across a variety of industries from $4 million in revenue twenty-nine years ago to over $1 billion today; further, in the worst ten-year

---

22 Alex Libertas, "Holochain: Interview with Founder Arthur Brock," *The Daily Chain*, April 10, 2019.

recession in Brazil's history, the company's proceeds grew 600 percent, profits were up 500 percent, and productivity rose 700 percent.[23] How?

Instead of assuming as CEO that he is the most motivated, qualified, invested, and experienced person to make decisions for the good of the company (old school), he realized that employees are inherently motivated and more than capable of making their own decisions when empowered to do so (new school). So that's what they do: from designing their own jobs and choosing their length of vacation time to selecting their supervisors and defining salaries. Ricardo even regularly abdicates the role of CEO temporarily to individual workers, so each has a turn at understanding what it's like to be in that position. It's a vision that rewards the wisdom of workers, promotes work/life balance, and holds individuals responsible, while rewarding the company with strong financial results and economic value as well.

Inspired by imagining what would happen to his company if he were hit by a truck, Ricardo decided that he would no longer manage with a focus on what might go wrong but would instead direct his attention and energy to the best-case scenario. Sure, if employees are allowed to set their own salaries and are given unlimited vacation, a small number of people will abuse the system, but the vast majority will make the right decisions. So Ricardo chose to create policies and practices that served the majority.

As liberating as this sounds—and as successful as this has proven to be—Ricardo still finds that many adults struggle to embrace a structure with no rules they can benchmark themselves against. As a result, he believes we need to begin learning these practices much earlier and has turned his attention to reinventing education.

---

23 Chuck Blakeman, "Why Great Leaders Beat Super Managers Every Time," *Colorado Biz*, January 11, 2016.

Changing these kinds of behaviors is not easy, but there is hope. In 2014, not long after he took the role, Microsoft CEO Satya Nadella began convening an annual weeklong gathering (either remotely or in person) of all Microsoft employees, including a three-day hackathon where they were asked to set their regular tasks and projects aside and work in small teams of their choosing to create something new—whatever they wanted, but something that would add value or make a difference in some way. Since its inception, more than sixty thousand team members in four hundred cities and seventy-five countries have participated. Due to growing interest, they now also invite corporate customers to join in.

Satya implemented the hackathons in an effort to shift the entire organization to a more collaborative culture and to break down the silos that had become entrenched at Microsoft. He didn't just start with his leaders, and the mandate wasn't to create a specific number of new ideas but rather to empower *everyone* to participate. All ideas were shared internally rather than externally, giving employees a safe space to experiment and begin rebuilding trust with their coworkers, as they could see the faces behind the work.

It was also a brilliant way to incentivize curiosity by redirecting all that pent-up energy many disillusioned employees start to feel when they lose faith in their organizations or believe their employers are doing the wrong things. Instead of letting that rumble become a toxic drain on resources, this assignment released employee energy to power new momentum. It also made visible the need to work across silos and shore up one's own capacities by learning the skills and cultivating the relationships needed to create the solutions envisioned. Now an annual event that all look forward to, these hackathons make clear that "innovation" is everyone's role and actively support the shared mindset needed to succeed.

Having powered new momentum and restored the trust needed to drive big changes, Microsoft is now one of the most valuable companies in the world, under Satya's leadership. And, not inconsequentially, the company also consistently ranks as a great place to work.

Not all bold moves are as grand as these mentioned above. In my own experience, shifting Nestlé from thinking about how to sell more frozen meals to how to rebuild trust in industrial food was also an audacious move. One they pursued at the right time by addressing changes in consumer sentiment and patterns of spending in a much bolder way. The data told a compelling story about what the future needed and what they—as one of the largest, best-resourced food companies on the planet—were in a unique position to contribute. The opportunity was clear; the bigger risk was *not* taking this on.

Fast-forward to the rise of plant-based proteins, ghost kitchens, and all the other enormous disruptions taking place in the prepared foods industry, and you can see why we all need to be willing to reimagine ourselves in order to stay relevant. We had little idea at the time of what was just a few years over the horizon, but with a vastly different mindset and goal, this Nestlé business unit was better prepared than its competitors to adapt.

AUDACIOUS IN ACTION

Leadering embraces audacious, human-centered action over incremental, bureaucratic steps by framing authority in an entirely new way and embracing co-creation and collaboration with everyone from channel partners, to vendors, to clients, to those uncommon partnerships previously unimaginable. It requires a confidence to disrupt ourselves and reshape our own industries. We have seen many examples of audacity in this book so far—from Martha Stewart and Eileen Fisher to CVS and IKEA—and the work is happening all over the world.

As we described earlier, to feed nearly ten billion people by the middle of the century without further endangering the planet, the food system has to fundamentally change. Approaching the problem as a design challenge, global architecture firm Sasaki Associates worked with developers CP Group to propose a 250-acre agricultural district in China that would take advantage of cutting-edge technology: vertical hydroponic farming interspersed with urban living and civic spaces just on the outskirts of Shanghai.[24] While landscape design isn't a new practice, what is particularly audacious about their plan is that the Sunqiao development is intended not only to improve air quality in this dense urban center and provide the city with a beautiful, green aesthetic attraction, but also it has been intentionally designed to integrate vertical farming to help feed the city's twenty-four million people. Alongside goals of minimizing water, pesticide use, and transportation waste, the Sunqiao developers are rethinking urban food security and bringing the farm right into the city.

The proposed design recalibrates assumptions of what landscape architecture, urban livability, and farming could be. CP Group is guided by a clear purpose and values, bolstered by a commitment to the Sustainable Development Goals.

This is the beauty of the moment we are in. Marrying exponential technologies with a massive transformative purpose opens entirely new solutions and frontiers. Audacious Leading challenges us to see more holistically as we redesign.

---

24 Leanna Garfield, "Shanghai Is Getting an Entire 'Farming District' with Towering Vertical Farms and Seed Libraries," *Business Insider*, April 18, 2017.

In Japan, Toyota has decided the best way to understand how autonomous transportation integrates within a smart city is to build an entire one from scratch and learn. This prototype community will initially welcome two thousand residents (all employees of Toyota) and sits on a 175-acre site in Higashi at the base of Mount Fuji. Named "Woven City," the focus is on converging technologies, including high-speed connectivity, robotics, shared mobility, smart homes, sensor-based AI, and more, in a living laboratory designed to better understand the dynamics in this kind of community of the future.[25] While technology is an integral part of the equation, there is an equal focus on ensuring the highest quality of life for residents. Streets will be separated into fast transportation hubs where all vehicles are powered by hydrogen fuel cell technology with zero emissions, through to pedestrian-friendly linear grids over three square blocks that move people through parks, not sidewalks or streets. This provides a wide variety of intersections between various kinds of inhabitants: humans, animals, vehicles, and robots.

Attempting to see the *whole* makes an audacious idea visible and opens a new world of learning. What other audacious advancements might we look forward to ahead?

Elon Musk's Neuralink is a brain-to-machine interface that would allow humans to control external devices using only their minds. Early successes of this audacious goal show a monkey has been able to control a computer with its brain.[26] Even as far back as 2004, Google co-founder Larry Page was talking about his similar vision for the future of search. "Eventually, you'll have the implant," he said at the time, "where if you think about a

---

25 Woven-City.global, 2020.
26 Isobel Asher Hamilton, "Elon Musk Says He's Tested His Brain Microchip on Monkeys, and It Enabled One to Control a Computer with Its Mind," *Business Insider*, July 17, 2019.

fact, it will just tell you the answer."[27] The statement was very controversial at the time, with many claiming he and fellow Google co-founder Sergey Brin were out of their minds (uh, no pun intended), but as we're starting to see, what ten or twenty years ago seemed distinctly science fiction is now becoming a scientific reality.

As often happens, Elon is not the only one thinking about this. Driving his own mission to create a brain-to-machine interface is Bryan Johnson, the original creator of Braintree, the software that later became Venmo once he sold to PayPal. Bryan believes that in order for humans to keep up in the increasingly tech-advanced world, we need an enormous upgrade. With his new wealth, Bryan and his team of neuroscientists, physicists, and engineers developed Kernel. What started as a chip that could be implanted in our brains has become a noninvasive wearable that will allow us to keep up with machines by absorbing and assimilating data more effectively.[28] With an eagerness to expand neuroscience advances, Bryan has begun offering Kernel as a platform that provides "NaaS": neuroscience as a service, which along with a world-class "full-stack neuroscience" team is able to offer "neuroscience studies delivered at the touch of a button."[29]

Bryan also created the OS Fund, a $100 million fund to invest in entrepreneurs commercializing breakthrough discoveries in genomics, synthetic biology, computationally derived therapeutics, advanced materials, and diagnostics that, in his view, would fundamentally shift the "operating system of humanity" as he "seeks founders who see beyond our lifetimes" and "want to author a better future for humanity."[30]

---

27 Stephen Levy, "We Are Entering the Era of the Brain Machine Interface," *Wired*, April 22, 2017.
28 Kernel.co, 2019.
29 "Hello Humanity," *Kernel*, 2020.
30 OSFund.co, 2019.

Many of the experiences that we've taken for granted are being reimagined—from how we buy a chair (remember the earlier example of bioengineered furniture parts that assemble themselves in our homes?) to where we're able to vacation. Highly immersive VR applications are now digitally transporting those with limited physical mobility, environmental concerns, or other financial priorities to the destinations of their dreams.

This has inspired Japan's All Nippon Airways (ANA) to launch an ambitious effort to sell trips that won't involve a plane at all, and instead will use robotics, haptic technology, and what they describe as fast communication to create a "new mode of instantaneous transportation" that lets people carry their "presence, consciousness, knowledge, and skills" to remote locations.[31] At first glance, this might seem cannibalistic to their airline business, but by leveraging their broader identity as a travel company (rather than simply an airline), ANA wants to lead the market in developing an entirely different type of travel experience never before possible.

Fascinated by how to meet escalating expectations for exploration and adventure, audacious entrepreneurs are thinking literally above and beyond when it comes to reimagining the travel experience: from underwater theme parks[32] to low-orbital space visits and eventually as far out as Mars. Virgin Galactic went public this year, saying it has the cash to begin flying tourist trips to the edge of space sometime soon for a cool $250,000 a pop.[33] Blue Origin, Jeff Bezos's space firm, said it would fly people on its New Shepard suborbital rocket in 2020.[34] SpaceX's Starship rocket aims

---

31 ANA-avatar.com, 2019.
32 Michael Bartiromo, "'World's Largest Underwater Theme Park' Opens in Bahrain, Features Sunken Boeing 747," *Fox News*, September 30, 2019.
33 Catie Perry, "Want a Ticket to Space? It's Yours...for $250,000," *Fox Business*, October 3, 2019.
34 "New Shepard," *Blue Origin*, 2020.

to be fully reusable and able to launch as many as one hundred people at a time on missions to the moon and Mars.[35] In case you feel like an orbital stopover, NASA is opening the International Space Station (ISS) to tourists sometime in the next year or so, while a Houston-based startup called Orion Span has proposed a four-guest space hotel called Aurora Station that would open in 2022. In what might be the most ambitious space hotel of all (at this moment), Gateway Foundation, a startup in California, is proposing the space equivalent of a cruise ship, built using artificial gravity and including sports arenas, gyms, concert venues, restaurants, and accommodation for one hundred guests.[36]

Back here on Earth, AI is increasingly at the center of many innovations and is radically changing entire sectors. A new solar energy tech company called Heliogen, founded by serial entrepreneur and inventor Bill Gross and backed by investors including Bill Gates,[37] has developed cutting-edge solar technology using AI-driven mirrors to concentrate energy. Able to exceed temperatures greater than 1,000 degrees Celsius, Heliogen is a remarkable breakthrough in concentrated solar energy that could replace fossil fuels used in heavy-emissions processes, such as making cement, steel, glass, and petrochemicals:

We've made great strides in deploying clean energy in our electricity system. But electricity accounts for less than a quarter of global energy demand. Heliogen represents a technological leap forward in addressing the other 75 percent of energy demand: the use of fossil fuels for industrial processes and transportation. With low-cost, ultra-high temperature process heat,

35 Michael Sheetz, "Elon Musk Says SpaceX's Starship Rocket Will Launch 'Hundreds of Missions' Before Flying People," *CNBC*, September 1, 2020.
36 Kate Baggaley, "Huge Space Hotel Promises Fake Gravity and 'Supersized Basketball,'" *NBC News*, September 14, 2019.
37 Heliogen.com, 2019.

we have an opportunity to make meaningful contributions to solving the climate crisis.[38]

According to the company, Heliogen's technology is on track to ultimately produce temperatures up to 1,500 degrees Celsius—hot enough to split carbon dioxide and water to make hydrogen and other fossil-free fuels.

Audacious Leadering, however, does not require a technological breakthrough. *Every* organization in *every* sector can start putting this new imperative of the 1PR into practice right now by thinking boldly and systemically.

Robert Smith is the wealthiest Black investor in the U.S. whose net worth is estimated to be $5 billion. Believing that Black communities and minorities have been starved of access to the typical banking, technology, education, and healthcare infrastructure the white population takes for granted, he has committed to channeling 2 percent of his annual net income for the next decade to empower minority-owned businesses and entrepreneurial ventures with access to the capital they need.[39] He argues that investing directly is a fast way to advance economic justice for Black Americans, and he has shared a concrete plan with the nation's business leaders outlining that an investment equal to 2 percent of net income over the next decade would be a small step toward restoring equity and mobility in America. He's challenging other leaders to do the same.

And global conglomerate Siemens has announced a new policy that allows staff to work anywhere, several days a week.[40] Due to a global staff survey

---

38 David Hodari, "Bill Gross, 1990s Dotcom Trailblazer, Is Now Betting on Green Energy," *The Wall Street Journal*, October 6, 2020.
39 Nathan Vardi, "The 2 Percent Solution: Inside Billionaire Robert Smith's Bold Plan to Funnel Billions to America's Black-Owned Businesses," *Forbes*, June 19, 2020.
40 Justin Bariso, "This Company's New 2-Sentence Remote Work Policy Is the Best I've Ever...

in which employees expressed the desire for greater flexibility in their approach to work, Roland Busch, deputy CEO and labor director, released a statement outlining that:

The company is adopting a new model that will allow employees worldwide to work from anywhere they feel comfortable for an average of two to three days a week. The basis for this forward-looking working model is further development [of] our corporate culture. These changes will also be associated with a different leadership style, one that focuses on outcomes rather than on time spent at the office. We trust our employees and empower them to shape their work themselves so that they can achieve the best possible results. With the new way of working, we're motivating our employees while improving the company's performance capabilities and sharpening Siemens' profile as a flexible and attractive employer.

To be clear, this is a swift declaration made by a member of the global Fortune 100 and one of the largest companies in the world, with around 380,000 employees in two hundred countries.

What all these examples demonstrate, including the UnitedHealthcare solution we opened with, is a willingness to disrupt current approaches and industries with bold systemic moves that consider the whole.

...Heard," *Inc.*, July 27, 2020.

CHAPTER SEVEN

Thrive (versus Die)

"With ideas it is like with dizzy heights you climb: At first they cause you discomfort and you are anxious to get down, distrustful of your own powers; but soon the remoteness of the turmoil of life and the inspiring influence of the altitude calm your blood; your step gets firm and sure and you begin to look—for dizzier heights."

—Nikola Tesla, inventor

A four-hundred-year-old postal service has been voted the most innovative company in Norway.[1] SVP of digital innovation at Norway Post (aka Posten Norge) Alexander Haneng enthusiastically shared a two-minute case study on Instagram crediting two approaches: they are focused on continuous learning, and they have buy-in and backing from senior management. As he enthusiastically shared in his video post, these Leadering practices led to the creation of an e-commerce marketplace where shops are able to promise fast delivery. As Alexander explains it, this isn't a part of their core business but rather a "sandbox for learning where they can test with shops and with customers what works and what doesn't—making changes every day."

This kind of thinking—and story sharing—builds on a decade of innovation that has incorporated robotic process automation to streamline and integrate differing IT systems as well as machine learning to enable chatbots to handle more than one thousand different customer inquiries, 24/7, in Norwegian, Swedish, and English, seamlessly transferring questions to a human if needed. This year, they are executing a swift rollout of parcel lockers nationwide.

While, clearly, Posten Norge has created a strong culture of innovation, they are supported by an even larger system, as countries with cohesive social safety nets are less afraid of trying and implementing these kinds of technological advances than those without. These forward-thinking nations are focused on protecting the worker rather than protecting the job, allowing both organizations *and* citizens to thrive.

Perhaps the most important takeaway from this entire book is this: Leadering puts people at the center of every decision and makes thriving the goal.

---

1   "From Horses to Robots and AI: How Posten Norge Took on the Future," *Avo Consulting*, 2020.

The new KPIs for this transformative era are still being defined, but by now it is abundantly evident that we need to drive bold innovation and shift from a relentless focus on short-term financial growth to results that factor in social equity and access, environmental and ecological stewardship, technological safety, and our collective physical, emotional, and mental health, now and in the long term. As we've discussed throughout this book, to accomplish this, we need to reorient our focus from outdated ways of framing our work to investing in these new, empowering practices:

LEADERSHIP	LEADERING
PREDICTABILITY	Curiosity
EFFICIENCY	Empathy
SILOS	Ecosystems
EXTRACTION	Contribution
INCREMENTAL	Audacious
ROI	Value
WORK FOR ME	Work with Me

Survival is not guaranteed. Nor is longevity an excuse to stand still. Inspiring case in point: a nine-hundred-year-old city is considered to be one of the world's most livable, progressive, sustainable, and child-friendly cities on the planet. Considered an environmental economics and solar research hub, Freiburg, Germany, is now inspiring other city planners around the world to learn from their groundbreaking projects.

Using the two-question compass, I have honestly never encountered an organization or team that wasn't in a position to more audaciously answer the call to what the future needs and expects of it, unleashing a powerhouse of momentum and engagement. With Leadering as our North Star, organizations of all sizes and industries are able to uncork the inventiveness and compassion necessary to cross the liminal gap—safely and with confidence—as they continue to create sustainable value for all stakeholders.

It can take time to "change the way we change," as Unilever puts it. These are practices that require constant reinforcement and congruent incentives. To thrive in the unchartered territory ahead, we can begin by focusing less on planning and more on preparing.

PREPARATION OVER PLANNING

A reliance on efficiency planning works well when you know exactly what you need, but when you can't foresee the future, how can you plan for the unexpected? Margaret Heffernen, professor of practice at the University of Bath School of Management in the U.K., coaches us: today it is less risky to be prepared for multiple eventualities than to efficiently only focus on one...and then get it wrong.

In her TED Talk, "The Human Skills We Need in an Uncertain World," she references the Coalition for Epidemic Preparedness Innovations (CEPI), who are developing multiple vaccines for multiple diseases because it's impossible to know which diseases we'll encounter in the future and what vaccines will be needed. As Margaret reflects, is it efficient, knowing that some of those will never be used? No. But is it robust? Yes. Because we should not depend on a single solution. (Remember the banana crisis?)

She goes on to say:

Epidemic responsiveness also depends hugely on people who know and trust each other. But those relationships take time to develop, time that is always in short supply when an epidemic breaks out. So CEPI is developing relationships, friendships, alliances, now knowing that some of those may never be used. Preparedness, coalition-building, imagination, experiments, bravery—in an unpredictable age, these are tremendous sources of resilience and strength. They aren't efficient, but they give us limitless capacity for adaptation, variation, and invention. And the less we know about the future, the more we're going to need these tremendous sources of human, messy, unpredictable skills.[2]

Investing in relationships and building our networks of "PYNKrs" make us much better prepared when an unexpected moment to act suddenly arises.

Who would have guessed that Walmart and Microsoft would discuss joining forces to buy the short-form video app TikTok in just a matter of days? Because Microsoft CEO Satya Nadella and Walmart CEO Doug McMillon worked together on various projects for years building trust and a solid relationship, they were able to spring into action together.

Rather than go all in on one uncertain future—building a solid plan to a specific destination—Leadering asks us to simultaneously commit resources to a *range* of likely possibilities, so we are ready to act as the opportunity makes itself clear.

While Leadering is a radically new and empowering belief system, there are tangible ways—both big and small—in which we can prepare ourselves, our teams, our organizations, and even our kids to thrive in this 1PR.

---

2   Margaret Heffernan, "The Human Skills We Need in an Unpredictable World," *TED*, 2019.

PREPARING OURSELVES FOR THE FUTURE

The new Leadering practices organizations are learning to cultivate also apply to us as individuals.

This matters, because the future isn't taking shape around us, it *is* us.

THE POWER OF NOT KNOWING...YET

Confronting our own blind spots and our long-reinforced, ego-driven habits have become critical business skills. These can be difficult because, whether you are an experienced corporate executive or a startup founder who just closed a big round of funding, as a leader, you are expected to "know it all" at all times. I was listening to a joint interview recently with the founder and CEO of Airbnb, Brian Chesky, and successful hotel entrepreneur (and my inspiring PYNKr pal) Chip Conley, whom Brian invited into Airbnb when it was early in its growth cycle.[3] Chip gave Brian insight into the hospitality business, while Brian and his team educated Chip on the digital business landscape. Chip describes it as being both mentor and mentee, simultaneously. It was such a smart Leadering move, as each had significant wisdom and experience with which to fill in the missing pieces of the other.

In this interview, Brian admitted how difficult it is for business leaders to appear vulnerable, unsure, or in a state of learning. This is especially true for executives in public companies who have to deliver a positive growth story every single quarter. As such, Brian was grateful Chip had introduced him to the work of influential Stanford psychologist Carol Dweck,

---

3   Commonwealth Club, "Airbnb's Chip Conley and Brian Chesky: Modern Elders and Millennials at Work," *YouTube*, October 3, 2018.

who is helping executives see the difference between having a growth mindset, which is primed for learning and evolving, versus a fixed mindset that (in its simplest description) believes what you know is locked-in and immutable.

Learning he could choose to adopt a growth mindset took Brian off the hook of always having to "know." In the same way, we as leaders can embrace the invitation—and permission—that Leadering gives us to dump the outdated belief we aren't leading if we are still gathering information. "I don't know...yet" is a powerful, liberating phrase. Expecting to have 100 percent clarity 100 percent of the time is dangerously limiting as it freezes us in our tracks. Presenting our honest selves—rather than our facades—draws resources and equally inquisitive collaborators to us.

Moving out of a posture of having to always *know* also encourages us to seek out and learn from all levels of tenured experience, appreciating that even the most recent recruit may know or see something no one else has. Increasingly, I see C-level executives seeking to learn from entry-level hires who can help them understand the ways things are shifting, like the etiquette of hosting an AMA ("ask me anything") session on a fast-growing social platform like Reddit. Or why in the world an online payments platform like Venmo added a social layer that makes everyone's transactions visible to everyone else.

Being unafraid to ask others for help with learning is essential for thriving.

THE NOW-CRITICAL SKILLS OF SELF-CARE

As much as we can learn from others, there also is growing support for the practice of mindfulness; regularly turning inward to reflect on our feelings, beliefs, and tendencies is no longer seen as fringe. This practice allows us to explore new terrain with less expectation and respond thoughtfully, rather than react out of fear.

We must also prioritize self-care and time out. It's why we started this book with a deep breath. As we are in a mode of continuous learning and doing—managing today's expectations while we build the runway to tomorrow—it is literally impossible to get it all done in a day, a week, or even a month. Presidential historian Doris Kearns Goodwin advocates for taking time for renewal and reflection, observing that each of the four most influential presidents she has studied ensured he took time to relax, connect with his family, and create the space needed to see the large problems the nation was facing from a fresh vantage point. Leadering knows it is important that we do this as well.

Earlier, we discussed the high levels of anxiety and loneliness that permeate culture, our offices, and increasingly ourselves. While it may seem that we have no time in this race to keep up, intentionally making time to take a walk, get enough sleep, connect with others, eat well, and even write in a journal ensures we avoid burnout. From a performance perspective, trust that when you care for yourself, you are better able to absorb new information, connect the dots for greater insight, and deliver more meaningful results.

You are also setting a powerful example for your team (and your children).

PREPARING YOUTH FOR THE FUTURE

To have a healthy, resilient society, and more adaptive, inventive talent, we need to focus not just on the adults in our workforce—we also need to nurture more secure and creative children.

It starts immediately. Neurological research shows the clear line between providing quality care for the first five years of a child's life and building the foundation for learning, self-control, and the deep sense of psychological safety that makes it possible to innovate, collaborate, and experiment.[4] It is vital all children have access to this, because investments here have a steep and undeniable payback for both employers and society for decades ahead.

I am frequently asked how we can ensure our kids are equipped for a world in so much flux. I am always grateful when this is raised, as I am genuinely concerned about the levels of anxiety and sense of futility many youth are feeling. A mother in the (virtual) audience for a professional keynote I gave messaged me afterward to share that her fourteen-year-old son recently told her there was no bright future for him. Similarly, another woman I met at an event last year told me two of her son's classmates had missed several weeks of school due to anxiety-related stomach ailments—and they are only in fourth grade!

The introduction of SEL (social-emotional learning) into our schools is a fantastic response to this crisis. However, having spent six years co-creating large TEDx events with teens, and then building the Career Fair For the Future for youth ages fifteen to twenty-two,[5] I believe there are some very tangible things we can all do to help reinforce the preparedness and emotional wellbeing of our children.

First, we must ensure they hear a positive narrative of the future. Yes, things are changing. And that is exciting, as breakdowns create breakthroughs. Today's youth *must* be able to believe in a future that *is* safe and

---

4   "Early Moments Matter for Every Child," *UNICEF*, 2017.
5   CareerFairForTheFuture.com

abundant, and that where it needs oversight, they are empowered to act: with their attention, their purchases, their time, and their advocacy. They should be taught how to share "power with."

Second, we can shift our focus from pounding specific vocational curriculum into their heads to ensuring they have the confidence that they can thrive no matter how technology or society changes. Today, both technical skills, such as coding, and soft skills, such as team building, are sought, but who knows what the specific needs will be ten to twenty years from now? Kids need to cultivate a more evergreen collection of capacities that will empower them to thrive in an unknown future—and I believe these include curiosity, empathy, agency, grit, and integrity.

CAPACITIES TO PREPARE FOR ANY FUTURE

We need to model the message that youth (and everyone!) can be the architects of what is being built right now. That as new opportunities emerge, they will be able to respond effectively and confidently. Specifically, this means actively encouraging these five traits. In an era of "snowplow" and surveillance parenting and *Hunger Games*-style college admissions, this is not at all easy for adults to commit to. But it is so important we understand how we can help kids in these ways:

- **Curiosity:** This is by far the number one thing every single leader and innovator on the planet is advocating for, because a world that is in constant creation is a world that requires constant learning. We must help kids hold on to their innate sense of curiosity and teach them that what they each see and wonder about is as unique to them as a fingerprint. The twenty-first century will have no use for cookie-cutter thinkers; it needs and expects those who can observe, question, and seek out greater understanding. Encourage their questions, encourage them to teach you about their passions, and reflect back for them what makes their ideas so interesting.

- **Empathy:** It is vital we are able to see things from another's point of view. Study upon study confirms the need for "social perceptiveness" or social intelligence—basically being able to read how another feels—as a critical leadership skill. And this isn't just a kind thing to do; empathy is the place from which all innovation must be centered. Today's children are exposed to so much difficult news and suffering, but we can help them learn more about why these things they care about are happening and how decisions and circumstances impact lives.

- **Agency:** How do we develop a sense of confidence and responsibility that we can take action versus just stand by? This is all new territory and we have to believe we can "figure it out." Kids need to be encouraged to solve the problem themselves by applying their curiosity and trying, sometimes "failing" as they learn. Agency is trusting yourself, believing you have something valuable to add...and then doing it without needing anyone else's acknowledgment for validation first.

- **Grit:** In a culture of instant gratification and Instagram influencers, it can be challenging to appreciate that things don't always come so easily. But as any entrepreneur or innovator can attest, creating the new requires the ability to persevere in the face of difficulty or rejection. While we often describe this as tenacity, someone like Michael Phelps has shown us that sometimes grit is also having the courage to remove the mask of superhero and ask for support as you struggle through something especially difficult or painful. While agency is important, our children need to know they are never, ever alone.

- **Integrity:** This is what we lean on in a moment of ethical ambiguity, which, in this increasingly complex and fracturing world, we will all encounter ever more frequently. As the amount of data collected allows us to know much more and be much more precise in our actions, the moral ambiguity of each choice will continue to rise. I also encourage kids to apply their agency and confidently (and respectfully) raise a key question if they sense or believe something they are witnessing or contributing to is wrong. Even (or especially!) if they are the only person with their specific perspective or background in the room. They should be encouraged to believe their perspective and values matter. And they should always be tenacious in fighting for the rights and inclusion of those who cannot advocate for themselves.

When we learn to honor and express these capacities, we become less fearful of the future. By recognizing opportunities in the challenges in front of us, we feel prepared to successfully navigate and even solve any problem we encounter.

Our children literally *are* the future, yet as we look at dismal health projections of obesity and truly alarming rates of anxiety, depression, suicide, and loneliness, we are currently failing them. Doing so is not only cruel, but we are putting our own future in jeopardy, as the costs for ignoring their wellbeing will take a giant toll on society—both economically and on any kind of global scale of competence.

Our kids deserve to believe in the future. And they will need a broad range of skills and capacities to thrive in a vastly different-looking world in which they will increasingly set their own course. Leadering plays the long game.

PREPARING OUR TEAMS FOR THE FUTURE

Almost every leader I speak with briefs me with similar language: as they're managing transformations within their companies, they're constructing a bridge at the same time they're trying to cross it. Or they're building the plane while they're flying it. Or they're putting wheels on the car while they are racing it. Pick your metaphor. Leaders are trying to build structures and quickly adapt processes for a future that can't even be imagined yet. As the prime minister of Iceland, Katrín Jakobsdóttir, validated when interviewed recently by Katie Couric, "Right now, everyone is learning by doing."

This, as we all know, can get exhausting. Even the most visionary folks I have met have experienced challenges motivating their leadership teams or directors to have the same sense of momentum and enthusiasm, because they are often suffering one or more of the following:

- **Change fatigue.** Even before the pandemic, it seemed like we had been "transforming" forever. Mobile, cloud, social media, and even the internet have all required we learn new tasks and shift our work. Just when we think we've grasped what the future needs, wants, and expects, the ground shifts from underneath us...again. The global move to Zoom delivery of remote work / learning / medical care and all the rest has certainly amplified this existing issue.

- **Skepticism.** Sometimes the things we are told are going to change the world never do (or haven't yet). How can we believe this time is any different? And given the frequent C-suite turnover these days, should we really buy into a new vision yet again?

- **Constant urgency.** When the need for every change is outlined with impressive urgency—everyone clamoring that the iceberg we are standing on is melting—we can easily lose perspective. The tyranny of the urgent can cause to us either live in a state of constant panic or become inured and numb, unable to distinguish that which is truly critical.

- **Confusion.** Even if we believe transformational change is necessary, we often have no idea how to navigate this new landscape. We don't feel prepared or clear on the next steps, so we freeze...if it really matters, it will make more sense sometime later, we figure, like it did in the past.

- **Fear.** In the face of so much change in business model and delivery, there is a growing concern about job security. And whether at a conscious or subconscious level, this sabotages transformative action.

And I'll add one more that few of us are able to express out loud...

- **Imposter worries.** A Twitter query recently asked, "What is the biggest threat to humankind?" and along with all the biggies around climate change and volatile geopolitical actions, someone answered with a very human reply: "imposter syndrome." At first, I scoffed at this reaction, but then it sunk in. I began to consider how true this statement might be. If we worry we don't have what it takes to keep up and don't really trust ourselves (or each other), how can we even begin to navigate ambiguity and change?

In our desire to always feel competent, most managers are searching for updates to the how-we-do-this "operating manual" they have been guided by all these years. They have a hard time accepting there is no longer one at all. That in its place, instead, we are building dynamic capacities to absorb continuous information and chart the course in real time.

Letting go of a "this is how we've always done things" approach requires that we unlearn decades of education and workplace expectations. As we've mentioned, it also requires that what we are asking of individuals syncs up with what the organization is providing in support and encourages—either directly or indirectly. We exist inside systems that signal which way is safe to proceed. To encourage people to change, we have to look at the way the system itself delivers innovative, audacious, and caring actions, including:

- **Incentivizing Collaboration.** Recent Stanford research shows how workplace competition often backfires and works at cross purposes to the behaviors that will lead to twenty-first-century success.[6] The opportunity, then, is to rethink approaches that nurture cross-collaborators. And encourage those who invest time cultivating these relationships.

---

6   Beth Jensen, "Rethink Competition in the Workforce," *Stanford Graduate School of Business,* December 3, 2019.

- **Incentivizing Curiosity.** Self-directed learning and the ability to absorb new information have become crucial thriving skills we want to encourage. We need to replace "We tried that, and it didn't work" with "We tried that, and here is what we learned." How is continuous learning actively supported? How do you encourage experimentation in safe ways? And how do you react when a new or pilot initiative "fails"?

- **Incentivizing Agency.** If a team member wants to explore a different department—or organization—for six months, are the structures of our organizations flexible enough to accommodate their interest? Are titles the only way one is guaranteed access—or acknowledgment? How can you actively encourage and support those willing to be the accelerators and cultural change agents?

- **Incentivizing Discourse.** When we work in diverse teams, we won't always get our way. We think of great innovations or great documents and accords—say, in the case of the Declaration of Independence—as having been crafted with perfect agreement and consensus. In reality, a tremendous amount of compromise goes into building the ideas that become cornerstones of the present and future. How do you build space for an inclusive and respectful environment that makes room for necessary dissent?[7] And then how are difficult decisions within our organizations effectively made?

As companies as diverse as Gravity Payments, Unilever, and Patagonia are demonstrating, when people inside and out of our organization are aligned in a shared purpose and incentivized by supportive structures, they are

---

7   Amy Gallo, "Why We Should Be Disagreeing More at Work," *Harvard Business Review*, January 3, 2018.

empowered to create their best work and, together, design and implement transformative solutions.

PREPARING OUR ORGANIZATIONS FOR THE FUTURE

Leading asks us to take a critical look not just at the tasks or productivity of our teams but at the real outcomes we are focused on together and the behaviors we incentivize to achieve them. It recognizes the need to reduce the stress on organizations as they take on digital transformation by building a wholly new, yet comforting, set of adaptive capacities and approaches.

FROM TRANSACTION TO TRUST

We've entered an era in which we no longer just get to sell something and move on. Every encounter has an afterlife and the opportunity for a more meaningful connection. And this goes for everyone we engage with—internally and externally. Because the only way we become more effective at sensing, adapting, and responding is to actually build the kinds of relationships that extend beyond commerce and encourage us to safely exchange information and ideas.

Jerry Michalski, the connector, curator, and catalyst behind the think-and-do tank Relationship Economy eXpedition (REX), describes the nature of trust and relationships this way:

> *Smart companies are building authentic relationships with their customers, no longer treating them as consumers. Smart governments are figuring out how to trust their citizens by opening their data and their budgeting processes, among other ways. Less enlightened incumbent companies, trying to keep their hold on markets and consumers, are using the old methods*

with greater force and accuracy. They're exploiting the world of big data to surveil and manipulate. The problem is that such behavior isn't trustworthy. In the Relationship Economy, trust is paramount. Whom you trust and who trusts you are primary assets.[8]

Ideally, we can nurture relationships with a variety of stakeholders for mutual benefit. This includes those we would have historically considered "targets," such as our customers as well as our "vendors" and even, in some circumstances, our competitors. In short, we won't thrive with a mindset focused only on what *we* need. Or by ignoring the potential available when we learn and build together. As we get clearer on our core purpose and unique value, we can more comfortably cultivate and manage broad ecosystems. And as we more actively co-create the future with our network of stakeholders, our teams and our organizations will become increasingly borderless—replacing old hierarchies and chains of command with trust, shared values and purpose, and a commitment to mutual—even transcendent—benefit.

TAKING RESPONSIBILITY FOR OUR CHOICES

Earlier, we discussed the concerns some Google employees had about selling AI technology to the U.S. military. Similarly, there is growing concern among Amazon team members about its sprawling environmental footprint. Distrust and negative externalities grow when we don't pay attention to the amplified impact of what we create. So, where does that leave us in this era of exponential tech? At a recent event, I met a young founding CTO of a company that was building an AI technology for store surveillance cameras. The AI was originally designed to detect whether someone had walked into a store with a gun, but users quickly realized the technology

---

8 JerryMichalski.com

was even more helpful in reducing fraud by detecting people who claimed to have an "accidental" fall, when they actually engineered it.

This prompted a question: "If a retailer using this technology asks you to do something else more ethically ambiguous with the footage, such as identify specific kinds of people who were walking through the store, would the CTO give that information?" This CTO responded that he personally didn't think it was a good idea for retailers to use the data the camera collected this way—but if their competitor created that ability for their customers, his company would too. His answer signaled that he didn't believe the potential misuse of his technology was his responsibility; he was content to build it and let others deal with the ramifications.

He is not the first person I've heard say those same words, so when we had a private moment, the young CTO and I discussed the responsibility he had to educate his clients on how to use this technology with integrity, that if you build something that can be misused, it is important to dissuade your clients from exploiting it in ways that erode trust, both for them and for you. When a competitor makes a long-term choice that you don't feel is right, don't bury your values to follow them.

This same conversation happened as a team of us were scoping out a new AI application to help call-center employees at a large bank respond with more insight to incoming calls; the question is not whether to use this capability but how? By accessing and synthesizing vast amounts of data about how our customers make a decision, we will eventually know them better than they know themselves. This will give us the ability to empower or exploit. Or, as Jerry Michalski puts it, "to serve or to stalk."

This choice seemed like a no-brainer to me. But my colleagues pushed back, saying it was the client's decision, not ours, to determine how such an algorithm would be used. Again, I countered: if we build this, we need to educate our clients on its best and highest use; we should even name the product in such a way that clearly signals the intention to hold our customers well with this approach. And by the way, not just because it feels right ethically but because of the mounting business imperative of building and sustaining trust.

As we pointed out earlier, this thinking must also extend to our supply chain partners. We have seen photos and heard stories of factory workers in places like Bangladesh that toil under appalling conditions for virtually no pay to make garments for the fashion industry or computer components. Similar abuse is beginning to happen to those who label data for machine learning around the world via Mechanical Turk, for around ninety-seven cents per hour.[9] We must build cultures and teams that *expect* ethics and values to be part of the discussion. As we build new processes, we must strive to understand what is at stake and the implications of the decisions we choose to make. Leadering means caring about the conditions in which this work gets done and that people are compensated fairly, so we do not repeat the exploitive supply chain lessons of the past.

Inherently, the flip side of greater agency and freedom bestowed in decentralized, collaborative, and self-leading ecosystems is a broader accountability. Responsibility falls on everyone involved along the end-to-end value chain: individuals need to hold themselves accountable, companies must make their intentions clear, and we as buyers, talent, and investors will actively consider whether or not to do business with these organizations.

---

9   Andy Newman, "I Found Work on an Amazon Website. I Made 97 Cents per Hour," *The New York Times*, November 15, 2019.

BUILDING CONGRUENCE (VERSUS CONSISTENCY)

As we've noted several times, current leadership behaviors are often carried out in a hierarchy, where people with bigger titles and more experience at the top hold far more responsibility than those "at the bottom." The expectation is that leaders know how to get the right things done and therefore are tasked with instructing those with less experience. However, this doesn't work as well in environments of constant change and in which everyone is learning. Past experience becomes less relevant (and is often an unhelpful anchor) to building what needs to come next.

At the same time, leaders often ask how they can get their people to be bolder, take more initiative, be more innovative, or even be more vulnerable about the challenges they face in their roles. What these leaders often fail to appreciate is that we work and live inside systems. And these systems determine whether adopting these new behaviors is smart to even try. Often, the metrics by which employees are measured disincentivize the things we say we care the most about, such as learning, experimentation, and collaboration.

What we put resources toward and how we align our incentives—financial and social—determines whether stakeholders across the board can trust that the things we say matter actually do. Historically, leaders focused on building consistency across groups and geographies to minimize cost and drive more efficiency. But as the landscape shifts and we focus on relationships and building trust, it is much more important that all parts of the organization stay responsive to the situation and context they are facing, while all staying focused on the same North Star.

Once you are clear what your North Star is, each micro-action you take then intentionally aligns toward manifesting your vision. The future is formed in the countless decisions we make every day—from how we source the materials we need, to how we structure our procurement contracts, to how we name our conference rooms, to how we build teams with diverse perspectives and incentivize our people to learn and experiment.

As leaders, we must be sure we walk our talk, both in operations and culture. We can be aligned (congruency) without being uniform (consistency).

PREPARING FOR A DISTRIBUTED FUTURE

Preparing ourselves, our teams, our organizations, and this next generation of citizens and leaders for this fast-moving future ensures we have the capacities necessary to adapt as radically new solutions are offered. Said another way, as our mindset shifts, new terrain becomes visible.

We have spent a great deal of time in this book advocating for a new way of leading the organizations that currently exist. But if "management" is dead and leveraging large, complex ecosystems will become the norm, then perhaps there is a bigger question for us to be asking as leaders: Beyond the culture of a company, what should the structure of an organization itself be in the future?

In 2015, consulting firm Wolff Olins interviewed forty-three global CEOs, as well as over four hundred students in their twenties who represent the next round of employees, to find out where they believe things are headed. In their report, they show how leaders are beginning to create the "uncorporation":

> *Employees today are uncorporate individualists. For a CEO, this makes life almost impossible. How do you make an uncorporate culture, yet still meet corporate targets? How do you liberate people, without unleashing*

chaos? How do you give people a purpose, without imposing an ideology? How do you lead, when everyone's their own leader? And how do you do it all fast?[10]

Similarly, Deloitte undertook two years of research and discussions with hundreds of clients to devise underlying strategies that work together to make organizations "irresistible" for workers:

The employee-work contract has changed: People are operating more like free agents than in the past. In short, the balance of power has shifted from employer to employee, forcing business leaders to learn how to build an organization that engages employees as sensitive, passionate, creative contributors. We call this a shift from improving employee engagement to a focus on building an irresistible organization.[11]

In response to these needs and expectations, we are seeing a slew of options popping up in business literature to describe how to organize the company of the future; some are trying Holacracy[12] or Wirearchy,[13] or creating democratic workplaces,[14] while others are building Exponential Organizations.[15] There are seemingly infinite approaches, but what is clear is that there is no longer a single "best practices" way to structure enterprise output.

Excitingly, however, there are several encouraging models and fresh frameworks taking shape. Here are some interesting ones worth exploring.

10 "Impossible and Now: How Leaders Are Creating the Uncorporation," *Wolff Olins*, 2015.
11 Josh Bersin, "Becoming Irresistible: A New Model for Employee Engagement," *Deloitte*, January 27, 2015.
12 Holacracy.org, 2019.
13 Wirearchy.com, 2019.
14 Rea Regan, "Workplace Democracy: What Is It and How Can You Create It?" *Connecteam*, August 23, 2020.
15 Jonathan Jeffery, "What Is an Exponential Organization?" *Entrepreneur*, October 29, 2019.

TAKING CUES FROM MOTHER NATURE

"I'm not trying to copy nature. I'm trying to find the principles she is using."
—R. Buckminster Fuller, architect, inventor, author

As we pay closer attention to the vital patterns nature has cultivated over billions of years of constantly changing decentralized environments, we are inspired to imagine radically new ways we, too, can coordinate, adapt, and sustainably steward our resources.

"Stigmergy" is the term that identifies how birds flock and how ant colonies self-organize through a combination of positive and negative feedback, amplifying actions and learnings that are beneficial, while suppressing those that aren't. Wikipedia describes stigmergy as "a consensus mechanism of indirect coordination between agents through complex, seemingly intelligent structures, without the need for any planning, control, or even direct communication between the agents."[16] (Which, fascinatingly, also describes the internet-supported collaboration that actually *is* Wikipedia.)

Trees have built ecosystems that foster and rely on various internal cooperations and external codependencies to fully function and thrive as a whole.[17] They are a surprisingly intelligent, coordinated experience of interdependent systems ("tree families") that communicate via scent talk, support mutual growth, share nutrients, "agree" to bloom together and take communal action against pests—all of which contributes to a resilient ecosystem in which other organisms like mushrooms and fungi play vital roles.

---

16 "Stimergy," *Wikipedia*, 2019.
17 Peter Wohlleben, *The Hidden Life of Trees: What They Feel, How They Communicate—Discoveries from a Secret World* (Vancouver: Greystone Books, 2016).

As such, trees are incredibly adaptive to their environment. Just as no two organizations are the same, the ecosystems of trees differ widely—from a waterlogged mangrove, to an epically tall redwood forest, to an oasis of desert palms. While there is an ingrained natural intelligence that knows how to convert sunlight into food and transport water from its roots to its leaves (well, for the most part—redwoods actually pull moisture from the clouds!), they each conform to thrive where they are. Without—you guessed it—a playbook or anyone telling them what to do.

Is it possible our human organizations can take cues from nature to flourish in similar ways? How would our thinking and our approaches need to shift to ensure a healthy coherence (rather than total chaos) in decentralized environments?

SELF-MANAGED ORGANIZATIONS

Reinventing Organizations by Frederic Laloux is one of the most transformative and influential management books of the decade.[18] With an appreciation of how culture and technology work in tandem to form organization structures, he walks us through a cleverly color-coded history of these frameworks and introduces us to an evolving next-gen level he describes as "Teal."

Frederic profiles a range of organizations—from schools and manufacturing companies to tech startups and a neighborhood nursing company—that are all decentralized and intentionally designed to sense and shift direction faster in response to problems and opportunities. As he describes it, thriving Teal organizations come with three breakthroughs that are fundamentally changing leadership as we know it:

---

18   Frederic Laloux, *Reinventing Organizations* (Millis, MA: Parker Nelson Publishing, 2014).

- **Self-management** that works in fluid systems of distributed authority and collective intelligence.

- **Valuing wholeness** and inviting employees to drop their masks and bring all of who they are to work—our outer passions and responsibilities as well as our inner emotional maps and responses.

- **Evolutionary purpose** that allows the organization to take in new information and shift the ways in which it creates and delivers value to its stakeholders, creating ongoing relevance, direction, and momentum.

These qualities amplify why cultivating a capacity for Leadering is so important. It sets us up to thrive through this kind of radical transformation.

This isn't just theoretical. As we are beginning to see, building faster, more responsive, and innovative organizations in these ways leads to marketplace success.

Red Hat, the largest open-source software company in the world, is a prime example of a decentralized organization. Though Red Hat works with tech titans such as Cisco, Microsoft, and Dell, it operates on the transformative effects of openness: from the community, through the technology, and into the organization "at the deepest and highest levels." With a long executive history at BCG, Delta Airlines, and now IBM, former Red Hat CEO and current board chairman Jim Whitehurst shared in his book, *The Open Organization*:

> *Rather than the CEO dictating what the peons must do, they instead become the catalyst that encourages open organizations to largely self-organize. Projects of all kinds, beyond just software, naturally emerge throughout*

Red Hat until it's obvious to everyone that someone needs to work on it full-time.[19]

Note: Red Hat's market value is reportedly up 300 percent under Jim's leadership as CEO.

Replacing an outdated bureaucracy in which nurses were burning out with a more humanistic approach, Dutch social care network Buurtzorg was founded by a group of nurses thirteen years ago with the mission of delivering high-quality community healthcare in a whole new way.[20] Since then, the system has revolutionized the way healthcare is offered by deploying teams of up to twelve self-directed nurses—responsible for between forty and sixty people within a particular area—who prioritize their own workflows via a distributed network of iPads rather than a centralized system of control.

Voted "Best Employer" in the Netherlands for the last four out of five years, the organization now operates with 950 teams and fifteen thousand nurses in twenty-five countries. In the Netherlands alone, this approach has led to 40 percent savings for the entire Dutch healthcare system. Not only that, but client satisfaction rates are at an all-time high, with recovery rates doubled, and staff report almost 90 percent satisfaction and contentment levels. As a result of their innovation, new applications are in development with Apple to offer the same kind of care across mental health as well as children and family services.

Something important is starting to happen here that we should be really curious about. The implications are vast as we open to new and more responsive ways to organize for the work ahead. Our experiences working

---

19 Jim Whitehurst, *The Open Organization* (Boston: Harvard Business Review Press, 2015).
20 "Buurtzorg's Model of Care," *Buurtzorg*, 2020.

(and learning) so differently in 2020 have primed us to be more comfortable considering new approaches.

Time for another big deep breath...are you ready to get to work?

THE *REALLY* BIG SHIFT FROM WINNING TO CARING

"Some people believe it's naive to think we can make love our new bottom line. What I believe is naive is thinking that human civilization as we know it will survive another two hundred years if we do not."
—Marianne Williamson, author, spiritual leader, and politician

While all these ideas on how to approach the future may have your head spinning, the best way to navigate complexity is actually quite simple: when you design processes and solutions with people's needs at the center, the decisions of what to do (or not) become clear. The result is a more resilient, sustainable business that draws customers and creates raving fans.

Caring for others is not a philanthropic action. It's the driver of twenty-first century success. It harnesses our enormous and potent new capabilities and technologies to ensure we all thrive. That we all have access to dignified housing, healthy food, ongoing education, and a legitimate sense of personal safety. That our unique skills and curiosities are cultivated and given outlets for expression. That the technologies we advance are working for us, not against us. And importantly, that we stop measuring our success with outdated yardsticks that only extend a quarter of a year ahead. Ironically, in this world of nanosecond processing, we must take a much longer view of our decisions.

It is so encouraging to see the world's most prominent CEOs make the commitment to put caring for people and the planet ahead of strictly profit-taking.

WINNING	CARING
POWER OVER	Power With
SHAREHOLDER	Stakeholder
GDP/GROWTH FOCUSED	Creates Sustainable Value
IGNORES EXTERNALITIES	Prioritizes Externalities
LINEAR / EXTRACTIVE	Circular / Regenerative
EXPLOITATIVE TECH	Empowering Tech
SHORT TERM	Long Term
DOMINATES	*Generates*

It is even more inspiring to see organizations such as Microsoft put caring into action by experimenting with better ways to support their team members and customers with the practices, products, and services they are advancing. And it is very reassuring to see Salesforce truly put caring at the helm as, in January 2020, they welcomed their first-ever chief ethical and humane use officer.[21] Though Salesforce has had some pushback against the ways their products have been used by Customs and Border Protection, CEO Marc Benioff is an outspoken critic of the practices of his tech titan peers. Creating this new ethics role helps ensure Salesforce thoughtfully considers the potential externalities and ripple effects of the choices they make going ahead.

As we continue to advance conversations on the shape of capitalism and the role of business in a shifting society, it is encouraging to see many

---

21 Lauren Feiner, "Salesforce Hires Its First Chief Ethical and Humane Use Officer Following Benioff's Criticism of Facebook," *CNBC*, December 10, 2018.

challenging the orthodoxies and assumptions of the past around linear, consumptive growth and the meaning of "value." We are rethinking how we apply the tools of markets, public spending, and even debt—potentially to rebuild structures that should be better serving people and the planet.

A consistent thread in the work of those already practicing Leadering follows these actions; putting people at the center of economic decisions flips many long-held beliefs and offers a more hopeful path to healthier organizations and societies as well as sustainable, inclusive stewardship and distribution of resources.

LEADERING IN ACTION

I am often asked who is practicing Leadering; whom do I admire? Here are six leaders I continue learning from:

Paul Polman—former CEO, Unilever. Paul Polman ushered in an entirely new era during his ten years at Unilever, becoming the face of sustainable capitalism and ditching quarterly reporting in favor of more robust long-term planning, which better supported sustainability goals.[22] He developed an ambitious plan to double Unilever's profitability while halving their negative impacts on the environment. The plan involved embracing a circular-economy approach to their supply chain and committing to ensure 100 percent of their plastic packaging would be fully reusable, recyclable, or compostable by 2025—an action they're on target to achieve. Paul has since gone on

---

22 David Gelles, "Paul Polman, a 'Crucial Voice' for Corporate Responsibility, Steps Down as Unilever CEO," *The New York Times*, November 30. 2018.

to establish a new sustainability consulting firm called Imagine, focused on urging business leaders to take action on global issues, creating scale at speed.[23]

Satya Nadella—CEO, Microsoft. Despite being a career-long veteran of Microsoft, Satya has still been able to completely transform the software behemoth in the six years since he has been CEO.[24] He has enabled the organization to break down silos and foster the kinds of collaboration necessary— inside and out—to support the big business strategy shift they needed in a world of cloud computing. He exudes humanity as he describes the inspiration he gets from his wife and special-needs daughter, humbly recovers from an interview blunder,[25] or enthusiastically interviews a customer on LinkedIn video snippets. While Microsoft is learning to navigate the challenging waters of technologies such as facial recognition, the company seems genuinely interested in how to take better care of the talent it attracts, demonstrating how that is congruent with being one of the world's most valuable companies.

Indra Nooyi—former CEO, PepsiCo. It is not always easy to pull a company into the future. Indra received her share of resistance as she worked to prepare PepsiCo for a world increasingly focused on health and wellbeing by investing in better-for-you foods and beverages. Yet, with her at the helm, PepsiCo's revenue doubled in twelve years to reach $63.5

---

23 Imagine.one, 2019.

24 Ron Miller, "After 5 Years, Microsoft CEO Satya Nadella Has Transformed More than the Stock Price," *TechCrunch*, February 4, 2019.

25 Kara Swisher, "Microsoft CEO Satya Nadella on Women Pay Gaffe: 'I Answered That Question Completely Wrong,'" *Vox*, October 9, 2014.

billion, half of it coming from the healthier product categories (up from 38 percent in 2006). Eleven years ago—ahead of even Kickstarter—she spotted the rise of social media and community involvement among youth and audaciously redirected their entire Super Bowl advertising budget to instead launch Pepsi Refresh, a community social-impact platform where people could outline and vote to support projects to refresh their communities to make a better world.[26] With her Performance with Purpose stance, Indra was way ahead of her peers in recognizing the need to create value with each choice the organization made versus transfering it philanthropically after the fact.[27]

Darren Walker—president, Ford Foundation. Established in 1936 by Ford Motors founder Henry Ford and his son Edsel with the simple mission to "Advance Human Welfare," the Ford Foundation ranks second behind the Bill and Melinda Gates Foundation as one of the largest and most influential private foundations in the U.S. (and around eleventh in the world). In 2010, Darren left the Rockefeller Foundation to take the helm and has become a strong advocate for rethinking the role of philanthropy and its relationship within a capitalist system—encouraging foundations "to reject inherited, assumed, paternalist instincts—an impulse to put grant-making rather than change-making at the center of our worldview."[28] Darren clearly sees both the historical mechanisms that have created

---

26 Larry D. Woodard, "Pepsi's Big Gamble: Ditching Super Bowl for Social Media," *ABC News,* December 13, 2009

27 Emily Pidgeon, "Indra Nooyi Reveals 8 Lessons She Learned as CEO of PepsiCo," *CEO Magazine,* July 18, 2019.

28 Darren Walker, "Toward a New Gospel of Wealth," *Ford Foundation,* October 1, 2015.

the inequities his foundation is working to address as well as the ways capitalism must be reformed to more effectively spur innovation and distribute productivity. Under his leadership, the Ford Foundation recently became the first nonprofit foundation in U.S. history to issue a $1 billion social bond in the U.S. taxable bond market, to increase grant-making to stabilize and strengthen nonprofit organizations in the wake of COVID-19.[29]

Jacinda Ardern—prime minister of New Zealand. The world's youngest female head of government—stepping into her role in 2017, at age 37—and new mother, Jacinda Ardern, has spearheaded multiple initiatives that have transformed the country of New Zealand, earning her a huge 62 percent approval rating among citizens. In addition to her 2019 announcement that her government would no longer measure wealth and economic growth using GDP only, Jacinda introduced a wellbeing budget with all new spending to go toward five specific wellbeing goals: bolstering mental health, reducing child poverty, supporting Indigenous peoples, moving to a low-carbon-emission economy, and flourishing in a digital age. When a mass shooter took the lives of over fifty people worshipping at a mosque in Christchurch, her response was swift, ushering in gun reforms in less than a month. The first-ever New Zealand prime minister to march in a Pride parade, she joined a crowd of more than twenty-five thousand in Auckland that called for more support for LGBTQIA people with mental illness.[30]

29 "Ford Foundation Announces Sale and Pricing of Landmark $1 Billion Social Bonds," *Ford Foundation*, June 23, 2020.

30 Eleanor Ainge Roy, "Jacinda Ardern Becomes First New Zealand PM to March in Gay Pride Parade," *The Guardian*, February 18, 2018.

Jesper Brodin—CEO, IKEA. IKEA serves around one billion people globally per year, and their annual catalog is more widely read than the Bible. At that kind of scale, IKEA CEO Jesper Brodin's bold commitment to reduce more greenhouse gas emissions than its entire value chain creates—and to hit that milestone in just a decade—represents an opportunity to make an enormous difference. The company aims to be climate positive by 2030. As part of the plan, they are phasing out single-use plastic this year (2020).[31] They also run a range of "Good Cause Campaigns," from creating safe spaces for vulnerable children to play (developed by partnering with top NGOs such as Save the Children and UNICEF) to providing IKEA's team members with the opportunity to volunteer their time to assist refugees. Their flat-packed "Better Shelter" housing design for refugees won the Beazley Design of the Year 2017, plus the company prioritizes employing local artisans, especially women, to contribute their skills to IKEA's home furnishings collections, thereby giving them the chance to earn a sustainable income.[32]

We each play a part. No one is able to sit on the sidelines of this new world unfolding. Nor should we want to. There is so much news we can celebrate, even as we remember we are only 1 percent in. Imagine what is truly possible as we reorient our mindset to be in a better position to give what the future needs and expects from all of us.

---

31   "IKEA to phase out Single-Use Plastic from Its Home Furnishing Range and Restaurants by 2020," *Ikea*, June 8, 2018.
32   Tim Nelson, "IKEA's CEO Shares His Plans for Changes at the Company via LinkedIn," *Architectural Digest*, October 18, 2019.

Leadering is a belief that we all deserve to be better held: by each other, by the systems we design, by the stories we tell, and by the technologies we advance.

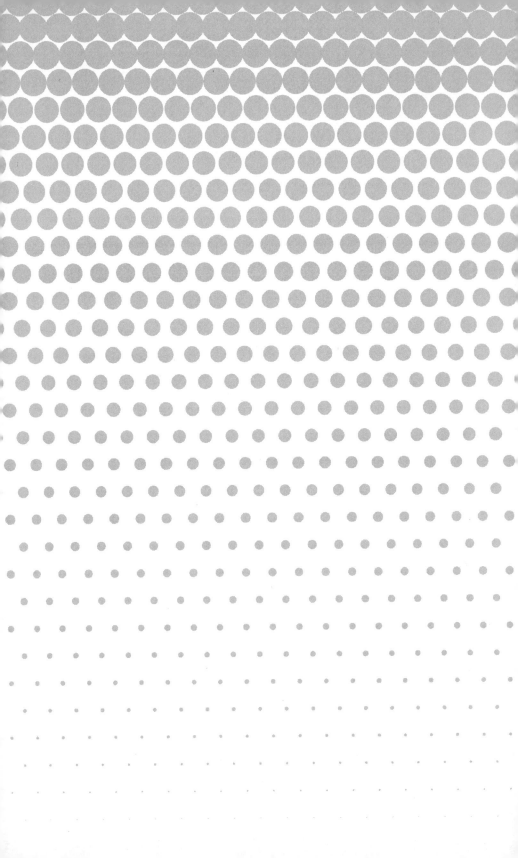

Answering the Call to Leadering

"Your playing small does not serve the world."

—Marianne Williamson, author, spiritual leader, politician, and activist

This quote has guided my work for decades and became the focus of my consultancy. I was thirty-one years old when I first read it. Having been told most of my life that I was "too much"—too curious, too sensitive, too passionate, too impatient (read: too ambitious?), and, on occasion, too smart for my own good—it was as if the heavens had finally opened and I was granted full permission to throw it all into the ring. I realized that not only does playing small not serve the world but that I had a *duty* to stand as tall as possible.

I was also pregnant with the first of my three children and becoming aware of my responsibility to them and to all those who entrust us with not only their care but also creating a safe and thriving future. Playing big became my mantra. All in my world heard me evangelize this invitation; I even themed the first TEDx event I created (one of just a handful in the world in those early days) "Play Big."

Twelve years ago, my business was rebranded Play Big Inc, and each day I am learning what it means to do so. I learn from many of the business leaders we have profiled throughout this book. I learn from the thought leaders, entrepreneurs, and technologists pushing us to reconsider and reshape the stories, structures, and tools that frame our behaviors. And I learn from the guides who encourage me to go inside when I become afraid and make peace with whatever old demon or shadow still makes me question whether I have permission to share my beliefs or ideas.

As we are continually reminded, playing with a whole and open heart, with both confidence and humility—and with an awesome imagination—is a call, not a final destination. It is why we have each had the unique experiences, insights, and teachers we have been gifted (even the dark ones). We all are here for one purpose: to put our curiosities, passions, ideas, enthusiasms, and voices to work in service of each other and this planet we collectively inhabit. Our playing big serves the world.

And it is time for us to step in and step up.

USING YOUR NEW COMPASS

As we shared in the opening, futurist Gerd Leonhard believes society will change more in the next fifty years than in the past three hundred; even if he is off by a century, that is big change. Radical solutions are just around the corner. The work of business leaders is to see them, because the enterprise of the future will require our attention in *all* these areas simultaneously:

- Actively addressing climate stability
- Accelerating talent development and upskilling
- Acknowledging and addressing deeply held systemic biases
- Investing in digital transformation and the swift adoption of new tools
- Transforming business models and approaches to deliver consistent revenue generation
- Cultivating a more resilient, agile culture that can confidently sense and respond
- And, critically, throughout all this change, fortifying the wellbeing and emotional resilience of ourselves, our teams, and society overall

Your first call to action: *Take personal responsibility for the value you want to create.* Take time to understand who you are and what matters to you. How do you want to create value? Leading requires a significant amount of self-awareness; you have to dig deep to understand your values and how you are bringing them to the work you do. You need to learn to trust yourself as you commit to what you want to create. As a human, as an organization, and as an industry.

Your second call to action: *Embrace the joy in navigating new terrain.* As we've said before, for decades we have relied on collecting proven best practices as the path to success; now we get to use a compass—one uniquely calibrated by your values, your talents, and the diverse community around you eager to collaborate as you explore unknown territory. The excitement of discovering something new—that gets you closer to your massively transformative North Star—is one of the most gratifying human (and team) experiences.

This is how we rebuild systems that serve us. It is also how we rebuild trust. Shifting one's mindset from extraction and profit creation to contribution and value creation has powerful results. Simply put, realigning focus back to the needs of stakeholders—both short term *and* long term—will be the key that unlocks future growth. By taking better care of ourselves and others, we can create the psychological safety needed to release each other from fear of change and empower the full expression of the many things we long to create.

This holds even more true for our technology-fueled future. Change must walk hand in hand with compassion. We must make sure we build the kinds of things that will be good for people and the planet—and that we, and our children, will be proud to look back on fifty or a hundred years from now.

And the third call to action: *Always put people at the center of your decision-making and acknowledge the systems in which they operate.* Otto Scharmer, of MIT and the change management method Theory U, said that "Leadership is about being better able to listen to the *whole* than anyone else can." Leadering takes this concept to the next level. It asks us to listen to the whole *and* to then create the systems, services, and products that will support us. It puts people at the heart of our business decisions, believing that this is not only the most humanistic stance but also that market forces (really just more people making choices) in an ever smaller, more tightly connected world will reward those who do.

This orientation gives you the courage to build more audacious solutions. It mandates you to rethink risk. It ensures the viability of your business, as you are now playing the long game. A human-centric view makes it much easier to identify what is right, prioritize what matters most, and draw extraordinary resources to yourself.

TRUST YOUR IMAGINATION

This book raises many questions and has hopefully encouraged you to conjure even more. Leadering recognizes that questions are the rich fodder needed for redesigning outdated approaches and inventing bold new opportunities. So, as you dive in, let's reflect again on this critical question: Do we have the right yardsticks in place to measure the success of our endeavors and ensure the initiatives driving our economic efforts are pointed in the right direction?

Measuring the wrong things sets us up for colossal failure. For example, on an individual level, how do we go from only focusing on current performance to appreciating a person's ability to be adaptive (AQ)? Even common measures pushing us to increase jobs (including dangerous, dirty, and demeaning jobs) obscure the potential for more meaningful work.

Here's another mind-bending thought: Will advances in renewable energy, 3D printing, food technology, AI, and robotics drive consumer costs *down* in such a way that we can have a higher quality of living on a lower income? Right now, a think tank called RethinkX is working on exactly that. They predict costs falling ten times across key sectors including transportation, food, energy, materials, and information—as well as production processes simultaneously becoming more efficient by an order of magnitude—so that "within ten to fifteen years, everyone on the planet could have access to the 'American Dream' for a few hundred dollars a month," as stated on their website. If you recall, at this moment, we can print a house within twenty-four hours for $7,000, have an AI give us a reliable medical diagnosis, share our cars, and grow food faster, supported by renewable energy, so is it such a stretch to imagine we may not need the same income to live a good life? Given the environmental and ecological benefits, isn't "positive degrowth" something worth shooting for?

Similarly, as technology improves productivity and shifts what work looks like, what should we consider a basic human right? As we mentioned earlier, a universal basic income (UBI) is being trialed in cities of all sizes across the U.S. and around the globe. What about universal basic transportation? Or medical insurance? Or education? Or housing? Or childcare? Importantly, what metrics and measures will incentivize better, healthier economic investments and behavior as we focus on repairing our planet and strengthening the human cloud at the center of the growing digital one?

Are we ready to rethink our understanding of "work" itself? Our tendency to focus on job growth as a measure of social and economic prosperity only values the time and energy that is directly compensated by others. If we can zoom out and rethink how we distribute productivity and incentivize our unique curiosities and talents by making them visible and acknowledging their value, it seems clear there is plenty of "work" ahead for every curious and community-engaged person.

All systems, approaches, and institutions will be reimagined and redesigned. What beliefs will guide and inform these huge changes? What future do *you* want?

Today's leaders are currently inhabiting the undefined liminal space between here and there. Between the old and the new. Between what exists now and what will be created for the first time ever. For some who really like security, that news is unsettling. They are waiting nervously for someone to tell them what to do and how to do it.

But for the rest of us, this is such an exciting moment. Starting right now—today—we can begin applying the new Leadering mindset to wonder, navigate, contribute, connect, and be audacious.

We get to create what has never existed before and find new solutions to old, hard problems, adding huge value to people's lives.

And we finally get to put our spirit of caring to work. No longer do we—or our employees—need to be bisected, striving to win at the office and then focused on caring when we get home. As the world becomes more technologically advanced and enhanced, we actually get to *become more human*. More whole.

PLAY BIGGER...AND BREATHE

"What frightens many people is not being seen as the 'expert' and yet how can you create and innovate when you are not willing to let go and explore the unknown? There is no roadmap or blueprint where the creators of a healthy world are headed, and that is exhilarating to the pioneers among us."

—Ayelet Baron, award-winning author,
former Cisco global strategist

You are awake to what's needed. You appreciate the possibility in wonder. You actively cultivate curiosity and connection. You no longer find comfort in a worn-out playbook because you now have the tools and faith to explore new lands.

Find your North Star and begin building something *you* are really proud of. Something the future needs uniquely from you.

Just remember to also take a big, long inhale. *Often.*

Thank you for all you already do to make this future bright. I hope you feel inspired and ready now to play even bigger!

Thank you for Leadering.

With love and gratitude,
Nancy

Acknowledgments

This book would never have happened without the input and excellent support of my best friend and business wingwoman, Emma Pezzack. She and I are appreciative of the adaptive, patient, and very talented support of Kathryn Irwin, Emily Gindlesparger, Bailey Hayes, and the team at Scribe Media, Heidi Toboni, Sunni Brown, Danyelle De Jong, and Peter Corke.

I am an insatiable learner, and my ideas have been shaped by the work and thinking of Arthur Brock, Riane Eisler, John Hagel, Nora Bateson, Matthew Schutte, Jerry Michalski, Douglas Rushkoff, Doug Lenat, Elliot Kotek, Shawna Butler, Yarrow Kraner, Chip Conley, Jeremy Heimans, Henry Timms, Elatia Abate, Erica Dhawan, Jeff Leitner, Byron Reese, Jacqueline Novogratz, Sasha Dichter, Hugh Forrest, Annie Hardy, Shaku Selvakumar, Amber Allen, Patrick Spear, Trey Holder, Jeff Sharpe, Michelle Khafif, Rosie von Lila, Josh Adler, Nyla Rodgers, Al Merschen, Tom LaForge, Paul Rector, Parker Thomas, Bob Wright, Chris Riley, Peter Vander Auwera, Carol Reese, Craig Webber, and my colleagues at Singularity University, TEDxAustin, TEDxYouth@Austin, the Career Fair For the Future, Retail Tomorrow, and KUNGFU.AI.

A huge thank-you to all those I've interviewed for the Femme Futurists Society and the hundreds of clients I have had the pleasure to work and learn with, including Keith Brannen, Frank Higgins, Seth Foster, Leagh Turner, Cynthia Keeshan, Kelley Haggart, Adrian Barrow, Jeffery Chapman, Adel Mekhail, Claire Capeci, and Debra Dickson. I am so appreciative that Mike Humphrey called me out of the blue one day to encourage me to become a keynote speaker and for the teams at BigSpeak and other agencies around the world who continue to make that possible.

A heartfelt hug to my dad, Lou Patierno, who instilled in me the combination of curiosity, responsibility, and empathy that infuses all my work. To my brother, PJ Patierno, who makes sure my thinking stays sharp and includes multiple perspectives. And to my lifelong friends who champion and support all my enthusiastic ideas and are up for long discussions when I dig excitedly into a new concept, thank you for always being by my side, Jim Hart, Susan McElhenney, Anne Martino, Suzanne Johnson, Margaret Keys. And Kelley Knutson.

I would like to also thank the inspiring women who have directly shaped the leader I have attempted to be: Betsy Lembeck, who led by example to balance work and motherhood and gave me the courage to create my own schedule, even in the nineties corporate world. Brené Brown, who knows her shit, leads from the heart, and owns her style as she reminds us all to open to our shared humanity. Jacqueline Novogratz, who reminded me of the importance of solving big problems with dignity, humility, and moral imagination, and who introduced me to the power (and joy) of audacity. Marianne Williamson, who gave me permission to play big, embrace complex ideas, and put love smack-dab in the center of all my work. And Arianna Huffington, who nearly ten years ago encouraged me to write and then sent me overnight a copy of her book *On Becoming Fearless*. My deepest affections, gratitude, and love.

Index

Page numbers in *italics* refer to illustrations.

vulnerability
  and empathy, 149
  hiding vs. embracing, 128–129
  Leadering with, 133–134, 252–253
  questioning ideas and, 130
  as state of learning, 252–253
  and team performance, 127

W
waking to need for Leadering mindset, xiii–xvi,
  6–11, 17–50
  with big shifts reshaping business (*see*
    shifts reshaping business)
  by broadening view of future, 40–41
  description of active stance of, 48–50
  with dynamic not static model, 39–40
  with guide for personal strategy, 41–43, 78,
    152–153, 211, 250
  with move into First Productivity
    Revolution, 21–24, 23
  by navigating liminal gap, 43–46, 44, 212,
    250, 288–289
  outdated leadership model and, 6–7, 36–39
Walgreens, 55, 153–154
Walker, Darren, 34, 278–279
Wall Street Journal, 37
Walmart, 3, 196, 251
warm data vs. cold facts, 47
waste, 164, 184, 186, 188, 204
water, access to, 162
Watson (IBM), 59
Watson, Robert, 161
wealth
  inequality in, 33–36, 124, 150, 158, 161,
    165–167, 202–203, 222–223
  redistribution of, xv, 35–36, 104, 150, 189, 288
  survey about accumulation of, 34–35
weapons, retail sales of, 215
weapons-related technology, rejection of, 168,
  216
Webb, Amy, 172
wellbeing
  of children and youth, 255, 259
  connections with self and others for, 117,
    119–120, 129, 147, 285–287

human cloud for, 121, 122
  of societies, 124, 159, 180, 221–226, 279, 285,
    288
  of workers, 19, 193–196, 225–226, 286
wellbeing budget of New Zealand, goals for,
  279
WeWork, 121
"What if…" as essential question, 8, 54, 57, 192,
  233
"What If Mother Nature Rebuilt the Internet?"
  (Giordano and Schutte), 231
Wheatley, Margaret, 83
Whitehurst, Jim, 272–273
Whole Foods, 179
wholeheartedness, 133–134
wholeness of self at work, 128–129, 133, 272, 289
Wikipedia, 228–229
Williamson, Marianne, 274, 283
Wing drone delivery service, 55
winning vs. caring, 275
Wired, 201
Wolff Olins, 268–269
women
  algorithm bias against, 87–88
  inclusion demands by, 95
  record unemployment rates of, 214–215
  struggle for equal rights and opportunities
    for, 34, 35, 36
  in top leadership positions, 92, 93
"Wonder Project, The," 151–152
wondering mindset, 8, 53–80
  about emerging innovations of companies,
    54–57
  about pace and significance of shifts, 57–60
  about strategic issues and concerns, 70–73
  about ten emergent technologies, 60–70
    (*see also* technologies reshaping
    society)
  in conversations across boundaries, 78–80,
    100–102, 151–152
  importance of, 105–107, 237, 256–257, 262
  RIFF model for, 73–78, 75
work, future of. *See also* jobs
  with alignment of company's values,
    199–201, 203, 215, 216, 267–268

alternative models for, 50, 188–192, *191*, 288
reskilling of workers in, 70–71, 196–199, 212
wellbeing of workers in, 19, 193–196,
  225–226, 286
worker-leader relationship in, 236, *249*,
  267–268
work environments, social relationships in,
  119, 120–121, 125–128
work locations, flexibility with, 244–245
work schedules, problems with, 193, 195
workday or workweek, shortened, 54, 56, 194,
  195–196
workers. *See* employees
work/life balance, 193, 196
World Bank, 116–117
World Changing Ideas, 150
World Economic Forum, 21, 23, 28, 222

World Wide Web, 68
Woven City (Toyota smart city), 240

Y
Yes I Can (VR mental therapy program), 64
young people
  audaciousness of, 219–221
  capacities for empowerment of, 256–259
  mental health of, 118, 255
  nurturing sense of safety in, 254–256
YouTube, 98, 144

Z
Zara, sustainability practices at, 204
ZestMoney, 28
Zuckerberg, Mark, 167, 172

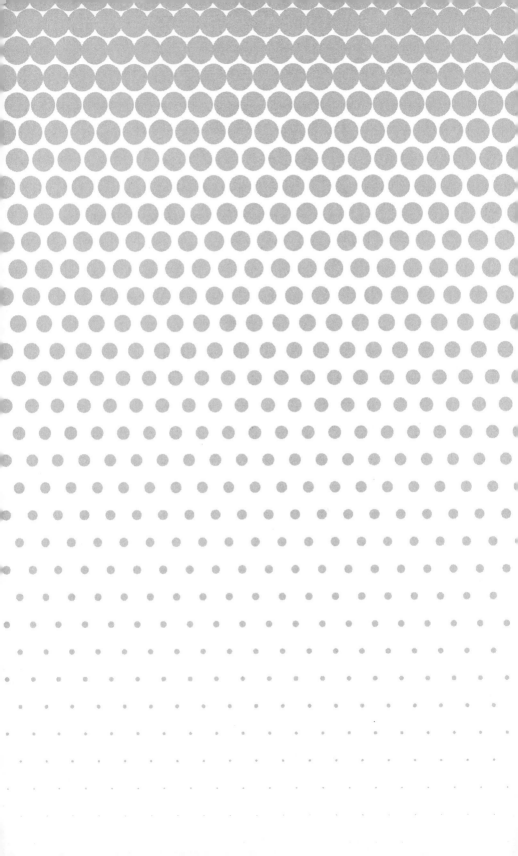

About the Author

Described as endlessly optimistic, Nancy is a strategic futurist, global keynote speaker, corporate strategist, and gatherer with a drive to help enterprise organizations and visionary leaders transform to meet the escalating expectations ahead.

Recognized as one of the world's top female futurists, she has spent her career building, shaping, and evolving a portfolio of $50 billion worth of major global brands and has delivered over eighty keynote talks around the world. Nancy's expertise and experiences range from artificial intelligence to frozen foods to reinventing the internet. And all her projects have a key common denominator: transitioning away from the extractive operating systems and outdated business thinking that no longer hold up to create the more sustainable, inclusive, and dynamic solutions the future demands.

With an early career at three of the top global advertising agencies and as a fifteen-year founder of her own strategic inspiration company, Play Big Inc, Nancy has a rich history of advising and learning with both iconic companies and horizon-technology startups, helping them transition to the new economy of collaboration, contribution, and trust.

The world's first TEDx licensee, a Singularity University lecturer, creator of the first Career Fair For the Future for college and high school students, and recent co-founder of the Femme Futurists Society—a growing collection of interviews with leading futurists around the world—Nancy has joined forces with KUNGFU.AI to advance the organizational structures and new approaches necessary to effectively harness the significant technology innovations heading our way...and ensure a safe and thriving future for us all.